Education Towards Freedom

Frans Carlgren

Education Towards Freedom

Rudolf Steiner Education: A survey of the work of
Waldorf Schools throughout the world

Floris Books

Translated by Joan and Siegfried Rudel

First published in German in 1972 as *Erziehung zur Freiheit*
Ninth edition 2005

First published in English in 1976 by the Lanthorn Press
Third edition published in 2008 by Floris Books

© 1972, 2005 Verlag Freies Geistesleben & Urachhaus GmbH, Stuttgart
This edition © 2008 Floris Books, Edinburgh

All rights reserved. No part of this publication may be reproduced without the prior permission of Floris Books, 15 Harrison Gardens, Edinburgh.
www.florisbooks.co.uk

British Library CIP Data available

ISBN 978-086315-651-9

Printed in China

Contents

Foreword	7
Rudolf Steiner and his ideas on education	9
The Child during the Pre-School Years	29
The child as sense-organ	29
The first three years	34
The kindergarten years: little material, much imagination	42
Some Basic Features of the Method	53
The rhythm of the day	53
Block period lessons	54
Artistic activities	55
The spoken word	55
The use of textbooks	56
The role of art	57
Drawing forms	59
A relationship with colour	63
Handicrafts	69
Free artistic creation	73
Physical education	76
Eurythmy	79
Monthly assemblies	82
The world of language	82
The temperaments	84
Differentiated religious instruction	98
Concerning the idea of freedom	101
The First Eight Years of School	105
The right time to begin	105
The class teacher	108
Authority or freedom?	111
The need for images	113
Pictures before letters	116
Fairy tales in Class One	120
Introducing arithmetic	124
Fables and legends in Class Two	129
The Old Testament in Class Three	131

Stories relating to individual problems	134
The ninth year — a turning point	136
Environmental studies	138
The human being and the animal world	143
Botany	149
Environmental studies	154
History	159
Drama	162
Geometry	165
The twelfth year	167
Science	167
The Stars as we see them	173
The Last Four School Years	**176**
Puberty in today's world	176
Contrasts in Classes Seven and Eight	181
From Class Nine to Class Twelve	181
Mathematics and geometry	187
Physics	193
Chemistry	200
Technology	205
Biology and the study of the human being	208
History and sociology	213
The arts in the upper school	214
The history of literature	217
Drama in the upper school	223
Music	225
Painting	226
The School in the Modern World	**231**
The industrialized school	231
The independent school	232
A worldwide school movement	234
Education towards freedom	238
Further Reading	**240**
Waldorf Schools around the world	**243**

Foreword

In the forty years since this book was first published much has changed in the world of education. Whereas a generation ago school and childhood were not a major social concern, we now live in time of vociferous debate and constantly changing perceptions. Nothing can be taken for granted in a world where "secret gardens" are a cause of suspicion, and transparency and accountability are seen as an important aspect in all areas that carry responsibility, especially in those that concern children. Children's rights have thankfully come of age within a less deferential and more openly questioning culture. Schools are taking on new role as centres of community and life-long learning with all the risks such reform involves: an increased number of stakeholders; a tension between control and prescription on one hand and autonomy and creativity on the other; arguments about the content and width of the curriculum; the challenge of new classroom techniques incorporating new technologies; and concern about the actual conditions of childhood today. Parenting is seen to be of ever-growing complexity in a world that is turbulent and at times insecure and career paths are increasingly flexible and unpredictable.

The first 1976 English edition of this book, published in a large hardback format whose vibrant illustrations spoke volumes, stated that there were at that time 220 Waldorf Steiner schools worldwide. The 1986 edition spoke of 370 and the 1993 edition of 600. All these figures were slightly out of date because of the time between writing and publication. There are now more than 1000 in over 60 countries and 1600 recognized early years settings, and by the time you read this there will doubtlessly be more. Each of these schools has been built from personal initiative, communal endeavour, devotion to the needs of the child and hard work. Now the Waldorf inspiration is to be found beyond schools, such as in *favelas* in Latin America, charter schools in the deprived inner cities of the USA, township kindergartens in Cape Flats, prison schools in California, self-sufficient communities in the Egyptian desert and orphanages in Nepal. Many ideas have been incorporated into mainstream practice; for instance it is a method utilised by maintained primary schools in the canton of Bern. Why has this phenomena come about in one generation?

In the new vocabulary of education, words like creativity, citizenship, emotional learning, childhood well-being, personal, social and health education are current, alongside assessment, testing, benchmarking, outcomes and key competencies. One aspect depends on an implicit freedom for the teacher to use their vocational skills in areas that are basically immeasurable, while the other seeks to control the quality of education to which every child is entitled through measurement and rankings. Steiner education strives to bridge the divide by allowing the child to grow into freedom and working with a methodology that stresses the importance of age-appropriateness, while at the same time creating a secure environment of warmth and care within which the individuality of the child can find its own potential. Simultaneously it views teaching as a learning profession where we can all do better for each child by working both individually and inwardly, and together as an institution that supports our own development and competencies.

Education Towards Freedom has been a milestone in this development and still has a contemporary feel, despite the multitude of changes that have occurred in the intervening time. It gives expression to what is universal in Steiner-Waldorf education in a form that is both inspiring and clear. Its continued relevance speaks of what all parents wish for their children and in many countries this is becoming more available to them regardless of financial or social circumstances. At the root of all educational activity are ideals and imagination and a book that is able to express that is a gift to us all. It may on one level be considered a classic text yet it also manages to encompass the future. The tasks ahead are formidable and the Steiner-Waldorf educational impulse is entering unknown waters. However with clarity, vision and courage, together with a sense of humility and self-questioning, there is a way, as this book shows, that serves our children's humanity and brings out the joy of learning.

Christopher Clouder
European Council for Steiner Waldorf Education
June 2008

Kindergarten	age 3–6
Lower School	
Class 1	age 6–7
Class 2	age 7–8
Class 3	age 8–9
Class 4	age 9–10
Class 5	age 10–11
Class 6	age 11–12
Class 7	age 12–13
Class 8	age 13–14
Upper School	
Class 9	age 14–15
Class 10	age 15–16
Class 11	age 16–17
Class 12	age 17–18

Note: In North America 'Grade' is used for 'Class'

Rudolf Steiner and his Ideas on Education

A short biography

Rudolf Steiner was born in 1861 near the border of Austria and Hungary in what is now Croatia, the son of a station official on the Austrian railways. After he had passed the final examinations at school, he went on to the Technical College at Vienna where he studied mathematics and science. He also attended lectures at the University on Philosophy and Literature as well as Psychology and Medicine. During this time too he became familiar, both through experimental research and study, with Goethe's methods of scientific observation. At the age of twenty-one he was asked by Professor Kürschner to edit and provide a commentary on Goethe's scientific works, which were to form part of a comprehensive publication called the 'Literature of the German Nation.' Seven years later in 1889, he was invited to join the Goethe-Schiller Archives in Weimar, as editor of part of Goethe's scientific works for their first complete publication in the Sophien Edition. Alongside his work at the Archives, he was busy with his own philosophical writings and in 1891 submitted at Rostock University the thesis for his PhD, taking as his theme the theory of knowledge. Two years later appeared his most important book on philosophy, *The Philosophy of Freedom,* sometimes referred to in English as *The Philosophy of Spiritual Activity.* After concluding his work on the Goethe edition, Steiner moved to Berlin, to become editor of the *Journal for Literature.*

As well as pursuing his studies and research work, Steiner had been engaged for several years in educational activities of one kind or another. From the age of fourteen he had financed his school career and later his university studies by giving private lessons in various subjects. After leaving college, he became the tutor of a boy who was suffering from a hydrocephalic condition and had been considered not to be educatable by more than one specialist.

Through his special way of training and teaching this boy, he achieved such remarkable results that two years later the boy was admitted into a class of his own age group at a normal school. Subsequently, this boy passed his school-leaving examination and successfully studied to become a medical doctor.

After moving to Berlin, he was from 1899 to 1904 a lecturer at the Workers' Institute of Further Education founded by Wilhelm Liebknecht.* His contribution in this realm of adult education has often been spoken of with great appreciation by his former students.

Already at the early age of seven, Rudolf Steiner had begun to have inner experiences of a nature that were later to determine his whole life. He began to experience a supersensory world as a concrete and ever-present reality. As his father was a free-thinker and no one around him would have had the least understanding for what would have been looked on as a figment of his imagination, he did not speak of these experiences. Although he was very sociable and in time came to have a wide circle of friends, for many years he spoke to no one of this facet of his inner life. Side by side with his manifold outer activities, he pursued in inner quietness the systematic path of

---

* An active social reformer of his time, 1826–1900.

Picture from ancient Indian mythology (Class 5)

spiritual training, which he later described in his fundamental writings, especially in the book, *How to Know Higher Worlds,* and in many lectures.

Anthroposophical activity

By about the turn of the century, Rudolf Steiner had achieved such a degree of conscious control over his faculty of supersensory perception that he was in a position to regard it as a real basis for spiritual-scientific research. He now took the decision, by no means an easy one, to speak of these things as opportunity offered to those people who were willing to listen. In the autumn of the year 1900, he began to give lectures to small groups. On October 8, 1902, he lectured to the scientific Giordano Bruno Society, of which he was a well-known and well-respected member. In this lecture he spoke openly of his future life task — to find new ways of soul-spiritual research based on scientific methods. A week later, a discussion on this theme was introduced by the Deputy President of this Society and in summing up Steiner's lecture, he expressed his regret that the audience had numbered only some 250 or 300 hearers instead of 'the 2000 or 3000 who are the representatives of the cultural life of Germany.'

At the time that Steiner took this step which was to prove such a decisive one for his whole future. He was held in esteem in German scientific circles and was on friendly terms with such well-known and eminent personalities as Eduard von Hartmann and Ernst Haeckel. He had, however, no illusions as to what reception the ideas he was now presenting might have in the academic scientific milieu to which he had himself hitherto belonged, a world which assumed as its natural right the authoritative decision as to what was or was not true science.

The reaction was as he had expected. From now on Steiner was regarded as a Theosophist. In actual fact it was indeed within the framework of the Theosophical Society that his main field of activity lay from October 1902 to January 1913, but at that time a parting of the ways came about. Within the established cultural life of Germany, however, he was for many years completely ignored.

From the year 1902 onwards, Steiner used on occasions for his researches a new term, which he was later to employ consistently. As this path of knowledge led to an understanding of the true nature of man, he named it 'anthroposophy' — from the Greek *anthropos* (man) and *sophia* (wisdom).

The fundamental results of his research were presented by Steiner to a small circle of enquirers, both in lectures and writings. Some of his most important and most widely read books belong to this period: *Christianity as Mystical Fact* in 1902; *Theosophy* and *How to Know Higher Worlds* in 1904; and *An Outline of Esoteric Science* in 1909.

It was in answer to the request from the continually growing number of his collaborators and students that Steiner in the course of time initiated activities which had their origin in the impulse of anthroposophy.

He wrote and produced four mystery dramas and created eurythmy — a new art of movement which aims at expressing in gesture and movement the living quality of the sounds of speech and music.

As a place where these various artistic activities could unfold more fully and, at the same time, as a focal point for the whole anthroposophical movement, Rudolf Steiner founded at Dornach, on the outskirts of Basle in Switzerland, a centre which was eventually called the Goetheanum, in honour of Goethe, the great German poet and scientist. Steiner, after his move to Dornach in 1914, designed the new building there and supervised its construction. He himself took part in the actual work. For example, the paintings inside one of the two large cupolas were his own creation and large parts of the gigantic wooden structure were carved by hand by members of seventeen different nations in accordance with his instructions, throughout the years of the First World War.

During these years there had been no special interest in anthroposophical circles for questions of social and educational importance, although Steiner had tried to draw attention to these spheres in various articles and lectures.

In his lecture of 1907, *The Education of the Child in the Light of Anthroposophy*, given in various places in Germany, almost the whole of his new ideas on education were expressed in a germinal form. Contrary to his usual custom, he revised the shorthand report and had it published in book form, adding a postscript which merits quoting. He stresses the point that the cultural isolation of the anthroposophical movement can only be overcome when the spiritual impulses at its root can be consistently carried over into practical spheres of life, 'otherwise people will continue to regard it as a variety of religious sectarianism for a few cranks and enthusiasts. If, however, it performs positive and useful spiritual work, the anthroposophical movement cannot in the long run be denied intelligent recognition.'

Amid the enormous upheavals and catastrophes which the First World War brought, new avenues of possibility were opening, new demands were coming to expression, and thus the appeal contained in the words quoted above found a ready ear.

The social question

In the spring of 1919, Germany was threatened by civil war. The guns at the various fronts were silent but the Allied blockade continued. The economy was collapsing, epidemics were spreading, and starvation was rife. Unemployment, demonstrations and riots were the order of the day. Many people joined cultural and political movements which were radical in nature. But the more level-headed were often in despair: the Empire was about to collapse; how could class differences ever be bridged?

There was a confusion of voices expressing opinions about the future of Germany and the world. It was then that Rudolf Steiner decided, at the request of some prominent people in the government, as well as industrialists and scientists acquainted with anthroposophical ideas, to present openly his concept of a new social order. With this he emerged from his former isolation and in March his statement, 'To the German people and the Civilized World,' signed by a large number of leaders in the cultural sphere, was made public. In April, he published his book *The Renewal of the Social Organism,* and started giving lectures and talks. He spoke to industrialists in small lecture halls, and to huge crowds of workers in factories and smoke-filled taverns.

Some of the examples which Rudolf Steiner used in his lectures and articles on social issues may now seem dated. But many of them are even more pertinent today than they were then. Some basic aspects will now be considered. Since sociological factors are nowadays part of the necessary background to education, it might not be amiss to look at this aspect of Rudolf Steiner's concept of education as an art which he tried to realize in the first Waldorf School. He considered education and training to play important roles in the development of people and in the shaping of society. They must, therefore, be seen against this wider background.

The Concept of a threefold society

With the idea of a threefold structure of the social organism, Rudolf Steiner presented neither an abstract idea nor a political party programme. It was by taking into account the nature of human beings in conjunction with existing social conditions that he was able to set forth how a fundamentally new social order could come about and how current problems could be solved, both in society at large and in the individual human being. Three 'spheres of life' may be distinguished, each of which has its own particular characteristics: the spiritual-cultural sphere; the economic sphere; and the legal-political sphere. Since about the fifteenth century, when the modern states began to evolve, we have gradually become used to a largely centralized management of these three spheres. It appears to us that the obvious form of social life is the 'homogeneous state,' in which the responsible rulers have decision making powers not only in matters of foreign policy and the administration of justice but also in questions of spiritual and economic life. In many states, this power extends to the minutest details. We shall subsequently turn to the problems and dangers which are brought about by this centralization, not only in totalitarian states but also in those which are considered democratic. But it should be mentioned here that Rudolf Steiner was in favour of a threefold social order, which would regard and deal with the spheres of business, legal, and spiritual life as three coexistent spheres which are administered as independent entities. He was of the conviction (in conscious opposition to his as well as our contemporaries), that the situation of modern humanity demands such a decentralization of social life.

Liberty, equality, fraternity

Human needs, which according to Steiner's view can only be satisfied by a threefold social order, can be simply summarized. It is no accident that the words 'liberty, equality, fraternity' have been able continually to awaken enthusiasm in so many people not only during the time of the French Revolution but since as well. Upon closer examination, these three ideals are seen to correspond to deep instinctive feelings which we all bear within ourselves more or less consciously. As will be immediately made clear by a single example, each of these ideals can only be realized within a limited area of social life: before the law we can and must all be equal. However, to compel by law our spiritual and material needs to fit the demands of just such an equality would, as many examples from ancient and modern history substantiate, bring about a disastrous levelling. Rudolf Steiner strove for a clarification of the concept of equality in which he assigned these three ideals in a consistent way to specific functions of human society. The goals which form the basis of his work for the threefold social order can be expressed in three brief formulations: spiritual freedom in cultural life; democratic equality before the law; and social fraternity in economic life. The following examples illustrate this point of view and the fact that this is not mere theory but can be put into practice at almost any point of life.

Cultural life

Freedom is a basic condition for the existence of a creative spiritual life. We live in an age in which the tendency to overall planning in industry, necessary in its own sphere, reaches ever more deeply into the structure of education and research and thus into the whole area of cultural life. To an ever greater degree schools, universities and scientific laboratories are regarded and treated as factors in an international economic-political competitive struggle; curricula, the form of instruction, decisions concerning examinations, research programmes and methods are consistently adapted to the needs of industry, government or even the military machine. It cannot be contested that through this process the freedom of cultural life is endangered in those nations which consider themselves 'free.'

A child's upbringing and education play a decisive role in this context. The future of the human race appears already in its children. In the final analysis, all innovations and creativity in the world go back to individual achievements and the extent to which they are adopted by society. But the chances of the individual to unlock their inner sources depend upon the attention they receive from their parents and teachers. The most important task of the educator is to encourage the talents of the individual and allow them to bear fruit in society, not to exploit the new generation for the benefit of the one-track continuation of pre-established technical-economic paths of development.

According to Steiner's view, the human being should grow up free from the demands of the state and economic life, until as an active citizen they can take part in the shaping of these branches of society. When the demands of the modern industrial state influence the pace of work and the examination requirements of the educational system to too great a degree, the inevitable result is youth and student revolts (see also the section on the 'Industrialized School,' page 232).

The right of the coming generation to such a free education which allows their impulses and talents to unfold in a comprehensive way, so that they can someday reform the existing society, is probably the most important reason Rudolf Steiner gives for the establishment of independent schools and independent universities. These can be financed by gifts and donations as well as by legally established grants from the economics sphere of society. Teachers in the schools and universities form autonomous co-operatives which, by working independently together with their students and others around them, care for the rising generation of teachers and which autonomously decide on all questions relating to curricula, methods of teaching and other aspects of their common work.

This same independence must also hold good in the field of science. The misuse of power practised by government and industry in many countries (especially by the great powers for their military ends) offers proof in many instances that influential circles of politicians, or businesspeople, who have the financial means at their disposal, can (with respect to their special goals) 'order' researchers, research programmes, and even the outcome of research. Today this is widespread and can only be prevented in a radical way if the whole field of science governs itself independently and autonomously in a manner similar to that of education. It goes without saying that researchers who are so financed, and even if the grants which they receive have no specific conditions attached, remain dependent on their environment in many practical respects. But it must also be equally clear that the final decisions on the selection of projects and methods of investigation must be within the jurisdiction of the panel of researchers themselves.

One consequence of this independence would be that the institutions of education and research throughout the world would be free to interact and collaborate without regard for political boundaries.

These same possibilities for financial support, self-determination and international co-operation would appertain in a similar manner to all bodies of independent spiritual life (eg. religious communities, cultural institutions, the media).

It is no doubt evident from the above what an important role an autonomous spiritual life could play in modern society. Institutions are necessary in the complicated network of modern existence whose acknowledged task it is to represent and defend in all situations that which lies within the 'purely human' sphere, irrespective of economic or political interests. This task cannot be properly fulfilled without the guarantee of autonomy.

Law and government

Just as each person needs the institutions of a free spiritual life to fulfil certain purely individual needs, so also do they need the structure of the state to maintain due protection of those rights which must be held equal for all people. The authorities of the legal-political life, which are established through free democratic elections, face enormous challenges within a threefold social order, challenges which are relatively new. One must, for example, also see to it that the financial grants and contributions given for the advancement of education, research, etc. do not involve conditions which might endanger the independence of cultural life. Care must also be taken that independence in economic life, which we shall soon discuss, does not give rise to a concentration and increase in the means of power, which already lie in the hands of leading industrial circles.

Whoever considers these tasks insoluble should bear in mind that they mainly occur in those countries where the patterns of thinking, the formation of laws, and the exercise of government make possible, or even favour, a control or at least an influence on the common cultural life as well as on parliament and the general administrations. Once the necessity of a threefold social order is realized, laws can no doubt be made which gradually lead to an effective distinction between the political, economic and spiritual-cultural functions. Up until now such a thing has never been carried out thoroughly. Those areas for which the decisions of democratically chosen government bodies (rather than economic interests) must be the last court of appeal, are — according to Steiner's conception — those which are valid for work in general, for social welfare, and for the regulation of earnings. That the state makes it a principle to refrain from directly interfering in the matters of cultural life or of its undertakings, need not cause any weakening of the judicial functions to be fulfilled by the state. On the contrary, a government which is not involved through self-interest in other realms of the social structure, can arrive at objective, non-partisan directions and measures. Without any other means than those belonging to it as an administrator of justice, the state can offer decisive assistance in overcoming social conflicts and anomalies.

The economic system

In order to satisfy their material requirements a person living in an industrialized region is completely dependent on the achievements of other people. No matter how strongly the individual may feel that he or she works merely to earn money, it is quite clear that within the modern economic system he serves other consumers through his activity. In most parts of the world self-sufficiency is a thing of the past. Without assigning any moral connotation to the word, one can speak of a 'fraternity' that is the immediate consequence of modern processes of production.

Since we nowadays always want to buy a product where it can be produced most cheaply and easily, the economic system has the natural tendency to create a network of connections which embrace the entire world. However if this tendency were given the opportunity to develop freely, then, independent of all political boundaries, economic associations would form in which the participants themselves or their chosen representatives could consult with one another on production, distribution and consumption, as well as on the necessity and possibility of satisfying the existing demands. The associations could approach the given tasks according to circumstances; in some cases they would work more on a local basis and in others become worldwide. The essential point is that they develop out of purely economic considerations without being influenced by political demands. In this way possibilities will arise for completely new forms of economic relationships between the inhabitants of both industrialized and developing countries.

Whether the individual associations link up to form larger groups or not, all of them would be active in a common field of work, which is one of the three independent spheres of the threefold social order. Their activities would embrace the production and distribution of goods of all sorts, which serve to meet most diverse needs of society. Such a system cannot be carried out in nationalized industries. On the other hand government measures are necessary to guard against the difficulties which are associated with private enterprise in the traditional sense. Here Rudolf Steiner proposed a solution to the problem of ownership which in certain ways represents a middle road between Communism and capitalism. If one wants to avoid too strong an element of bureaucracy and bring into play the strength of individual initiative, then capable individuals must be given the opportunity to control capital freely and means of production during their most productive years. However, when they leave their posts, the right to take over and administer the undertakings which they have built up and expanded is handed over to other capable persons or groups. This would be done after an informed council of the free spiritual life has given its approval. Administration of law directed in this way would render it impossible for rich economic enterprises to be handed down through inheritance into unproductive hands.

Is a threefold social order Utopian?

The construction of a decentralized social order in which each person takes part in three independent spheres of life with their different institutions would, without doubt, cause profound changes in the social life of humanity. One especially significant result would be that the representatives of states and groups of states would not be able to count on the automatic support of worldwide institutions of the cultural and economic spheres for the realization of their own political and military aims. It is obvious that the authorities of the state must have at their disposal all means of assistance which they need to be able to attend to social justice within their confines. The legal functions of the state would then become more important than ever. But beyond that the state would have no further authorized power. Compulsory powers would be extremely limited.

Is it not then Utopian to believe that responsible politicians would ever co-operate in bringing about such an order of things?

Let us take a look at the present world situation. Despite the breakup of the Communist superpower, a number of centralized governments today possess war machinery of almost inconceivable strength. How this machinery of destruction will ever be dismantled, no one knows. The mutual threat of states and allied states rests on a monstrous conglomeration of political, intellectual and economic might which is always concentrated in the hands of a relatively few state functionaries. Local unrest and collapsing systems leave a vacuum into which step the economic and political interests of a small number of ruling people with subsequent increase of centralized powers.

Only when the functions of intellectual life (upbringing, education, research, formation of public opinion) and the functions of economic life (industry, agriculture, finance) are removed from the direct sphere of state power, can these dangers be avoided. One of the most widespread Utopian ideas in our contemporary society is that the worldwide wish for peace and security can be satisfied without such extensive decentralization.

If such a social change were ever to become reality, public opinion would have to be re-educated on an international scale, even in countries at present governed by a dictatorship. Much detailed information would have to be passed on, much time would have to be expended, and perhaps also much suffering endured.

In 1919 Rudolf Steiner hoped that the required social measures initiated through conscientious statesmen could be understood and then carried into effect peacefully and along democratic lines. But the hoped for reformation never materialized. And thus he predicted that the way of humanity would go through violent coups, revolutions and wars, so long as the requirement for a social order in keeping with the times was not fulfilled.

His descriptions of conditions to which one can aspire on the path to a threefold social order were quite down to earth. He constantly emphasized that individual measures could be formed quite differently from the way he himself outlined them. Contrary to many reformatory and revolutionary thinkers, he consciously emphasized that the ideas he wished to promote would not lead to a social paradise. He cherished no illusions about the moral capabilities of those with political and economic power or of people in general. The goal he worked for was no Utopia, but rather a system of society which recognizes the social and anti-social impulses of the human being. In its realization this society promotes just those social capabilities which, in spite of all weaknesses and egoism, can come to life when healthy forms of social life are developed on the basis of true humanity and a feeling for the needs of the time. Whoever wishes to understand Rudolf Steiner education in its full implications will have to come to terms with the ideas of the threefold social order. Because one of the fundamental goals of his art of education is the endeavour to awaken and to cultivate these social capabilities already in childhood and youth.

The first Waldorf School – a result of the threefold social order

Of the seeds sown by the Movement for a threefold social order after the First World War, only one really took root. That one, however, proved to have strong life forces. It was the first Waldorf School.

It all began on April 23, 1919, in the tobacco storeroom of the Waldorf-Astoria Cigarette Factory in Stuttgart, Germany. The workers were crowded together on benches and on chairs. Some were sitting on large bags of tobacco lined up against the wall at the back of the hall. The head of the firm, Emil Molt, introduced Rudolf Steiner as a 'social philosopher.' How could someone coming from abroad, from neutral, well-fed Switzerland, understand the needs of the common people in the midst of post-war misery and famine? The listeners were markedly reserved until the speaker turned to problems of education: 'All of you, as you sit here, from the sixteen-year-old girl apprentice to the workers in their sixties, suffer from the fact that your real personality has been buried because from a certain moment there was only the hard school of life for you, but no longer any real education.' He began to speak of something that did not yet exist but was a need of the times, namely a comprehensive school of twelve classes (grades), comprising primary and secondary school (public and high school in North American terms), and available to everyone, regardless of social background. Now he had won the hearts of his listeners!

Herbert Hahn who was present at the time called this moment 'the actual hour of the birth of the Waldorf School.'* The wish of the workers for such a school, so clearly expressed, created the basis for its formation. On the following day, some of the workers came and asked whether their children could attend such a school as Steiner had described.

For some time Emil Molt had already nurtured thoughts about a school. Now he wanted to act upon them. His first step was to ask Rudolf Steiner to take over the direction of the educational side. His aim was to open the school in September 1919. He bought an empty building overlooking Stuttgart, and which had previously been used as a restaurant. He had it renovated and acquired the necessary equipment.

Only two days after the lecture in the tobacco storeroom the first talk between Steiner, Molt and two future teachers took place. It was late at night. Steiner, as usual, had a day of intense work behind him. He came straight from a lecture to the workers at the Daimler works. 'Rudolf Steiner quickly shook off the last traces of fatigue. What he had to say to us became ever more fresh, ever more invigorating.' He made a number of suggestions for the initial preparations and commented in some detail on the timetable and curriculum he envisaged.

A course on Education for the People

In the course on Education for the People, given in May and June 1919, Rudolf Steiner formulated his ideas on the art of education. His impulse for a new form of education for all classes of people had nothing in common with the social ambitions or denominational interests normally associated with the term 'private school.' It encompassed everyone, independent of their world-view or position in society. The basic ideas of the course on Education for the People outlined the social intentions of the Waldorf School and proved to be all the more

---

* 'Rudolf Steiner and his pupils,' *Golden Blade* 1958.

up-to-date in the light of present-day tendencies to do away with traditional forms of schooling. A few passages serve to illustrate this.

The school of the future must be based on a more fundamental knowledge of human beings. 'If we start from this premise, nothing else can spring from it but a comprehensive school for everyone. For, of course, the laws of human development between about the seventh year and approximately the fourteenth to fifteenth are the same for all.' Later, education has to be more specialized. 'But above all ... a certain part of education must be the same for people of all classes ... Everyone must have the opportunity of the same *general* education, whether he is eventually going to do manual or professional work.' Up to the age of twenty everyone should be allowed to go to such a differentiated school in order to develop their powers of responsible judgment. 'When in the future the carpentry and engineering apprentices sit together in the same places of learning as those who may one day be teachers then the result will be an education that is at the same time specialized and "comprehensive."'*

In a lecture to teachers in January 1922, Rudolf Steiner enlarged on this idea when he proposed the inclusion of preparatory vocational training in conjunction with workshops in the schools for those young people inclined towards practical occupations. Teaching in such schools would include certain subjects common to all. 'Nobody should pass through this part of his life without acquiring some notion of what happens in agriculture, trade, industry and the crafts. These must be treated as special subjects, they are much more important than a lot of stuff crammed into the teaching of adolescents.' All the teaching, especially of history, geography and science, should be the same for all the students, 'but in such a way as to be always related to the human being, so that man meets and recognizes man as a being belonging to the universe.'

There is only one goal for such a school: the education of the human being. The first condition of reaching this goal is a fundamental reform of teacher training. 'Today, when a candidate for the teaching profession is being examined, he is very often tested on his knowledge of facts which, with a little application, he can later pick up from an encyclopedia or a textbook, should he not be familiar with them. This kind of test can be entirely omitted when examining teachers ... Conversely, present-day examinations should establish whether the person who is to teach and educate evolving human beings is able to form helpful relationships with the growing, developing pupils, and is capable of appreciating their needs.'

Preparations for the opening of the School

Rudolf Steiner regarded the right of the independent school to choose its own teachers as an essential condition for the independence of spiritual life. In the negotiations with the South German school authorities, as well as in his further activities on behalf of the school, he agreed to compromise regarding official curricula and regulations for examinations, but not with regard to the principle of the free selection of teachers. As soon as his plans concerning this point were accepted, he saw his way clear to start a school.

Now the foundation for the new education had to be laid. This was and still remains a knowledge of the human being approached from the three aspects of body, soul and spirit — a concept of human beings based on spiritual science.

On the morning of August 21, the teachers who

---

* *Education as a Force for Social Change.*

had been asked by Rudolf Steiner to undertake the teaching came together. Most of them, but not all, had had some pedagogical experience. Today it is regarded as essential for a future Waldorf teacher to have attended a course on Waldorf pedagogy, in addition to other qualifications. In the place of such a course, Rudolf Steiner at that time gave a fifteen-day course, and followed this up with further lecture courses during the School's early years.

Every morning from 9am to 11am, he spoke on the 'Study of Man': concentrated descriptions of the most important functions of the human soul in connection with physiological processes.

These lectures were taken down in shorthand and published (in English as *The Foundations of Human Experience),* as were almost all of the lectures given by Rudolf Steiner. This course of lectures is not easy to comprehend but it is of particular depth and value. It is something to return to again and again, a scientific basis for meditational study from which the teacher can profit throughout life. It contains the essence of Rudolf Steiner's pedagogical insight.

The hour-and-a-half long practical teaching course followed at 11am. In these sessions the curriculum from the first to the eighth class was presented in lively and comprehensive descriptions. These are the fundamental outlines of Waldorf methods of teaching.

The many lecture courses which Rudolf Steiner gave later on educational subjects can be regarded as elaborations of what he described here for the first time. *Practical Advice to Teachers,* as it was called in the English edition, is an inexhaustible source of practical advice to which the teacher can refer time and again.

During the seminars in the afternoons, those attending the course did speech training, made contributions themselves, and held discussions about the temperaments and other educational topics. During these seminars Rudolf Steiner made very detailed suggestions for handling human and practical problems in the classroom.

On September 6, a festival took place in which the first pupils of the school participated with their parents and met their future teachers.

Steiner's activities in the new School

On September 7, Rudolf Steiner opened the school. In concentrated form he outlined the pedagogical aims he had in mind and, in conclusion, stressed that the Waldorf School was not going to be a school embracing any particular philosophy saying, 'Anyone who says that anthroposophically orientated spiritual science is now founding the Waldorf School with the intention of establishing its outlook in this school is not — and I say this on the opening day — speaking the truth. It is not our intention to teach the growing human being our principles, the contents of our world-conception. We are not aiming at education for the sake of any special dogma. Our aim is that what we have gained from spiritual science shall become a living force in education.'

When the school started it had eight classes and about 300 pupils. It carried the name of the factory with which most of the parents, at that time, were connected, the 'Free Waldorf School.' Although he lived in Dornach, Switzerland, and was constantly burdened with many other responsibilities, Rudolf Steiner was closely involved with the work of the school.

Caroline von Heydebrand, one of the first teachers at the school, has given vivid descriptions of those early days:

At the beginning, teachers and children

alike had many difficulties. The children were presented with something completely new. Right up to the top classes, children from all social strata were included in all classes. The Waldorf School was the first in Germany to carry this comprehensive principle right through the whole school. There were pupils from grammar, secondary and elementary schools (high schools, junior high schools and public schools) in the classes. Boys and girls were together. The children were not used to this, nor were the teachers. Learning to live together presented problems.

Naturally, there were difficulties over discipline. One day, Rudolf Steiner — who on his frequent visits to Stuttgart spent much of his time at the Waldorf School — came into a noisy and unruly class. He began to tell the whole class a story …
He knew a city and in that city a school, and in that school a class, and in that class there were children of such and such characters, and they did such and such things. The children began to nudge one another: 'That's us … he means us!' But they did not resent this, for he had not said anything critical. He went on to describe how the children's behaviour would affect the teacher's health. At the end he told them how that class had improved. At that, the children were deeply satisfied. One always had the feeling when Dr Steiner was taking a class that an immensely deep sense of satisfaction was present. Peace spread over the children. They were quite natural, quite lively, but not particularly quiet. They did not try to give the impression of being particularly well-behaved. However, one sensed a quiet satisfaction which permeated the class.

When, in teachers' meetings, one spoke to Dr Steiner about one of the children in any of the classes, he would ask where the child sat in the classroom. He was able to recall everything about the child when he was told where the child usually sat — near the window, or in the centre of the third row, in a corner, or close to the door, etc. That was the case when the Waldorf School was still small. Later, as the School grew, he would ask to see the children singly.

In one class there was a particularly difficult boy. During lessons the teacher often had to hold his hands as he stood by his side. From time to time, one had to take him for a walk outside for a while, and then he would calm down. Dr Steiner's advice about this boy was that he should make shoes. The teacher at the Waldorf School who knew how to make shoes let this boy do repair work. He improved greatly and could be kept at the School until almost the end of elementary school … Often the advice Dr Steiner gave for the treatment of difficult children was of this nature. Hundreds of examples could be given. Many children at this School were cured by him or set on a healing path.*

Herbert Hahn describes a boy who had a kind-hearted mother but whose domestic circumstances were pitiful. He disturbed the lessons by his fidgeting and his almost pathological talkativeness. The class teacher was very worried about this child's development. Rudolf Steiner advised the teacher to put a question to the boy every day to

---

* Caroline von Heydebrand, *Rudolf Steiner in der Waldorf Schule.*

be answered on the following day, and to continue this practice over several weeks. The teacher, following this suggestion, became aware of a look in the eyes of the boy when he gave his considered answer to the question put to him on the previous day. Gradually, there was something quiet, open and serious in the boy's gaze, something which was not there at other times. The whole face took on the same expression. This went on for some time. 'And strangely enough, the fact that he was questioned day after day and allowed to give his answer the following day, had a healthy influence on the soul-life of this boy. Slowly, his self-confidence, hitherto weak, began to grow stronger.' He changed — and the change was permanent. The observations and suggestions made by Rudolf Steiner arose quite naturally from the day-to-day work. At teachers' meetings he would report in detail, in an objective and factual manner what he had observed about the character of specific children, and how these observations had led him to his diagnosis and to the required therapeutic measures. Many examples could be given. To indicate the way in which Rudolf Steiner proceeded, here is just one case.

Dr Eugen Kolisko, the school doctor, described a seven-year-old boy who had just come to the school and was causing special difficulties. He could hardly keep still and had a strong impulse to be destructive. In sudden outbursts of temper he would hurl furniture and other objects about with abnormal physical energy. It required the strength of several people to control and calm him. 'His walk was awkward, swaying without firm control. His face was pale and drawn with a drooping lower jaw, and a darkly scowling forehead. I do not believe that he had laughed much in his life. At the slightest provocation he would fly into a violent rage. His whole face was like a mask which the soul could not seem to penetrate.' Unable to take part in regular class work, he went to a special class. To the surprise of the teachers and the doctor, Rudolf Steiner was confident of his recovery. He described how formative forces active in every living organism (observable to supersensory perception), were only partially able to penetrate this boy's head. Steiner suggested a number of medical and pedagogical measures.

> After a few months, the boy was able to laugh, had developed a more human expression, began to wake up, stopped his tantrums, and finally proved to be a very lovable boy, something one would not have suspected possible before. After he had undergone treatment for three years, he fitted in quite well with the other children of his age. His parents were then transferred to another place. Today, at the age of about eleven, he is at another school with his own age group. I am convinced that without this treatment, it would never have been possible to include him in ordinary lessons. Rudolf Steiner saw him only once or twice, but what he observed on the first occasion and what he could say about him saved this child.*

The Waldorf School was founded definitely for healthy and 'normal' children. This is still the case in Waldorf Schools today. There was no selection and no 'confrontation' between teachers and pupils — discipline being created out of confidence and co-operation — in fact, independent children with initiative were particularly well-placed in this school. Pupils with special difficulties were transferred to a special class. This was directed by an extremely skilled teacher

---

* Caroline von Heydebrand, *Rudolf Steiner in der Waldorf Schule.*

whose work Rudolf Steiner followed with special attention.

Teacher-child relationship

For the times when the Waldorf School was founded, many aspects of its organization were unusually permissive. Rudolf Steiner was not in favour of compulsory homework in the lower classes. He recommended voluntary tasks, formulated in such a way as to stimulate interest. Not until grade six or seven did he regard compulsory work as being of any value. He rejected strict and enforced discipline. Occupation with paints and brushes, notebooks made by the children, reciting plays, songs and music made life in the classroom colourful and busy. Judged with an ordinary yardstick, the atmosphere in the school was rather easy-going. Especially in the higher classes, the pupils were free to a degree which was undreamt of by their contemporaries in state schools. Rudolf Grosse, who was later a Waldorf teacher for many years, joined the tenth class in 1922 at the age of seventeen. He reports on his first impressions:

> For a pupil coming, like myself, from the usual grammar school, everything at the Waldorf School was astonishingly new. When I came into the class, with which I was to become very closely connected, I met a group of young people who were utterly frank, straightforward and with an air of freedom about them. I was speechless with admiration. For each seemed to set his own standard of behaviour.*

In the lower grades there were, of course, some rules of discipline but they were as few as possible. On the whole, all the work in the school was held together by one force only, the direct relationship between the teachers and pupils. Where this contact was absent or had deteriorated, problems quickly arose, which called for renewed efforts on the teacher's part.

The upper school (high school)

Rudolf Steiner had noticed a growing rift between the pupils in the senior class and some of the teachers. He said that lessons had become lectures, with too little discussion and human contact. Gradually, as Steiner predicted, trouble broke out. One of the girls wrote a letter to Rudolf Steiner who then invited the whole class to talk in the teacher's room. Rudolf Grosse reports:

> He sat behind a large desk, and we were standing around him in a semi-circle. At his invitation, one spoke — then another. Four or five of the pupils spoke and to each one Rudolf Steiner listened quietly and seriously. He himself did not say a word. What had been troubling them? Well, for example, one teacher was lacking in authority. During the lessons, he could very easily be diverted from his subject. This the class exploited — and consequently they did not learn enough. In another instance, the complaint was that the teachers only knew them in class, but knew nothing about them out of class, etc. The talk lasted for less than half an hour and then we were dismissed in a friendly manner, without any discussion having taken place. When school began again after the holidays, we noted to our surprise that we had different teachers for two important subjects, and our lessons were as

---

* Rudolf Grosse, *Erlebte Pädagogik.*

we had wanted them to be for a long time.

Perhaps it should be added that the changes were made by Rudolf Steiner in full agreement with the teachers concerned.

As the preparation for the lessons included considering every single pupil, allowing a picture of each one to stand before the mind, the problem of over-taxing the teacher arose. How was a teacher to find time for all these tasks?

The Waldorf teachers in those early years were themselves learning. Rudolf Steiner showed them by advice and example how to prepare lessons and lectures carefully by strict self-discipline and well-balanced study, even under great pressure of work and time.

Culmination of events

During the years 1922–24, Rudolf Steiner's life culminated in a series of outstanding events. He accepted the pressing offer by a well-known lecture agency for two lecture tours through Germany's largest cities. During the first two weeks of his tour, he spoke in all to some 20,000 people. As interest in anthroposophy and Rudolf Steiner grew, opposition also increased. The second tour, in May 1922, put Steiner in some dangerous situations. In two cities, Munich and Elberfeld, agitators at the meetings endangered his life. The instigators, the kind of people who later adopted National Socialist ideas, saw in Rudolf Steiner a decisive threat because of his cosmopolitan social ideas, and his attitude toward establishing the freedom of the spirit of people. On New Year's night 1922/23, the wooden structure of the Goetheanum was destroyed by arson.

Parallel with these events, the anthroposophical movement, which had begun to work in many social, scientific and artistic fields, out of the impulse for cultural renewal, passed through its own inner crisis. This was largely due to the fact that some of Rudolf Steiner's collaborators had taken responsibilities upon themselves which they could no longer cope with, either practically or spiritually. Finally, over Christmas 1923, he decided to renew and reorganize the whole anthroposophical work, by founding the General Anthroposophical Society, of which he became President.

The Waldorf teachers felt much involved personally in these events — while work at the school had to continue undisturbed. They were capable of these superhuman efforts only because they were helped by working with Rudolf Steiner. The comment of Rudolf Grosse (as mentioned before, at that time a student in the upper school) is quite revealing: 'Looking back on the achievements of those teachers, one can only describe them as outstanding. I have known no other body of teachers so unreservedly devoted to their educational tasks as that original college of teachers of the first Waldorf School.'

Between October 19 and November 13, 1925, the Württemberg school authorities carried out an official inspection of the Waldorf School. Their extensive report recognized and praised the methods used in the school. Their comments on the teachers was that this 'college of teachers, intellectually and morally of so high a calibre, bestows upon the Waldorf School its special character and its considerable level of achievement.'

In all of these events, Rudolf Steiner himself was the main enigma. It was often noticeable that the treble pressure of the tremendous burden of work, harsh public attacks, and the inadequacies of those who collaborated with him, was hard for him to bear. However, he lost neither his creative powers to produce results, nor his self control. On the evening of Year's Day in 1923, only hours after the catastrophic fire had wiped out the Goetheanum, and the ten years of his architectural and artistic effort, he entered the improvised lecture hall, commented briefly on the sad event, deeply moved but quiet and composed, and then proceeded to give the lecture on a scientific subject as previously announced for that evening.

During 1924, when he was already seriously ill, his work culminated in a continuous sequence of important lecture cycles, courses and discussions. Of the many and varied fields of practical social work for which he then laid the foundations, the biodynamic method of agriculture and the curative educational treatment for children and young people with special needs soon became especially prominent. All who met Rudolf Steiner during that year agree that he radiated more than ever his infectious enjoyment of life and his spontaneous kindness.

Work with the college of teachers

Rudolf Steiner let the teachers know that he thought each day of every pupil. When he was in Stuttgart, the college of teachers felt the high degree of responsibility with which he regarded his work in the Waldorf School. The minutes of the teachers' meetings report the concentrated work done on the everyday problems of teaching — questions of timetable and curriculum, methods of teaching, always with the needs of the individual pupil in the foreground. Rudolf Steiner was extremely well informed in every detail relating to the current work being done in the school. During this phase of the foundation of a new pedagogy, the role of leader was rightly his. The quick grasp and detailed knowledge he brought to difficult queries on special subjects, such as history, literature, history of art, science and mathematics was simply amazing. Yet he never let his superior ability overawe his colleagues.

Under the leadership of Rudolf Steiner, the meetings of the college of teachers became a continuous seminar. He trained the teachers especially to see a challenge in every single child, a divine mystery which the teacher had to penetrate through the art of education, permeated with love, until the point when the young person found their own self.

He was not concerned just with this mystery in the child as an individual. Time and again, and not merely in empty phrases, Rudolf Steiner in lectures and addresses expressed his thanks and that of the teachers, not only to the parents who had entrusted their children to the school, but also to the higher powers who had sent these children down to earth. To his way of thinking, every child is a gift to which one can lay no personal claim. For a few, brief years one is permitted to guide and to care for them until they go out into the stern school of life with powers to choose their own path. The aim of all education must be self-education.

The pupils

The objective love and interest which the pupils received was repaid with affection and love for their school. When Rudolf Steiner, speaking at school festivals, used to ask, 'Are you fond of your teachers?' the answer was a thunderous 'Yes.' This was not the result of mass suggestion. The generous gratitude later shown by former pupils to their school and the teachers proved clearly that their assent had come from genuine feeling.

During the last year of his life, Rudolf Steiner experienced how strong the link was with the pupils when the members of the first graduating class expressed heartfelt desire to keep in touch with him and with the teachers through personal conversations, by asking advice on studies and careers, at old scholars' meetings, and by personal visits. Experience showed that generally speaking the love of former pupils for their school continued, but that in their thinking the young people consistently went their own ways. 'There was sufficient proof to show that the teachers had fulfilled their duties in a purely pedagogical sense through the fact that few former Waldorf students later found their way into anthroposophy.'*

Rudolf Steiner once spoke in Oxford on August 19, 1922, in the lecture course *The Spiritual Ground of Education,* of the 'three golden rules' which should form the fundamental attitude of every educator. By his own example he showed that they could be put into practice. He said, 'The three golden rules must be embraced by the teacher's whole being, not held merely as a theory. They might be summarized thus — to receive the child in gratitude from the world it comes from; to educate the child with love; to lead the child into the true freedom which belongs to man.'

The social aims of Waldorf education

As we have seen, the actual objective of the movement for the threefold social order was to call forth and foster specific human capabilities necessary for a relatively harmonious social life on earth. It is a matter of arriving at the social qualities which can be called the 'inner organs' for freedom, equality and fraternity. Already after the First World War, when Rudolf Steiner was forced to give up the hope of realizing a threefold social order corresponding to these qualities, the possibility arose of founding a way of education through which social capabilities could be fostered.

The following statements may seem arbitrary. However, they give in concentrated form what is to be taken up in detail in the rest of the book and originate from a genuine observation of real life. Rudolf Steiner was the first person who indicated in an all-embracing manner the fundamental laws underlying the life of the human soul, which is here the fundamental issue. But everyone who is willing to take the trouble can test and confirm the validity of these laws in their own environment as well as in life in general.

The urge to imitate predominates in the pre-school age. Not only the visible actions, but also the thoughts and feelings of the people who constantly surround the child, are transformed into a component of his or her own life and actions through his imitative faculties. The moral qualities which the child absorbs in this way from the environment are decisive for his or her future existence. If children at this age are neglected, above all by a lack of real inner contact with their parents, then they will always remain imitators — unstable, dissatisfied people, who not infrequently run after the most primitive examples which they finds before them in life. In extreme cases — and these are apparently becoming more common in many industrialized nations — such children may become morally defective. Psychiatrists and criminologists can quote many cases of people who, through childhood neglect, are compulsively under the control of their more or less animal-like instincts. An awareness of the uniqueness of each human individual and respect of that individual's rights to personal integrity is based on one's capacity

---

* Rudolf Grosse, *Erlebte Pädagogik.*

to hold back to a certain degree one's own base impulses. Generally speaking this attitude is to be found only in adults whose own inner life and soul-qualities were cared for and fostered when they were children.

At about the age of seven a new tendency comes to the fore. The child wants to go to school, wants to learn — but actually only in a certain way: its inner wish is to follow its teacher, and to trust completely all the teacher says and does. In other words, the child needs what Rudolf Steiner calls 'a figure of authority.' Real authority is never gained by harshness or mere force. The only lasting respect is that which arises in the child through affection and inclination as if of its own accord. In the case of those children who found sufficient nourishment in their early years for their imitative impulses, this need for authority arises as a matter of course. If this need is not satisfied, then even here one cannot make up for these deficiencies in such people in later life. In the case of children who have been allowed to make all their own judgments and decisions at too early an age, a certain insecurity arises. Their mistrust and their constant desire to challenge do not reflect spiritual strength but rather inner weakness — such people remain unproductive. Because the need for dependence on someone else was not satisfied in early childhood, these people, especially in their teens, often seek out special 'substitute authorities,' such as pop singers, movie stars, or political dictators. The lack of stability which often prevails makes it very hard for them in later years to work with other people in a natural and harmonious way.

During the period of puberty a further need awakens: the urge to test and to learn to understand the external world as well as all aspects of our existence. In other words, young people have reached the age at which they are sufficiently mature to develop really profound interests. For this to happen they need people who can give them help in an unauthoritative manner yet through warm spiritual contact. Such people can show them the way to knowledge and activity through which life can become meaningful even in the midst of the bleak and impersonal atmosphere which characterizes so many areas of the modern work-a-day world. If they become bored with school or start out in a profession which offers them no room for their thinking and individuality, they become vulnerable to many dangers — especially if they live in a large city. For young people who have received a sufficient inner vitality and security through their education, the need in these years for a deepened knowledge of the world and of people generally arises. To sum up, the social capabilities which can be fostered in the ways described above are as follows.

Through imitation in the pre-school years:
　— a feeling for the freedom and integrity
　of other people;

Through authority in the primary and middle school years:
　— a feeling of security in life and with
　that the ability to participate in democratic
　co-operation;

Through close, unauthoritative human contact with instructors during the process of learning in the teenage years:
　— a deepened interest in the world and for
　the life-situations of other human beings.

In a lecture series which he held in Dornach in August 1919, *Education as a Force for Social Change,* Rudolf Steiner points out the broad implications of what we are discussing. He describes how the foundations can be laid in early childhood for participation in a free cultural life, in the middle school years for respecting an egalitarian sense of justice and in the adolescent years for contributing to a really social economic life.

The arrangement of the present book has, therefore, arisen from a consideration of the needs and possibilities which arise at the three age levels briefly described here. The development of the growing human being is depicted in three main sections:

The child during the pre-school years;
The first eight years of school;
The last four years of school.

There are in addition chapters dealing with general educational principles and the modern world.

The Child During the Pre-School Years

The child as sense-organ

When a new-born infant sucks its mother's breast, its whole body often quivers the moment milk flows into its mouth. It is not only the mouth that feels it; the child reacts as if its whole body were the organ of its sense of taste. During the first years of a small child's life, we observe the same phenomenon in other instances: the whole body moves whenever it suddenly sees or hears something. Even if nothing bad happens afterwards, the consequence of strong stimulation can be overpowering and can precipitate a violent fit of crying. Even the most subtle feelings and gestures are perceived by the child. Many parents will have experienced how difficult it is to conceal their own fluctuating moods from their children. Even if one tries to conceal one's irritation it is noticed at once by children, who suddenly behave more violently or obstinately than previously. For example, the following happened to one father.

After being drawn into an exceptionally irritating incident through the fault of others, he came home. He had to pass through a room in which his three-month-old daughter was lying. Usually she laughed when he leaned over her. This time when he opened the door he was still full of anger. He tried to conceal this and behave as usual. Nevertheless, as he bent down over his little daughter, she began to cry immediately.

Imitation

It is a well-known fact that children imitate their environment. No doubt everyone has observed how little children imitate grown-ups: their gestures, the movement of their hands and feet, even how they clear their throats. At first, children imitate quite unconsciously and only gradually does imitation become a conscious process, coming to expression when children play at being such things as buses, or animals in the zoo, or mothers and fathers. The need to imitate is incredibly deep-seated. When it is inhibited by unsympathetic adults, the consequences can be dangerous. A typical example of this is cited by J.A. Hadfield in his *Childhood and Adolescence:*

> At present I am treating a fourteen-year-old boy with antisocial tendencies. When he is together with other children at school he becomes violent and often has sudden outbursts of crying. His behaviour pattern came about through his being continually prevented from doing what would have given him pleasure. In particular, he was always stopped from joining in with his parents' activities. His mother was a bulldog-type, and the boy had a similar disposition. He was in a continuous state of war and rebellion because he would not easily give up what he had set his mind on. When his mother planted out flowers he was ordered from the garden. He resisted that and was beaten. He began to hate his mother and eventually everyone. How easily all this could have been avoided if his mother had only allowed him to partake in what she

was doing, and if she had shown him how to dig without damaging the plants. After all, all he wanted to do was to imitate her.

Hadfield points out the significance of imitation when he says further: 'Abnormalities arise especially when children copy the bad example of their parents. Arrogant parents make arrogant children.'

For children, imitation is as important as breathing; in fact one might even say sense impressions are breathed in. Imitation could be regarded as the out-breathing process.

The moral effects of impressions in childhood

Rudolf Steiner calls the period from birth to the seventh year the 'age of imitation.' He emphasizes the fact that the actual words spoken to children in the way of exhortation or explanation are of little importance compared with what is happening in their physical surroundings. When a grown-up scolds them, the anger in the voice makes a much deeper impression than the actual words that are said. Steiner hardly ever expressed himself in such forceful terms as in a lecture of August 13, 1924, when he said:

> What you say to a small child, what you teach him, does not make much impression on him. It is what you are, whether you are good and manifest this goodness in your behaviour which is of vital importance, or whether you are irritable and subject to outbursts of temper. In short, all that you yourself do reverberates within the child. One can say that he is a sense organ reacting to every impression to which he is subjected. It is therefore essential to realize that small children do not learn what is right or wrong through their intellects but through all that happens around them. This is transformed in his organism into body, soul and spirit. The child's future health even depends on the behaviour of those around him. The tendencies he develops later depend on the behaviour of those who influenced his earliest years.

Rudolf Steiner was certainly one of the first educationalists who argued the decisive significance of early childhood for the individual's later inner development. In more recent times, doctors, teachers and psychologists, and especially the protagonists of pre-school education, have become aware of the enormous importance of this.

Some results of psychiatric research

One of the pioneers in the field of child psychiatry, John Bowlby, was commissioned by the World Health Organization to investigate the child in relation to its environment. An enlarged version of this report was published under the title *Child Care and the Growth of Love*. Basing his remarks on numerous reports by British doctors, Bowlby declared that the most frequent reason for child neglect is not large families, bad housing, working mothers or other external factors, but has to do with the kind of attitude adopted towards the child. His description of the circumstances in which the children concerned in the study grew up was frequently shattering. Every teacher knows that very often it is in the well-to-do home that the psychological neglect of children is evident.

Bowlby gives some examples of the drastic effects of psychological neglect:

> Psychological treatment was given over a period of some six years to eighty girls in a small home for delinquent girls between the ages of twelve and sixteen. Half were successes and half failures. Response to treatment was related neither to intelligence nor to heredity. Its relationship to the girls' early family experiences, however, was striking.

According to Bowlby, deprivation during the first years of life has just as devastating an effect on the child physically and biologically as the physical disease of rickets. On the basis of comprehensive observations for his studies, he pointed out the basic significance of the presence of the same mother figure being responsible for the child during the first years of its life. This mother-figure need not necessarily be the natural mother. Bowlby asserted that mother love is decisive in the development of the child.

The American child psychiatrist, Professor Selma Fraiberg of the University of Michigan, has devoted a great part of her life to the study of diseases of non-attachment. In her moving and humorous book *The Magic Years,* she has presented a wealth of observations on this subject. She sums up the result of her research about the development of the young child as follows.

> We have come to know that those psychological qualities which we would call characteristically human, are not part and parcel of the original make-up of the small child …
> They are not instinctive reactions, nor are they acquired by way of natural development. Truly human love, for instance, which is more than self-love, arises as an outcome of human family-life and through the genuine bonds of feeling such as grow between members of a family. Human intelligence depends to a great extent on the ability to use meaningful symbols. Speech, in particular, is not simply the product of a superior human brain and speech-organ, but is acquired through early contacts based on real feeling. Self-consciousness, too, the concept 'I,' that is an awareness of one's personal identity, arises through this early soul-contact between parents and children. Man's triumph over his instinctive nature, his readiness to restrain his own inner drives and to set them certain limits, or even to act against them when they conflict with higher aims and intentions, is something which has to be *learnt*, and which is only learnt through the unfolding of love in the early years of development. Even conscience — that highest achievement in the cultural evolution of humanity — is not just a part of our constitution, but a product of parental love and education.

Physiological effects of childhood impressions

The effects of sense impressions in early childhood do not only work psychologically. They also have physical effects. Perhaps the most striking examples of this are children who have been brought up by animals. The 'wolf-children' of Midnapore, who were discovered in 1920 by the Rev. J.A.L. Singh, were at that time approximately two and eight years old. They displayed a number of peculiar characteristics:

The incisors were longer and more pointed than is usually the case in human beings. The oral cavities were blood-red. The children could squat on the ground but were unable to stand. Their knee and hip joints had not adapted themselves to it … The eyes were almost round. During the day they found it difficult to keep their eyes open, but at night, after twelve o'clock, they were opened wide and shone in the dark as do the eyes of cats and dogs. At night they were able to see considerably better. They showed no fear of the dark, but rather of light and fire. (J.A.L. Singh, *The Diary of the Wolf-Children of Midnapore.*)

The children were captured and taken along to the missionary station where they were looked after with meticulous loving care. The younger girl died one year after her discovery; the older child lived nine more years, learned about fifty words, and toward the end of its life showed clear signs of intelligence as well as spiritual growth.

This is a shattering example which shows the strength of the physical effect inherent in early childhood impressions. The physiological peculiarities which appear in children reared by human beings as a result of their early experiences — and not as a result of inherited tendencies — are naturally much less noticeable. But they are there. Rudolf Steiner emphasized that:

In the later periods also, growth takes place; but throughout the whole succeeding life, growth is based on the forms which were developed in this first life-period. If true forms were developed, true forms will grow; if misshapen forms were developed, misshapen forms will grow. We can never repair what we have neglected as educators in the first seven years. Just as Nature brings about the right environment for the physical human body before birth, so after birth the educator must provide for the right physical environment. It is the right physical environment alone, which works upon the child in such a way that the physical organs shape themselves correctly … What goes on in his physical environment, this the child imitates, and in the process of imitation his physical organs are cast into the forms which then become permanent. 'Physical environment' must, however, be taken in the widest imaginable sense. It includes not only what goes on around the child in the material sense, but everything that takes place in the child's environment — everything that can be perceived by his senses, that can work from the surrounding physical space upon the inner powers of the child. This includes all the moral or immoral actions, all the wise or foolish actions, that the child sees … The physical organs shape their forms through the influence of the physical environment. Good sight will be developed in the child if his environment has the right conditions of light and colour, while in the brain and blood-circulation the physical foundations will be laid for a healthy moral sense if the child sees moral actions in his environment. If before his seventh year the child sees only foolish actions in his surroundings, the brain will assume such forms as adapt it also to foolishness in later life. *(The Education of the Child.)*

Coming at a time when the significance of early childhood experiences were still not fully realized, such a statement as Rudolf Steiner's must have seemed incredible. The extraordinarily prolific material which has been gathered on this subject in the course of the last few decades by researchers and educators, however, thoroughly confirms his descriptions of the child as a sense-organ.

The first three years

The first three years have a special significance for our whole life, not just for the years of childhood. That we do not remember these years consciously does not alter this fact at all. This time in our life, although hidden from memory, is vital to our human existence, to our whole life-journey. At no other period were we so exposed to the impressions of our environment. Never again will we be so absorbed in our own bodily processes. Never again, through our own oft-repeated efforts of will, do we achieve such core abilities as these three: walking, speaking and thinking, which we shall then apply every day for the rest of our lives.

Walking, speaking and thinking

To learn to observe and understand what actually goes on when children practise these fundamental functions is one of the most important tasks of all people who educate and bring up children. From such insights we can gain the strength to bring forth the understanding patience, the tender warmth and the perceptive security which the child needs as a living atmosphere and which is even more important than hygiene.

Walking reminds us of the physical phenomenon of gravity: our long body-form with its high centre of gravity and the insignificant supporting area of the soles of our feet are no guarantee that we will be able to walk. Our vertical bearing is a continual complicated balancing act. Children are greatly astonished as they become aware of this new ability for the first time at about the end of the first year. Their triumphant attitude not only reflects the joy adults experience on this occasion. This delight comes from within and joyously bears witness to the fact that this is one of the great events in our life. The whole organism is orientated anew in space.

The fact that we later can recognize a person immediately by their bearing, their gait and their gestures shows how much they reveal of their character in their movements. The hidden secret of the will becomes visible.

After a few months the next phase of development usually begins. The newly-gained view of their surroundings now awakens a particular need. The child goes forth like Adam in the Garden of Eden and gives names to things. The sounds of desire and comfort, the inarticulate expressions of pain and joy as well as repetitive childish babbling begin to converge into a meaningful unity. The child often learns several hundred words within as short a period as six months. Three and four-year-old children already command a number of complicated grammatical rules, whose logical significance they do not appreciate until much later. Through direct practice, they know perfectly well how to handle gender, number, case and tense, how to apply adjectives and how to use primary and secondary clauses. Never again in life can one enter into a new language so quickly and with so little effort. Speaking reveals the relationship of human beings with things and

'When I cross the road.' Self-portrait of a four-year-old girl (Gothenburg, Sweden).

In many drawings of small children, perceptions of the world around them are interwoven with the experience of their own physical organism. A child who suddenly begins to draw people with enormous noses may have a cold and therefore a stronger awareness of its nose.

with the nature of our environment — a relationship which is rooted in feeling. Thinking is awakened by language. When a two-year-old looks about at the dinner table and calls out, 'Daddy spoon, Mummy spoon, Johnny spoon, Mary spoon — everybody spoon!' she has made a great discovery. All spoons have something in common which lies hidden in the name of the object, in the secret of the word. This is known as 'concept.' Learning to walk and speak are events which are played out in the physical world and which are characterized by a certain dramatic quality. The first attempts at thinking, on the other hand, show the first signs of the ability to detach oneself from the environment and to become quiet and contemplative.

The German child-psychologist, E. Köhler, has given a fine description of a two-and-a-half-year-old in the first moments of reflection: 'When Anna doesn't completely understand something and thinks about it, she stands quietly and places her hands on her back. Her eyes grow large and she looks into the distance; her mouth tightens up a bit and she is silent. After this exertion a certain tiredness takes over. Her expression changes. Nature provides for relaxation.' (Cited by K. König, *The First Three Years of the Child*). Thinking opens the door to all experiences of consciousness and self-consciousness; it is our most important means of orientating ourselves in the world and remaining alert.

The precise age at which children learn to walk, speak and think can vary a good deal. However parents need not let themselves become alarmed over this. One need only feel concern if the actual sequence is different. To understand this we may consider the following: what we want, we conceive of in a waking state; however if we indulge in feelings we are still in a dream-like state. Since the will develops entirely in a state of consciousness similar to that during sleep, children whose will is particularly strong seem to be half asleep and develop quite slowly in their early years. Later, sometimes not until they become adults, they show their true strength. Many children do not want to expose themselves either to criticism or ridicule. For this reason they can be reluctant to begin speaking.

One fine day they can suddenly express themselves almost flawlessly and with a remarkable vocabulary.

Walking, speaking and thinking follow one after the other. Gestures and movements are transferred to the speech centre of the brain and the entire physical organization of the head. This relationship becomes obvious when we try to make left-handed people use their right hand. If a left-handed child is too forcefully trained to use her right hand, she will soon start to stutter. Life is first of all gesture and this carries over into the motor-apparatus of speech. For the educator there are three primary rules to bear in mind: when teaching a child to walk, accompany all offers of help with *love;* when teaching a child to speak, take pains to speak the *truth* yourself; do not confuse your child through haphazard commands, be *clear* in your own thinking! Because 'To produce confusion in the environment of the child through unclear thinking is the actual cause of nervousness in our modern society.' (Rudolf Steiner, lecture of Aug 10, 1923.)

Actually there is only one thing which can cause serious development disturbance in normal, healthy children: lack of contact with other people. If children grow up in institutions instead of in a family, most of them learn to sit, walk, speak and think later than others do. Through a lack of contact with others they can become hindered or confused in their entire development.

The assertion that the 'walking instinct' is innate is based upon the observation that a newborn child whose trunk is leaning forward a bit and whose feet are resting on a flat surface will attempt to take small steps. However, this reaction more or less disappears, during the first half year. First the child must struggle to acquire the ability to lift its head, to crawl, to sit and stand, before it once more can learn the art of moving its feet forward along the floor. Alfred Nitschke studied an almost three-year-old girl who had an unusual manner of walking, but in whom doctors were unable to detect any pathological abnormality. Upon closer investigation he found that the little girl was imitating her father who walked with the help of an artificial limb. At a children's home in Teheran with insufficient staff it was ascertained that 60% of the one-year-olds could not sit and 80% of the three-year-olds could not walk. One child, who had never had the opportunity to imitate people who walked upright, would probably never learn to raise itself, like the wolf-children.

Even if we know that imitation is of such salient importance for the development of small children, in practice we often lack the trust and courage to bring children up in accordance with this principle. We attempt instead to interfere with the development of the child by other means.

Unnecessary interference

Small children are lovable. Many of the nice and pleasant things with which we keep them busy consciously or unconsciously influence the learning process of young children in a definite direction. For example we stretch our fingers towards them and help them learn to sit and stand. But if we do this before their bones and muscles have developed sufficiently, damage to the bones and back may result. We may also notice that the same people who at one time buy a suitable picture book out of pedagogical enthusiasm in order to teach the child as many new concepts as possible in a short time, at another time speak to the child in babbling baby language because it sounds so charming. In this way, however, we actually slow down the child's development. Small children want to develop and orientate themselves in real language. Often the children themselves are not particularly enthused at hearing infantile expressions. A well-meaning aunt described a dog to a three-year-old as a 'woof-woof.' After long, gloomy reflection the child said dryly, 'It's called a dog.'

On its own, the child may for a while chatter away in charming baby talk. Eventually, however, imitation leads the child along the right path. Still, an adult must never babble! We should keep our way of speaking free from sentimentality and pretence. Through imitating cultivated speech the child develops truthfulness, clarity and style. As a result, both the inner life and the organs of speech develop harmoniously.

Can prohibitions be avoided?

There are other ways in which adults may thoughtlessly interfere with the development of small children.

Little children can cause enormous difficulties. Mothers are often exhausted and frequently have no help. Our complicated everyday life is full of things that are breakable or dangerous. How are we to prevent children from pulling down the tablecloth, taking books off the shelf, knocking pots off the window sill, lighting matches, chewing cigarette butts or starting the car when the key has been left in the ignition? Not only psychologists know that constant warnings and prohibitions can lead to dampening initiative in a child, and in extreme cases cripple it forever. Of course, one possibility is to cover the wall sockets with safety plugs and to hide as many breakable and dangerous objects as possible. But there are always certain risks which cannot be avoided; furthermore, life in the living room would become empty and unnatural if we were to remove all objects not suitable for young children. Neither is it a good idea to allow children to handle the remaining objects in any way they please.

In his book on punishment in the education of the child, the Waldorf teacher, Erich Gabert, gives an example of how this stage of development of the small child can be dealt with. A child is to be warned against burning itself on the stove: 'During the weeks before the stove was to be lit again, a little game was played with the child and repeated several times ... An adult placed his hand near the stove, withdrew it quickly without touching the stove, and then cried, "Oh! That's hot! We don't touch that." The child does the same again and again until an aversion for the stove is taken for granted.'

Such preventative games can, of course, be devised ad infinitum. But do we have enough time?

The individuality of the small child

When we consider how far we should go in our concern for the small child we are ultimately led to the greatest and most profound question: what demands do the individuality and nature of the small child make upon us? There are very few people who can remain aloof to the unusually deep effect children have on us during the first few years of their life. It is not simply a question of those characteristics which, according to biologists, arouse our protective and tender instincts: soft hair, round bodies, awkward movements, etc. All of these charming characteristics may be found in puppies and kittens as well. We can be moved by a sense of devotion when confronted with a very small child. We feel that we stand before something which surpasses our normal powers of comprehension.

The situation of the small child is actually a paradox. At an age when tasks such as dressing oneself, making a bed, eating with a knife and fork etc. present almost insuperable difficulties, these children effortlessly have experiences which enable them to learn two of our most demanding accomplishments: speaking and thinking. There is no animal that can walk in a completely upright position, that is able to carry on a conversation about inner experiences, that can disassociate itself from the outside world in order to think about the world conceptually and formulate its conceptions in words. However, a child learns all this at an age when it is more helpless than any animal. After having studied the developmental phases of the growing human being for many years, the well-known American psychologist, Arnold Gesell, summarized his findings in words filled with a deep reverence for the underlying law of development he had discovered:

> Those parents and teachers who consider children to be so easily malleable that they can be moulded only through persistent external influences have not yet advanced to an understanding of the true nature of the psyche. The psyche can be compared to a plant, but not to a lump of clay. For clay cannot grow — it is shaped entirely from without. A plant, on the other hand,

receives its form from within, more precisely from its inner forces of growth. It is these forces to which this book wishes to draw attention.' (A. Gesell, *The Child from Five to Ten.*)

Arnold Gesell might not associate himself with Steiner and his work — but it must be said that both describe the same forces; one describes their physical manifestation, and the other their supersensory phenomenon. Steiner portrays the child as standing in a different relationship to the spiritual world during the first three years of its life from that of its later years. Mighty, supersensory forces work upon the child which are no longer recognizable in the same way once the life of the soul becomes more conscious. 'It is these forces that enable man to enter into a definite relationship with the force of gravity. It is also these forces that form the larynx, which in turn so moulds the brain as to make it a living instrument for thought, feeling and will.' Of course, small children as a rule do not experience the supersensory directly and consciously. To be sure, there are poets and philosophers who maintain with certainty that they had such experiences during their early childhood. But the intensive connection with the spiritual world need by no means be a conscious one. Steiner offers a dramatic image of a vestigial 'telephone' connection with the life in which the child found itself before birth. Later in life the human being is never again so directly 'subordinated to the direction of that spiritual world to which he belongs, as during his first three years.' *(The Spiritual Guidance of the Individual and Humanity).*

But to this spiritual world also belong — from children's points of view — their mother, father and the other people in their closest surroundings. That is the reason why their moods and thoughts so directly and so strongly influence the child. That is also the reason for the feeling of dependence, especially between the child and its mother to whom it is most profoundly bound and who has the most effect. That is also the reason why the child is so sensitive to impressions which come from strangers. This leads to several penetrating conclusions.

The circumstances through which children learn everything basic present themselves as deep wisdom. We must not interfere with these processes. We should only be present so that they may imitate us. We must try to become human beings worthy of imitation.

In this way the picture is completed which Gesell painted of the soul of a child as a plant; what the earth, the rain and sunshine are for plants, the child's surroundings and the adults around should be for the child.

Steiner's description of the first three years agrees with one of the most important discoveries of modern child psychiatry. When Bowlby and other researchers investigated the reaction of children to different forms of spiritual undernourishment, and the change from one 'mother-figure' to another, they found, as already mentioned, that the sensitivity of the child is decidedly greatest during the first three years and then later declines. They found that at this age the deepest of all the child's spiritual needs is to be cared for by one mother.

Experiencing the self

Sometime during the third year the child's behaviour often changes considerably. We all know that very small children like to speak of themselves in the third person: 'Charles wants more jam,' 'Ann is sad.' Gradually this changes and they begin to

speak of themselves as 'I.' Selma Fraiberg points out that among American children this change takes place approximately at the age of two-and-a-half. The basic causes for this often truly mysterious transformation have been described by Rudolf Steiner.

To experience oneself as an individual is something which many children recall as a dramatic event. A three-year-old girl who had just made this discovery, called out, 'I am I, I am I!' In all countries there are stories told by people who have had similar experiences in their own lives. Perhaps one of the loveliest is the one told by the poet, Jean Paul:

> One morning, as a young child, I stood by the door gazing at the wood pile on my left. All at once, like a flash of lightning from heaven, came the inner vision: 'I am I,' and remained as a radiant experience. I had for the first time, and for all time, seen myself as an individuality. A trick of the memory here is hardly imaginable, since no outside account could have added additional elements to an event which happened in the hidden, sacred depths of the human being and whose newness gave eternal meaning to mundane, everyday circumstances.

What happens is a kind of encapsulation. Part of the supersensory forces which formerly acted as a mediator between the child and supersensory world have separated themselves and become the child's 'inner being' and facilitated the experience of the self. The often irritable and stubborn little creative who now emerges, and with artfulness tries out the little word 'no,' frequently seems to be a totally new acquaintance to the parents. The age of defiance has begun.

To use an illustration from Genesis: for the first time man has eaten from the Tree of Knowledge and the portals of Paradise have closed behind him. But not completely; they are still ajar.

The kindergarten years: little material, much imagination

Of the inner capabilities which are at the disposal of an adult, creative imagination is one of the most important. It is no accident that large corporations have psychologists work out refined test methods in order to discover just this quality in prospective employees. Imagination, however, is not only necessary if one is to advance in industry. We need it in our everyday life. The path of life of a person without imagination is stuck in a rut which others have drawn out; such people cannot find their own way and are lacking in initiative and imagination. They are not free.

What actually is 'creative imagination'? Definitions are of little help in describing this quality which arises out of the most profound depths of the human being and brings us knowledge from the most distant heights. Imagination gives us the strength to transcend everything that is and to relate ourselves to everything that is and — through our own activity — to relate to what is in the process of *becoming*. Imagination points towards the future. It fits into existing reality but it also makes attempts to change what has come into being.

The foundation for this quality is established (or ruined) at an early age. Children are full of imagination, as are artists. Any field of artistic endeavour has preserved much of the spontaneous productivity with which all healthy children are equipped. Only as adults do we lose this precious innate gift under the pressure of life's trivialities and of the eternal hankering after advantage and convenience — much to the damage of our enjoyment of work and enthusiasm for life.

Parents who wish to cultivate such qualities as imagination and creativity in their children can do it in several ways. However, they can also unwittingly turn off the source.

What parents can do

A nursing infant has no need to be 'creative.' New-born children have as yet no means of expressing themselves, but at the age of two to three the first attempts show themselves. Give a child some chalk or pencils and a piece of paper on the table or wrapping paper on the floor and they will set to work: expression of the will and the unbridled desire to make movements visible as a picture. The archetypal motif will never be absent: the swirl. It is like the beginning of the universe. When a child walks, runs, jumps, learns to hop, the first graceful pirouette appears spontaneously. The parents' ensuing delight encourages the child further.

A child is sitting in her bed, babbling and chattering. One morning she suddenly sings her first little melody, monotonous and almost undecided, almost always in the framework of the five-tone (pentatonic) scale. If the parents understand how important such expressions are, their joy and attention will encourage their children. If the parents themselves can play the recorder or the piano, children will dance to it. Anyone who has not experienced the passion with which small children can dance has no idea of the intensity of their feeling for rhythm. Instead of simply noisy toys, children should have a small wind instrument of clay (like the old-fashioned clay-cuckoos), and perhaps a xylophone (preferably with a soft 'round' tone). At this stage they need lots of rhymes, songs, games and fairy tales.

A minimum of objects

One of the most important things is that children are not given too many objects, and above all, unfinished ones. Why?

One could call the present age the Age of Junk. It is the nature of the industrial process to produce many well-finished articles which can be used immediately for their special purpose and then thrown away. It is the nature of a child, however, to tire quickly of a specialized toy suited only to a specific purpose.

To present a practical example: three children, aged 7, 10, and 12, were in an environment in which for a long time there were few toys and playmates, but plenty of space outdoors. After using up the toys they had brought with them they started to build a grocery shop. An old toolshed became their shop. Two planks and a table with a missing leg served as the counter. Large round stones were converted into loaves of bread, small ones into beans and lentils, tossed-away jam jars with stuck-on labels were arranged as containers for their wares, various leaves were offered as lettuce and spinach, scraps of paper with writing on them were used as money. Another business, a ladies' hairdresser, was set up in an old glasshouse. In addition, a variety of different games followed: hide-and-seek, third-man-out, ball games. Even the adults were drawn in. The children refused to go on excursions because they wanted to stay at home and play. Undoubtedly, it was precisely this lack of toys which stimulated their gift for invention.

Even though it might strike a sore point in toy manufacturers, strictly speaking it would be better if children could grow up in an environment where there were no other toys than such things as boats made of bark, cows of pine-cones, and hand-made primitive dolls of wood or cloth. Such a pedagogical principle seems Utopian in an industrialized country. However, parents can try to persuade well-meaning grandparents, uncles, aunts, cousins and friends to choose toys which are durable and allow the imagination as much free rein as possible.

What the kindergarten can do

Here the kindergarten can be a great help. At most Waldorf Schools there are kindergartens and hardly a school is founded on Steiner's educational ideas where a solid basis for parent contact has not been considered.

Such a kindergarten contains as few finished things as possible. Naturally it has pencils, chalk, paints, brushes, and modelling clay; and, of course, beautiful chairs and tables as well, and several simple but beautifully formed toys. Above all there are stones, sea shells, comically-shaped twigs and stumps. With such objects a child can do almost any number of things. Of course, 'proper' things such as pictures, clay objects and decorative pieces of cloth, wool and yarn, paper and wood are very important, especially at the festivals of the year (Easter rabbits and chickens, Advent calendars, Christmas elves, Christmas manger etc.). But the most important items are those created 'just to pretend' during free play or in a group.

The children can pick berries, make jams, juices and all sorts of dishes, as well as imitate all imaginable household and handcraft activities. They can build food-stands and grocery shops, little one-family houses and blocks of flats. From chairs, benches and tables they can make ships

No steady Earth, no horizon, only a hovering man: drawn by a child of two-and-a-half.

and trains, cars and planes, and be carried off to unknown lands where there are crocodiles, lions and elephants. The departure from the train station or airport with baggage, customs control and waving goodbye is all like the real thing. They can also fly on magic carpets to Never Never Land to fight giants and dragons.

A kindergarten teacher built an unusual telephone which for all practical purposes resembled a real telephone. A few boys laid out a wire for the 'telephone' made of pine cones and other objects and explained excitedly, 'That's the cable!' Short, simple songs can be improvised: 'We'll bake a cake tonight — for everyone's delight.' The melodies made up lie within the pentatonic scale. Each new day brings a new song.

A kindergarten teacher delighted Rudolf Steiner with the following story. She had little more than wooden boxes and some cloth of different colours. Out of these she and the children built a group of houses on a village street. She now came wandering through the village as a hungry wayfarer. The children invited her to a table of bread and food contrived out of thin air. She praised the food and thanked them wholeheartedly. This game was especially popular and had to be repeated several times.

A few practical examples

When Susan was in the kindergarten she sat still with her fingers in her mouth most of the time. But she was a good observer. One day Agnes began an exciting tale. Two years ago she had taken part in a game in which a goat in the meadow was caught in a snowstorm and had to find his way home. He hit his head against the low stall door and suffered many other misfortunes. This time Agnes made up her own game: a flock of sheep has become lost and can't find its shepherd. The sheep sing sadly, 'The sheep have lost their way. Who will show them the way home?

Who?' Suddenly Susan wanted to join in — her fingers flew out of her mouth! She wanted to be the one to lead them home.

One day Peter brought along several pieces of paper that he had painted in magnificent colours. The kindergarten teacher asked him what he had. 'Fireworks!' Then he climbed up onto the table and tossed the pieces of paper all over the room. The others looked on and shouted with joy. Now they, too, wanted to make coloured pieces of paper. For a while everyone was immersed in this activity. As soon as the first children were finished, they climbed up onto the table, one after the other, and set off their fireworks. Quite peacefully they picked up the pieces of paper and took turns scattering them about the entire room. But the pieces of paper did not have the same meaning for each child; for one child they were a rainbow, for another a cluster of shooting stars. Up onto the table and down again, up and down; the children never tired of their game.

Are these merely childish games? No, they are at one and the same time real life and imaginary, fantasy and reality. In games the kindergarten teacher and the children find their element, their language and even the living pedagogical situations in which the adult can, when necessary, amicably intervene, arrange things, stimulate and appease.

Children and television

Children who eagerly watch television at home often have trouble getting involved in games.

Thomas has always been allowed to watch films on TV. His father has a gun shop. Of course, Thomas wants to do the same some-day, but his mother is against it. Thomas complains: 'I'm not allowed to shoot anywhere, not at home, not in the yard, not in kindergarten — where *can* I shoot then?' His self-confidence is weak. As is often the case, a good deal of insecurity is hidden behind his aggressiveness. He is afraid to jump down from the big stones in front of the kindergarten. The first time Thomas was productively occupied in the kindergarten was when he was given beeswax to use. At first the wax was very hard, then it became soft in his warm hand, after he had worked it awhile. Then he started to knead a basket and other 'friendly' objects.

It seems that Steven is an exception. He frequently watches television programmes, but is also frequently stimulated through direct human contact. His father is an artisan and they often do things together. He teaches him skating and skiing and lets him look on when he's working. Steven is quite inventive and can get other children excited about his games, be it Donald Duck or Wild West. He's come to know both from television and they occupy all his thoughts. After one year in the kindergarten other things occur to him; in his paintings different fairy tale motifs appear. Even his parents become more approachable — television loses its importance.

Young children who seldom or never have access to television maintain their imagination more easily and can create an inimitable childish replacement. They *make* their own television set with a frame of cardboard and moveable figures which they push back and forth, and they are happy with it.

What becomes of children who attend such a kindergarten? A certain sequence of events often occurs. After a child has attended kindergarten for a while, a satisfied mother phones and relates that her child has begun to play quite differently from before — not at all insignificant at a time when the problem of engaging children in meaningful activity has become more and more difficult.

Parents tell each other about such experiences at the kindergarten's parents' evening. Perhaps the celebrating of festivals is one of the most important elements which are gradually carried over from the kindergarten into the home — birthdays, the festivals of the seasons, religious festivals, and the saying of grace before meals. Life habits are developed which unite the children with the good and the beautiful elements of our culture in an obvious and cheerful manner.

The perception of the bodily organs and the drawings of young children

One of the most important suggestions that Rudolf Steiner made in the field of educating young children deals with their way of drawing.

We all know that when children draw or paint a human being they often put together the parts of the body in the most grotesque proportions: big noses, giant hands, and so on. In a course of lectures on education which Rudolf Steiner gave in 1920 in Basle, he described what we can learn from such pictures.

> If you take a number of drawings by children and try to see how they have drawn the arms and legs, then you will see that it comes from inner feeling, and what they draw in outline comes from observation. Their drawings derive from two sources of experience. Small children do not intellectualize — they draw experience, primitive observation, mixed with primitive feelings of their own organs. I believe one can always tell if the child has drawn from observation or from inner feeling: the outline of the mouth, for example, has been observed, *looked at*, by the child, whereas the teeth are, one can say, shaped by the inner feeling of the child's organs. (April 28, 1920.)

Rudolf Steiner then described how young children have a capacity for feeling or perceiving their organs that in ancient times was quite common and that in Greek sculpture, for example, was strongly cultivated. Their works did not grow essentially from the study of models, but out of the inner perception of their own bodies. Children who first begin to paint at the age of nine or ten do not develop their pictures of imagination from direct experiences, but rather from something which they have thought out: reason has begun to enter the picture. It is important that children be allowed to busy themselves with chalk and crayons at an early age, so that the specific soul-quality of imaginative experience is cultivated before it is dampened by the maturing of the intellect. To allow children to live out their organ-sensitivity in this way results in a harmonious interplay of soul experience and physical activity which is important for their whole life.

Eurythmy for young children

Of all the means of expression which can satisfy children's need to give form to their imagination, rhythmical movement is one of the most natural and archetypal.

Free play can develop into formed movements. To give an example: the children hear the fairy tale about the 'Three Billy Goats Gruff' who together manage to outwit the big dangerous troll. The kindergarten teacher sits in the centre and is the troll. Around her stand the children, who have been divided up into three groups. The smallest children are the smallest goat who trips along so

A child's experience of the hand is often expressed in drawings in which the hands are disproportionately large, or have a great many fingers. In drawing a house too the child's own inner experience plays a part — such a drawing shows the extent to which he feels at home or otherwise in his own body.

handsomely and lightly. The children who are a bit bigger are the middle-sized goat who walks with a steady gait and considerably more self-assurance. The oldest children are the big goat who stomps with heavy, forceful steps. Now all have to walk over the bridge under which the troll is hiding. With or without musical accompaniment each group must walk in its own way and with its own special rhythm. After the troll has been fooled by the first two groups, the big goat must give him a blow with its horns, so that he rolls away like a ball and never again in his life wants to see another goat. The children shout with glee.

It is important that not only the legs but also the arms are engaged in various rhythms. If the teacher wishes, she can let the children imitate a few simple eurythmical movements, completely without correction or artistic pretentiousness, perhaps a protective 'B' when the goats become anxious upon seeing their adversary, or an angry 'F' when the large goats chase away the troll, a relieved 'A' when they all finally come to the large and wonderful pasture in the mountain. (Eurythmy is described in detail in a later chapter, page 78). To 'play out a fairy tale' in this way is an activity which quite obviously captivates children.

One kindergarten teacher, who herself was a trained eurythmist, tells of her own experience:

> It sometimes happens that some of the youngest children find it difficult to join in such a game and watch from a safe corner. But when they come home — as their mothers tell us — they often carry out the game on their own; they had simply been shy. The somewhat older children are without exception swept along by the game.
> It was especially interesting to observe their reaction when they were watching a eurythmy performance. We performed some fairy tales, among others the humorous Russian fairy tale 'The Cock and the Mouse.' Even the children who watched a lot of television and often had difficulty in concentrating, sat completely still and watched for about twenty minutes. The mother of one such child told us later: 'To our surprise we noticed that during the first few hours after the performance the children sat quietly and peacefully, as though they had eaten a good meal and were digesting it. Then the mood passed and they were once again full of life.' A while later we repeated the first performance and we could see that the children still hadn't had enough of it. At the third performance some children cane especially well-dressed. They explained to us that they had made themselves 'especially pretty' so that the cock and the mouse would come yet again to visit them.

On one parents' evening we addressed the problem of television. During the course of the conversation we emphasized that young children are especially inclined to imitation and, therefore, always wanted to do whatever the parents did. All the parents listened with interest and showed a good deal of understanding. Now when the question of television came up, one mother suddenly realized that to some extent even the picture on the screen incited the child to imitation. She herself enjoyed sitting in front of the television and said with a sigh, 'Does that really mean we should sacrifice our own way of life for the children?'

How does it happen that a child draws a man like this? To depict the trunk as a big wheel gives us a glimpse of the imaginative way in which this four-year-old girl experiences the human body.

Does imagination cut us off from the real world?

If small children are constantly encouraged to live in the world of fantasy, are they not in danger of becoming cut off from the real world?

As we have just seen, a child picks up everything which is in her environment and which is expressed in the form of external gesture. If the people in her environment are ignorant of the world, then the risk of 'inner infection' is great. If they stand with both feet on the ground and have a good sense for the practical side of life, then this attitude toward life will correspondingly 'rub off' on the child. Here, as elsewhere, parents as a rule naturally play a central role. Through her whole attitude to life, the kindergarten teacher can make an important contribution as well.

Some Basic Features of the Method

The rhythm of the day

All children experience the rhythmic alternation of waking and sleeping and of active and passive states during the waking life. If this daily round as well as the greater rhythms of the year are taken into account in making a timetable and the general curriculum, then the whole education will be characterized by certain features, such as:

— A well-ordered daily programme
— Block period lessons which strengthen the powers of concentration
— Artistic activities for developing the will-forces
— The living world as a means of deepening the life of feeling

Let us begin with a comparison. Suppose an employee in a large store had to carry out such a daily routine as the following:

9.00 – 9.50	Manning the telephone switchboard
10.00 – 10.50	Selling in the perfumery department
11.00 – 11.50	Invoicing
11.50 – 12.30	Lunch
12.30 – 1.20	Negotiating for a bank loan
1.30 – 2.20	Tidying up
2.30 – 3.20	Window-dressing
3.30 – 4.20	Programming the store's computer

Nobody would dream of making such a schedule for an adult's working day. And yet in schools, we make timetables very like this for our children.

Rudolf Steiner describes in the lecture course, *Education as a Force for Social Change,* how destructively this kind of timetable works on the child's faculty of concentration. Waldorf Schools try to make each day an organic whole. It is easiest to think and concentrate during the early part of the day and so the morning starts with subjects that need knowledge and understanding and, therefore, call on the children's thinking powers. Each subject in turn is treated as a continuous theme for a number of weeks at the same time in the morning, the so-called 'main lesson' period. Then follow those subjects which require regular rhythmic repetition in shorter lessons, such as foreign languages, eurythmy, gymnastics, music and religion.

The later morning or the afternoon is a suitable time for subjects which mainly require manual dexterity and artistic practice, such as handicrafts, woodwork, gardening or scientific experimental work. Homework too should be aimed at increasing various skills through practice.

Thus each school day has a broad rhythm of inner absorption and outer activity, breathing in and breathing out.

However, smaller and quicker rhythms have to be woven into this broad and slow 'breathing' process. If memory and reflection are called on for too long a time, the children begin to look pale and tired. The circulation is stimulated and the children are refreshed when their feelings are aroused and their will is engaged again in some more active or artistic pursuit.

Especially in the younger classes, the teacher has to be aware of the effect he has through his way of teaching on the health of the growing child.

The act of 'forgetting' is an important factor both in harmonizing the actual teaching and in making the subject one's own. Rudolf Steiner repeatedly drew teachers' attention to this fact. There is an eloquent expression in the Spanish language, *'Hablaré con mi almohada'* (I will consult my pillow).

It is a general human experience that all that has happened to us during the day does not just disappear into nothingness when we fall asleep but undergoes a transformation. For children and teacher alike, the way in which things that have been learnt or experienced on the previous day rise up again into consciousness on the next is of great significance. This process of forgetting is important in education. It is especially obvious in manual activities, where having once learnt to do something we must forget the process of learning it. If we had to direct, with full consciousness, every movement we make in using a tool, we should never achieve real skill. In order to write fluently too, we have to forget how we learnt the individual letters.

There are two extremes. On the one hand 'fixed ideas' or obsessions are experiences that have not been sufficiently absorbed, and continually rise again in us. On the other hand, there is the inability to remember, and this shows either that the impressions have sunk down too deeply or else that sufficient interest has not been aroused in the child to make a real impression. Memory and learning depend equally on the right measure of forgetting and remembering. This is particularly noticeable in the younger classes. At the beginning of the day, the children wake up best if a few minutes can be spent reciting a poem, singing, playing recorders or doing some eurythmy movements. Then they will listen and take part as the teacher recalls the subject matter from the day before and leads it a stage further. Next they can become active again themselves, writing or drawing in their exercise books, modelling or painting. Sometimes the teacher may end the lesson by telling the class a story suitable for that age group.

Block period lessons

Roughly the first two hours of each school day are spent in one long 'main lesson.' While in the first class the subjects are less separated, later on three to four weeks are given up to a single subject such as arithmetic, grammar, geography, history, biology, chemistry, physics, or whatever else is indicated in the curriculum. Writing and reading are practised in connection with the subject of the lesson at various levels.

Since six months or more can pass before a particular main lesson subject is taken up again, the pupils have plenty of time in which to forget. The period between is as important as the night's sleep between one day and the next. It is interesting how easily the 'dormant' knowledge can usually be reawakened when the subject is taken up once more, particularly if the children were keen and enthusiastic about their original contact with it. In fact it is often to be observed that a certain maturing has occurred during the intervening time and the child's abilities have developed further.

No other way of working is so suitable for awakening the pupils' interest and enabling them to concentrate their thoughts and attention on a particular subject. In addition, it means that each section of the curriculum can be coherent and complete because the teacher can present both the general view and the details of a subject within an overseeable period of time.

Other subjects besides those given in the main lessons can also be treated in block periods. In some Waldorf Schools this is done with most of the afternoon activities, such as handicrafts and technological subjects, particularly in the older classes. Without experiencing it personally it can be hard to imagine how beneficial this way of working is, especially in our fragmented civilization with its jumble of changing impressions that make concentrated thinking and working ever more difficult. It is quite definite too that far less would be learnt in the main lesson subjects given the same number of hours, if these were to be spread over a longer period of time in two or three weekly sessions interspersed with other lessons.

Artistic activities

A common sight in Waldorf Schools is that of children drawing, painting, modelling, carving, doing handicrafts, making music, reciting, and rehearsing plays. Especially in the younger classes these artistic activities are woven into the lessons on every subject. One might think that the purpose was to train them all to be accomplished artists, or at least to encourage 'children's art' as something in itself.

However, the real purpose of these manifold activities is quite different. To express the typical movements of an animal in wood or clay, to create form out of pure colour in painting, to let light arise through the interplay of black and grey shades of charcoal on a white background, these activities are experienced as a challenge both to one's courage and one's patience. To work out the lyrical nuances in a choral or orchestral work demands enormous perseverance on the part of both teacher and pupils. The rehearsal of a play can be fraught with crises and catastrophes. Their overcoming through common determination often results in a renewed feeling of class-community. The feeling of satisfaction thus engendered is all the greater if the ultimate performance is a success.

All these are exercises for the will. There is no better way of training the will than to practise again and again something one finds difficult. Adults, if they really wish to, can always find a way of doing this. But children need tasks which give them pleasure and enjoyment as well. Art is an area of life in which repetition is not monotonous. If the teacher is able to deepen and renew the work through the impulses she gives, it need never lose its initial freshness.

The spoken word

There is a realistic rule to which there are virtually no exceptions. How often are children heard to attribute their proficiency, or lack of proficiency, to the excellence, or otherwise, of the textbook on which the lessons have been based? Almost never! It is nearly always the teacher's ability, or failure, to enthuse which is seen in direct relation to what the child feels he has learnt or failed to learn. This rule applies to all types of school. However refined and excellent the textbooks and technical aids may be, they are quite outweighed by a far more significant factor, the individual ability or lack of ability of the teacher.

This reality is taken very seriously in Waldorf Schools. The spoken and living word of the teacher is the real basis for all school work. The thread of continuity which runs through a main lesson block period cannot be found in any book. The teacher has to overcome the dangers of subjective presentations by awakening an interest in the subject itself. Textbooks are rarely used in younger classes, and later on only as incidental reading matter running alongside the content of the main lesson.

This method of working requires thorough preparation by the teacher but gives her much more freedom to go more deeply into questions and problems which arise and may be important to the class as a whole for one reason or another. The teacher's lively use of the spoken word enables pupils with very different degrees of ability to participate actively in the same subject.

The teacher may be tired and depressed when she is preparing her lesson or before she enters the classroom. But the living confrontation with the subject and with the children causes her 'private self' with all its troubles and worries to step aside, allowing inspiration to enter from sources outside her own being. She gains the strength to give her lessons the necessary variations in mood, the alternation between seriousness and humour, between inner tension and relaxation.

As modern human beings we are often slightly suspicious when feelings or emotions are discussed. What Steiner sees as true feeling is the ability to leave the sphere of our own emotions and 'feel our way' at least for a while into something which is quite outside our own self. If the teacher is able to do this, of course without actually pointing it out, he carries the children along with him. Thus he helps to develop what for lack of a better phrase we must call the 'feeling life of the children.' This is the most important aspect of all teaching, for the ability to 'feel our way' into the souls of others, to sympathize with their troubles and their joys, is the basis on which people can build their lives together. The best way of helping this to develop, especially in this age of telecommunication and technology, it to use the living word which goes direct from person to person.

The use of textbooks

One might ask whether children and young people might not become too dependent on the authority of the teacher if they have to rely only on what he has to offer them. The contrary is usually the case. The children are so stimulated by the living presentation that they turn to books of their own accord for further study of a subject. From quite a young age (Class 5 or 6), they can be encouraged to give short talks which they work out on their own. The literature they use for this becomes an interesting and indispensable source of knowledge in quite a different way from an obligatory series of textbooks out of which they would be given set tasks.

Instead of being dependent on printed textbooks, the children learn to make their own work books as they go along. All the illustrations are done without help except perhaps in the form of a rough sketch made by the teacher on the board. In the early classes, the text is usually dictated by the teacher after thorough discussion of the subject matter with the class. Then the children start writing their own accounts later on. Naturally not all of them find it easy to compose a clear and comprehensible text. But those who have difficulties quite often develop out of them a conspicuous ability to complement their own descriptions with quotations from their textbooks and other books. Early essay writing too lays the basis for the independent taking of notes during class in the upper school.

The role of art

To practise an art, we have to be able to deal with the basic materials: coloured paints, modelling clay, a movement diagram, a poetic work. We have to engage fully with the materials. This process often leads to a whole range of feelings: expectation, disappointment, anger, resignation, thoughtfulness, surprise, new hope, new efforts of will, intense joy at being creative. But it is not only in the soul that this is felt. It goes right into the physical body, into finger tips and toes.

Practising an art is particularly important in life today. In this technological age, life is full of physical actions which are carried out more or less automatically: switching on the light, turning up the heating, starting the dishwasher, and so on.

Some activities also require alertness and attention. You cannot relax for a moment while driving a car, working a crane, or drilling somebody's tooth. But the concentration you need is cool and requires attentiveness, consideration and reflection. Only one or two of your senses and very few of the great range of skills requiring physical dexterity are called on.

An artistic activity places you in quite a different situation. Nothing here is based entirely on routine. Full concentration is certainly necessary but it is very broad. Learning to drive a car may be very exciting but it cannot lead to such manifold and deep inner experiences, nor anything like the experience of pure bodily participation, which occur through modelling a form in clay, practising a piece of music on an instrument, or creating a part in a play.

In life today, there is a paucity of physical activities which require the full participation of body and soul.

Children and art

The intense bond between body and soul is one of the characteristic qualities of childhood. Adults are at pains to conceal their feelings and emotions, though they may not always succeed. But children do just the opposite. Instinctively they stamp their feet when they are angry or jump up and down when they are happy, and so on.

By allowing children to express their feelings through artistic activities, we give free rein to their deepest needs; but not just any free rein. Sometimes the inner involvement of children in creative, artistic activities is looked upon as letting them get something out of their system. If this were the case, we might just as well let them bang on an empty tin can, run round the house a few times, or go and smash some china in the park. But art is formative, both in the material world and in the world of the soul. Some artistic tasks might require a different inner attitude to the one we instinctively adopt. In this way a cautious child can be persuaded to be more daring, an exuberant child more circumspect, a weak-willed child more persevering, an obstinate child more adaptable, and so on.

The educational effects of artistic activities on children have frequently been observed and stressed. But it is not always realized how far-reaching and lasting these effects can prove to be.

The most deeply rooted habits and patterns of

A miner at work. From the local geography period in Class 4 (Bergen, Norway).

behaviour are those which form when a child is at the imitating stage of his development. Some of these change more or less naturally over the years with changes in the environment and in attitude to life. But others remain, and these are hidden beneath the threshold of consciousness and cannot be budged. One of these is a basic positive or negative attitude towards the environment and other people.

As teachers, we could help to make permanent in children another deep-seated instinct: to participate in everything they meet in the outside world, to occupy themselves with it and to try and give it form. There is no other form of activity which is more suitable for cultivating this instinct, even in early childhood, than artistic activity. Through this activity we learn to enter with all the qualities of our soul and with every fibre of our body into the battle with a problem which is important not because its solution will bring any material gains but simply because it is humanly interesting. Thus the basis is laid in children for the ability to take a real interest in the world around them in later life.

The effects of art in later life

'To take an interest' does not seem particularly remarkable. And yet the question of how we can pass on to children and young people the habits and occupations which can make their lives rich and purposeful is indeed one of the greatest challenges of civilization. For a teenager entering a stage of life when everything seems uncertain, it can be decisive for the whole of her future whether she has a real interest to which she can cling.

In the industrialized countries of the world the problem of what to do with increasing leisure time is gradually becoming more acute, both in our working life and in lengthening retirement as life-expectancy is increasing.

People who have an intense interest in the world at large, in people and events around them often remain lively and adaptable even at a ripe old age. Such people usually have an artistic disposition and a certain naive openness. Old people of this kind can be found everywhere; for instance Leonardo da Vinci and Goethe are among the famous, as well as many a robust old person among our friends and acquaintances.

It is by no means always the case that these people are professionally active in the field of art. But even their way of describing events often has an element of keen artistry. Their vitality is not always the result of good health, but may simply reflect their capacity to be interested in the outside world, or just their ability to conceal their aches and pains from those around them.

How is it that an artistic disposition brings with it the ability to produce and preserve vitality? Rudolf Steiner has pointed out an answer to this question. He described how artistic activities, in opening out a wide range of soul experiences and also an intimate interplay between physical and psychic activities, gradually bring about a change in the body. It becomes more approachable and receptive towards impulses which come out of our inner life. It becomes a pliable and harmonious organ on which the individuality can play with the help of the soul forces.

The earlier this process can begin, the better.

Drawing forms

No doubt we can all remember some of our earliest attempts to draw, let us say, a horse. Starting with the head we could draw a nice black line

Right from the beginning of Class 1 the children draw basic forms and patterns.

down the neck, down and up the front legs, along the belly, down and up the back legs, round the tail, and along the back to the tips of the ears where we started. But however nice the black line might have been, the result was not like a horse. So we would set to with the eraser, trying again and again and making more and more of a mess until finally the mass of ghostly horse outlines and the greyish smudgy paper would cause us to give up in despair. Even if we still pressed on to colouring in the horse, we would do so without any pleasure.

That sharp black outline killed something, not only in the picture but also in ourselves.

Of course, it is possible to learn to draw in this way. Thousands of artists the world over have done so and have produced superb works of art with the help of the outline. The most accomplished can simply dash off a few lines with amazing skill and produce a miraculous likeness.

But the fact remains that when we meet people in their houses or in the street we do not see them surrounded by a thick (or a thin!) black line from head to foot and back from foot to head. In reality there are no outlines, only colours which meet.

The real language of forms

We cannot learn to understand the real language of forms if we only look at the lines which arise as the result of a meeting of colours.

Wherever we look in the world we find geometrical shapes: the pattern of a snowflake, the hexagonal honeycomb, the many-sided crystal, the parabola of a trajectory, the spiral of a snail's shell, the regular pattern of leaves on many plants, the proportions of the golden mean as applied to the human body, the ellipses described by the orbits of the earth and other planets. And there have been artists who have surpassed all others in discovering the secrets of geometric relationships, weaving them into their paintings like an invisible skeleton, an imperceptible pattern which gives their work a stamp of supreme harmony: Leonardo da Vinci, Raphael, Cézanne, and many others.

To discover the geometric laws in the universe and in art can be a deeply joyful experience. The two different languages of art and of science can merge into one at such moments.

So that the older pupils of a Waldorf School can experience these moments in all their intensity, not only in mathematics but also perhaps in geology, physics, botany, physiology, astronomy and history of art, they have to have undergone thorough preparation.

The rediscovery of geometry in the outside world makes the greatest impression on those who have first become acquainted with its laws quite independently of any external experience. It is possible to construct the whole of Euclid's geometry without a single thought to its application in reality. Its laws live within the human being.

Forms from the very first day at school

Rudolf Steiner recommends that children should start to occupy themselves with geometry long before they are able to handle compasses and rulers. He pointed out that they could start on their very first day at school.

Having talked to the children for a while about their hands and how people use their hands for working, the teacher can then call each child in turn to the blackboard to draw, quite simply, a straight line. Then he can show them a semi-circle and again let each child in turn draw one on the

Carvings on a rune-stone as an example of form-drawing (Class 4, Stuttgart, Germany).

board. Thus the children have accomplished their very first geometrical construction, and the teacher has learned much about them by observing the way each one walks to the board, looks at it and draws on it.

But geometry need not remain confined to the hands. The children can be taken out to the playground where there is room to do geometry with their feet, walking and running in circles and spirals. Then they can return to the classroom and draw the same forms in their books.

In a eurythmy lesson in Class 2 the whole class can form a moving figure eight, crossing over at the central point by passing each other alternately. This calls for self-discipline, and indeed geometry can have the underlying element of creating order. It is good if the teacher, instead of telling a small boy where to stand, can say: 'Andrew, you are making a dent in our nice circle.'

Gradually the forms to be walked, stamped or run in eurythmy grow more and more complicated. In Class 6, when geometry is one of the important subjects, eurythmy lessons can supplement geometry lessons with moving geometry. While moving in forms is important, the drawing of forms has value on its own account. For instance, the children can be asked to finish incomplete forms: make your own inner or outer form; find the missing symmetrical form; make a mirror picture. The forms illustrated are based on suggestions made by Rudolf Steiner in various lectures.

Living forms

In drawing forms in this way the lines made are not hard outlines depicting the intellectually constructed 'edge' of something seen. They are the

Exercises in symmetry.

expression of an inner play of forces and therefore instead of destroying reality, they stimulate life.

An imaginative teacher can make unlimited suggestions and find endless variations, and drawing forms can become a favourite occupation with the children.

Is any other kind of drawing done in the younger classes of a Waldorf School? Not really. Everything else is done with painting: colour exercises, illustrating stories, even the first learning of letters and numbers. In Class 4 the children are led to perceive the forms they have been freely producing themselves in objects in the surrounding world, for instance the angles of a chair, or the curves of a vase.

The naturalistic copying of phenomena and scenes in nature and life is not encouraged before Classes 7 or 8. By then the children will have practised the basic techniques of artistic black-and-white drawing and a more thorough study of the physical environment with its perspectives and its light and shade will be justified.

A relationship with colour

Asked why an absolute amateur might want to draw or paint, many people might easily answer: 'To express one's feelings.'

It is quite true that through colours we can give our most excited moods a peaceful and harmonious expression. Somebody furiously angry might gain more satisfaction from splashing red paint all over a canvas than from smashing a window.

So for young children whose emotional life is as yet uncontrolled, the use of paints and chalks should be an ideal way of letting off steam. Rudolf Steiner did not ignore this aspect and offered ways of putting it into practice.

More symmetrical patterns. When the teacher draws only half the pattern on the blackboard and the pupils have to complete it in their own books, the special difficulties of some children come to light, and at the same time give the teacher an idea of how to help (Class 2, Stuttgart, Germany).

An excitable child should be surrounded and even dressed in red and orange colours and in contrast a placid child should be given blues and greenish blues. Steiner here seems to mean the contrast between sanguine and choleric children on the one hand and melancholic and phlegmatic children on the other. What is important is that the opposite colour is reproduced inwardly. For instance, with red it is green, or with blue it is an orange yellow. This can easily be seen if one looks for a while at a suitably coloured surface and then moves one's eyes quickly to a white surface. The opposite colour is produced by the physical organs of the child and brings about a suitable organ structure necessary for the child. If an excitable child has red colours in his environment, then he will inwardly produce the opposite greens. As the activity of producing greens has a calming effect, the organs take into themselves a calming tendency. (*The Education of the Child.*)

However, if one wants to make use of all the therapeutic possibilities of colours, it is not enough in the early school years simply to let the children express themselves and their experiences in colour.

Indeed, if in practice children today are allowed to draw and paint freely according to their temperament, it can often happen that in fact they become more and more involved in themselves and their emotions instead of being able to free themselves. Thus unruly choleric children might steep themselves in repeatedly painting burning cities, or melancholic children become more and more gloomy, painting morbid things like gallows scenes.

At best, if the teacher or another adult is able to guide the children to painting more healthy and happy scenes, the function of 'letting off steam' helps to reduce tension. But in the depths of the soul, not a great deal is affected.

Feeling what colours express

If we use colours only for self-expression, we never step outside the magic circle of our own inner life. But if we try to enter selflessly into the language of colour, new and unlimited horizons open up. Our inner life is changed and enriched.

In learning to know colours, there is no point in beginning by trying to study and copy an external scene. If we do this, form takes precedence over colour. It is better to start with the colours themselves by doing colour exercises. It is this kind of painting which is regarded as the most important for younger children in Waldorf Schools.

Crayons are not very suitable for colour exercises, since one cannot really mix them or make subtle nuances. But watercolours used on damp paper are relatively easy to use and the child has a feeling of space and flowing movement.

A painting lesson requires considerable order and discipline since all those wet paints and glasses of water for rinsing the brushes can be sorely tempting for a seven-year-old. But once the boy has stood in an orderly queue to collect his board, paper and brush, it can be a great experience for him to paint, under the guidance of the teacher, for instance a yellow patch surrounded by blue followed by a blue patch surrounded by yellow.

When the paintings have dried, they are hung round the room or propped against the walls and

A simple colour harmony from Class 1 and a colour exercise from Class 3.

carefully examined. Gradually the children begin to realize that there are colours which obtrude, for instance all nuances of red and yellow, and colours which recede, for example, blues and violets, while green is more neutral.

Slowly the children attribute a kind of personality to each colour, as though it were a being with quite specific gestures and characteristics.

> You can speak to the children in the language of colours. Just think how inspiring it is if you give the children to understand: this is a coquettish mauve, and there is a cheeky little bit of red looking over her shoulder; and both of them are standing on a humble blue. You must describe it quite graphically; it is formative for the soul … What is thus perceived as arising out of the colours can be put on paper in fifty different ways. (From a teachers' meeting with Rudolf Steiner on Nov 15, 1920.)

The teacher can do these exercises with the children over a long period, always trying to give them a feeling for the hues, tones, perspectives and spaces of colours. When they have learnt to allow the forms to arise out of the gestures of the colours, it will be quite natural for them when illustrating a fairy tale or legend to choose scenes in which people and things can grow out of the harmony of colours.

In helping children to come to terms with their temperaments, painting can be invaluable. Speaking in a very generalized way, one could say that if cholerics were allowed to choose their own colour exercises, they would spread dramatic shades of red all over the paper at the expense of the other colours. In the same situation, melancholics would paint something small and dark right at the top in one of the corners. Sanguines would hastily paint something small and bright and joyful somewhere on the paper and then start clamouring for a new sheet. And phlegmatics would spread something large and rather boring over the whole page.

It is more therapeutic to learn to use the whole sheet of paper in a balanced and economic manner and to do what the colours want and not what one's mood demands.

People visiting a Waldorf School or an exhibition of its work often ask, 'Why are all the paintings so similar? Why aren't the children allowed to paint what they like?'

The answer has partly been given above. Naturally, as in all teaching institutions, there might be a danger in one or two cases of slipping into a routine. But it should be stressed that most of what seems so similar in the way teachers approach and solve artistic problems comes about because in Waldorf Schools, painting follows a path of exercises dictated not by the individual teacher but quite simply by the nature of colour and by the necessity of taking the children's needs into account.

It is difficult to express in words what it can mean for people later in life if they have an early intense experience of colour. We are dealing here with inner riches which cannot be grasped with physical hands and with qualities and nuances which are too subtle to be described. It is quite clear that the whole world is different for someone who has begun to understand the quiet, entirely unintellectual and deeply penetrating language of colour.

Colour exercise in painting (Class 3, Stockholm, Sweden).

Handicrafts

The visitor to the handicraft classes in a Waldorf School will observe that boys and girls are mostly engaged in the same activities. She may also gather how important a part this subject plays in the general curriculum.

It is not only a matter of preparing young people for situations in later life where they will need this or that practical skill. The aim of the craft lesson goes far beyond this. It is concerned with fundamental human attributes, and was indicated by Rudolf Steiner as follows:

> When one knows that our intellect is not developed by the direct approach, that is by cultivation of intellectual pursuits themselves, but one knows rather that a person who is unskilled in the movement of his fingers will also be unskilful in his intellect, having less mobile ideas or thoughts, and that he who has acquired dexterity in the movements of his fingers has also mobile thoughts and ideas and can penetrate into the essence of things, one will not undervalue what is meant by developing the outer human being, with the aims that out of the whole treatment of the outer man the intellect shall arise as one part of the human being. *(The Renewal of Education,* April 26, 1920.)

In Class 1, the children begin to knit, and in Class 2 to crochet. Gradually they become able to make garments for themselves or others until by Class 7 or 8 they can make a shirt, a dress, a pair of trousers, etc. with a sewing machine. As they approach adolescence, students can also work with tougher material, such as leather and cane.

The attempt to create artistic form, even on a primitive level, runs like a thread through the whole subject, and comes to expression particularly in the making of toys from about Class 5 onwards. What the children have absorbed in their studies of 'the human being and the animal world' in Classes 4 and 5 appears in the way they make animals and dolls in handicraft lessons, clay-modelling and wood-carving.

Wax or clay modelling brings its own peculiar artistic problems. Details can be most vividly brought out. Nevertheless, they must remain subordinate to the overall concept, for the nature of the particular animal must be represented as a unified whole. When modelling with clay or wax, more material can always be added, and thus convex forms arise more naturally.

Wood carving goes in the opposite direction. Material is constantly being removed, and the concave form is more strongly experienced. Much concentrated energy is released when, for example, a twelve-year-old starts work with mallet and chisel on a big block of wood. Wood carving is usually started at this age.

Each material has its own special characteristics which come to meet the pupil and she experiences the nature of the different woods as she works with them. If the pupil, however, were to get used to throwing aside unfinished every article where she makes a mistake, she would never develop her real skill. It is an important step when, with the guidance of the teacher, she learns to correct her mistakes and bring her piece of work to some kind of conclusion, even if — as in the picture — the end result may be a spoon with a very small bowl on a disproportionately long, strong handle.

Above: Animals made in handiwork (Class 6, Bexbach, Germany).
Below: Movable wooden toys made in upper school woodwork.

*Above: Clay modelling is a voyage of discovery in the realm of three-dimensional form.
Below: Animal forms arise out of creative imagination (Class 8, Stuttgart, Germany).*

Above: Woodwork in Class 7.
Below: Clay modelling in the upper school.

Free artistic creation

The element of free artistic creativity developing more and more from Classes 4 and 5, was considered by Rudolf Steiner to be of great significance:

> The child should work out of its own will-forces, not according to anything prescribed to him from outside ... You can experience the fact that the children really bring things forth from within themselves if the teaching is alive. *(The Spiritual Ground of Education,* Aug 23, 1922.)

Naturally, the teacher must be present to organize things. If the lessons, however, proceed in a healthy manner, the teacher's role is fundamentally to help his pupils to fulfil their own intentions.

Art in a technical age

Living as we do in a technical age, we tend to make a sharp division between artistic creations and those that serve practical life. The former are usually hand-made and are expected to be 'beautiful,' the latter are factory-produced and their sole purpose is to be 'useful.'

Artists and technicians who are concerned with the design of practical articles often attempt to bridge this gulf. These problems come to expression especially strongly in the realm of architecture.

In other spheres, too, we are faced with this fundamental question. Can we afford to design our surroundings in such a way that they are not only technically practicable but also suit and serve the human needs of those who live and work in them?

An exercise in free form (Upper school, Amsterdam, Holland).

To achieve something in this field there is a need not only for efficient experts. There must also be a sufficient number of 'ordinary' people who take such an interest in these problems that they are prepared to accept the financial implications. Through an artistically orientated education in handicrafts, schools can make an important contribution in this direction.

From about the age of twelve, children show an increasing grasp of the fundamentals of mechanics. A boy or girl who is making a toy such as a dwarf with an axe, cannot help bringing together artistic and technical considerations.

In the later school years, more complex tasks of a similar nature can be set. There are no end of possibilities in this sphere of work.

Metalwork

If a young person shows the ability to work with a very hard material, it is important that he familiarizes himself not only with textiles, clay and wood, but also with metal. The creative possibilities which arise here can be interesting and stimulating to both boys and girls.

The pictures reproduced on the right show a silver bowl and an excerpt from a notebook, which describes how to finish metal objects of this type. Both the bowl and the notebook were made by two eighteen-year-old girls, partly during class time and partly as voluntary extra work.

In the hand-written text of the notebook it says, '... as an underlay use a piece of wood with a notch; then pound crenallations so that the bowl looks like a cake; then rotate the underlay slightly and smooth out the crenallations with a hammer. Now the object is heated until it is glowing hot. If working with silver, it must be heated until it becomes a glowing white. The next time crenallations are hammered out, it is best if they aren't placed in their former position. In this way one can produce a bowl quite quickly.'

Above: Copper work in the upper school (Bexbach, Germany).
Below: Extract from a notebook on making a silver bowl (upper school, Stockholm, Sweden).

Physical education

A sedentary society

An ever greater number of human activities nowadays are carried out while sitting. Machines have taken over most of our physical tasks. Essentially our participation is only in observing and controlling with our mind.

To compensate for this we need movement. How should this movement be stimulated? What form should it take? Should we, young and old, spend part of our free time exercising in parks, on sport fields, in the gym or the swimming pool? Many people see no other way to maintain their physical health at all. By moving in ways which neither fulfil a social need (as does a normal physical task) nor spring out of artistic activity, but only satisfy our physical needs, we arrive at a wide-reaching problem. Our activity becomes somewhat 'soulless.' What then happens can be quite clearly observed in those kinds of sports in which tackling, scrumming, or other forms of physical brutality are an essential part (ice hockey, soccer, rugby, boxing, etc.). A tendency towards animalization is reached, which can become crass, especially in the case of young people.

It will later be described how Rudolf Steiner wished to counteract this tendency through the artistic movements of eurythmy. In addition to eurythmy, there is also the special form of gymnastics as it is practised in most Waldorf Schools.

Count Fritz von Bothmer (1883–1941), gymnastics instructor in the first Waldorf School, worked out a system of gymnastics which has as its goal an in-depth experience of space and a cultivation of strength of will. This form of gymnastics is sometimes called spatial dynamics.

A graded system of exercises

After the rhythmical games and dances which have been practised in the first two classes, gymnastic instruction begins in Class 2. In keeping with the natural tendencies of young children, it consists in the first three years free and joyous playing on apparatus, gymnastic dances, and exercises in skill. The teacher strives to stimulate the children so that they can combine feeling and imagination in the exercises so that they never become simply bodily activities or competitive and 'show-off' sports. Activities used in crafts or characteristic animal-like movements are turned into rhythmical games. Climbing and jumping over the gymnastic apparatus becomes the acting out of stories in which adventures arise and in which helpful actions are performed. Ease and joy of movement stimulate the blood circulation and muscular activity. The child is refreshed and develops courage.

From Class 6 on, the struggle with the forces of gravity as they affect the physical body is addressed ever more consciously. The mechanics of the bones and tendons must be activated and mastered. Strength and decisiveness must be concentrated in passing through hazards and tests. With increasing awareness the will is engaged in springing and swinging, in order to experience the dynamics of space and the sense of balance.

All exercises involving athletics, ball or running games as well as practice on the apparatus in the advanced classes, are arranged with the thought of gradually achieving a conscious harmony between the light and the heavy, between self-imposed goals and the demands of group exercises. It is important, especially in view of the fact that boys and girls are taught together in many Waldorf Schools, that the teacher can allow

PE in the middle and upper school (Bexbach, Germany).

for individual differences of approach. At the same time, attention to each other and a concern for weaknesses is emphasized as a social element in this form of physical education. If one is successful in guiding young people in such a way that they do not necessarily strive for the victory of accomplishment in competition but are led to the joy in performance, which is attainable for each individual, then an essential goal of the gymnastic lesson is reached: self-assurance in moving through space; healthy strengthening of will and power of decision; social fairness and awareness.

A former student of Bothmer has vividly described how one can experience these exercises.

> In the upper classes we sensed the relationship of this subject to geometry. We felt the powers of the surrounding space working upon oneself, and we responded with the will through our own movement. Another experience was the perception of gravity in the body. Hardly had we become conscious of this gravity through the exercise 'fall into the point,' when — through a rocking motion in which the counter pull arose and through a powerful upswing — it was overcome. All of this affected us as a strengthened and healthy awakening.
>
> After the class we had not become merely fresher and warmer, as is usual after physical activity, but the greatest gain was this awakening of our inner self through the resistance of the body. What can now be put into words was then present as an inner feeling after such gymnastic exercises. Thus Count Bothmer succeeded in making gymnastics into a true educational method: the building of the body and the awakening of consciousness were united in the exercises. (Rudolf Braumiller.)

Eurythmy

What is eurythmy? We will approach this question by quoting a few passages from well-known poems:

Horchet! Horcht dem Sturm der Horen!
Tönend wird für Geistesohren
Schon der neue Tag geboren.
Felsentore knarren rasselnd,
Phöbus' Räder rollen prasselnd
Welch Getöse bringt das Licht!
(Goethe, *Faust,* Part II, Act I, Ariel Scene)

The fair breeze blew, the white foam flew,
The furrow followed free.
We were the first that ever burst
Into that silent sea.
(Coleridge, *The Rime of the Ancient Mariner*)

Säv, säv, susa
Våg, våg, slå
I sägen mig, var Ingalill,
den unga, månde, gå.
(Fröding, the great Swedish lyrical poet)

For every listener such verses are an expression of a phenomenon that characterizes all forms of poetry to a greater or lesser degree. The single sounds and words possess a value of their own well beyond their intellectual content, and appeal to a hidden realm of our inner being which lies below the threshold of consciousness.

We are not unfamiliar with the expression in movement of the contents of a poem, for example,

Eurythmy

in drama, mime, or various forms of choreography. Eurythmy, however, takes its start from the actual sounds of the language, namely vowels and consonants.

Pure vowels are often the expression of inner feeling, Ah!, Oh!, Ow!, etc. Words with strongly-accented consonants imitate happenings in the world outside, for example, rumble, clatter, whistle, rustle. In descriptive passages consonants tend to dominate, as is illustrated in the passages just quoted. But if one investigates the matter more slowly, one realizes that the vowel-sounds produce a certain atmosphere in the poem. In the scene from Faust it is especially the A and O sounds, in Coleridge the U as in blew and flew, in Fröding Ä and Å.

When we speak a sound it is accompanied by a kind of invisible gesture within us. It is this gesture which finds visible expression in the movements of eurythmy. Each vowel and consonant has its characteristic gesture. When we sing, too, similar unseen inner gestures accompany and correspond to the different tones. These also can be made visible as movement.

Eurythmy is thus 'visible speech' and 'visible song' — an art-form which did not previously exist and for which Rudolf Steiner laid the foundations. It is performed to the accompaniment of either recitation or music.

But how can one be sure that these eurythmic movements are not just arbitrary, but really do correspond to definite musical tones and sounds of speech? A merely theoretical approach will not lead far, and we can only become sure by our own experience in watching a performance, or, better still, by doing eurythmy ourselves.

In many countries there are schools of eurythmy, whose trained eurythmists put on public performances, or give eurythmy classes in Waldorf Schools or for the general public.

The value of eurythmy

What then is the value of eurythmy? This activity, this union of the inner experience of sound with bodily movements, leads as can no other subject to one of the chief aims of a Waldorf education: bodily movement penetrated by the forces of the inner life. In a lecture given in Stuttgart, Rudolf Steiner stresses the educational value of eurythmy by saying, 'Eurythmy can create forces of the will that remain throughout life, whereas a characteristic of other forms of education of the will is that the will weakens again later on.' *(Education as Force for Social Change, May 11–June 1, 1919).*

Eurythmy in Waldorf Schools

The eurythmy curriculum in the Waldorf School is wide and comprehensive. Beginning with simple rhythms and rod-exercises in the early years, it proceeds through more complicated rhythmical exercises and the simple beginnings of speech and tone eurythmy to elaborate representations of poetry, drama and music. In the regular school assemblies for children and parents, whole classes often perform what they have learnt.

One of the important elements in learning eurythmy is its social aspect; each member of the class has to be aware not only of her own movements, but of that of her classmates, especially when groups have to perform different movements simultaneously which must flow together in a harmonious whole. This aspect stands in striking contrast to the competitive and often aggressive movement patterns associated with team-games. It is no exaggeration to say that eurythmy exerts an ennobling and socially educative influence which has valuable results in later life.

A eurythmy performance.

Monthly assemblies

Monthly — or termly — assemblies occupy a central place in the life of a Waldorf School. The children show each other and their parents what they have learnt in class in the way of poems, songs, plays, music etc. This may sound simple but it is quite demanding in many respects. It is not only a question of choosing a suitable item and working at it with the class as a whole, but also of taking a real interest in what other classes are presenting.

Older pupils feel amused when in the presentations of the younger classes they recognize those themes with which they themselves once worked. The younger pupils feel respect for the things which are presented by the upper classes, and they often think: 'We'll be doing these things, too, one day!' For the seventeen and eighteen-year-olds the monthly festival is above all a review, and for the very young children a preview. For the pupils in the intermediate classes it is both.

When the pupils discuss their daily experiences with one another during classes and even during breaks, the most recent monthly festival is often an important topic of conversation. The feeling for what is genuine and original, which is always present in unspoilt children, can gradually transform itself into a true and mature power of judgment. The sensitive person can learn a great deal from watching the various classes as they appear upon the stage.

Today people often say that more transparency in their work is an indispensable instrument in making working life more democratic. Within the school there is probably no better means of informing the parents and the teachers about the daily life in the different classes than by these assemblies.

The world of language

Foreign languages already in the first school year, even in the kindergarten? Is this not too early? Is it even practical? While writing and reading in Waldorf Schools, as is well-known, make a slow start, in arithmetic the methods of teaching make greater demands than usual on the child. Why, then, two foreign languages as soon as the child starts school?

Should language-teaching be conducted by a direct method based on imitation, or be based on translation, sentence-analysis and grammar? Arguments on this theme still go to and fro. Long before these discussions began, Rudolf Steiner developed a plan of language-teaching. His suggestions throw light on this problem and point the way to a solution.

Early language teaching in Waldorf Schools

The fact that children are still closely connected with the environment during the first three school years (6 to 9 years) and imitation is still one of their strongest faculties, makes it obvious that only the 'direct method' should be used at this stage. After the fundamental psychological changes at about the age of nine (see page 136), however, language is part of the new experience of the world outside the child. At this point a consciousness for grammatical form can be awakened out of the child's experience of speaking the language. Two further observations speak in favour of an early start. The powers of thought that have begun to awaken as the result of the spoken word become still more enlivened through the new experiences of the foreign tongue. The speech-organs, still so pliable, take on a more differentiated form than they otherwise would. Both these aspects enrich the child's soul-life.

In language lessons in the first class, little games can be played. For instance, each child can be given the name of an animal and have to perform an action when that animal's name is called. Or singing games can be practised in the foreign language. The teacher can lead little conversations or tell a short story, using words the children have already learnt. In the third class, grammar too can be enlivened by rhythmical games.

The significance of grammar

The verb is the class of word which carries within it the greatest activity, so the learning of grammar should start with simple verbs. Classes 4 and 5 (age 9–11) should go on to the tenses and more complicated forms of the verb, as well as nouns, adjectives, exclamations, prepositions, pronouns etc. The principle is always to use many varied examples which need not be remembered and afterwards to write down and learn by heart the grammatical rules themselves. Every opportunity is taken to prevent boredom by bringing humour into the lessons. The learning of grammar should take up only a part of the lesson and, of course, should not take its examples from poetry, which should be experienced as an artistic whole.

Is it really necessary to treat grammar as something in itself? Rudolf Steiner calls it 'an inner skeleton.' It builds up a firm support in the child's inner being, just at this stage of development where consciousness needs to pass over into a stable self-consciousness. If this awakening process does not come about, not only does the pupils' own faculty of speech suffer, but their whole personality.

The living word

Although the learning of grammar is, therefore, important, it is not the heart of a language. The living word must always be the main thing, whether in conversation, description, recitation or the writing of essays and letters.

Every language has certain words which cannot be exactly translated, for example the German word *Gemüt*. These words or turns of phrase with their special nuances call for careful attention on the part of the teacher. Yet although on such occasions explanation is needed, the aim should always be to use, as far as possible, the foreign language throughout the lesson. The teacher greets the children in German or Spanish, and during the whole lesson only 'understands' that language. Especially in the younger classes it is not good to translate word for word. It is better for the teacher to tell a story in the foreign language first, and then let the children give a résumé in their mother-tongue or vice versa, rather than make an exact translation. When the children are older and approach the stage of taking examinations, of course, they must learn to make detailed translations.

The language teacher must always take pains to find little stories and jokes in the foreign language which illustrate the national characteristic in speech and behaviour alike. The different languages bring the character of different peoples to the fore.

Lessons in the mother-tongue

It is a great cultural achievement that so many children nowadays learn foreign languages. Yet it is often noticed that a real feeling for speech is gradually declining in adults as well as children and is especially noticeable in the use of the mother-tongue. In ancient Greece the practising of speech-choirs in preparation for religious festivals made a significant contribution towards a rich and wide use of words. In medieval times the traditional art of rhetoric and the study of Latin in the centres of learning exercised a strong influence on the use of language among all cultured people. In today's modern culture of the West, the terse and unadorned statements of sciences, technology and sport influence our use of speech. The decline in the ability to express oneself in words, whether in foreign languages or in one's own mother-tongue and a decrease in vocabulary is well illustrated by the following incident. A traveller on a Swedish train was listening to a boy of fifteen or sixteen trying to describe to his friends a film he had seen. It was clear that the film had been about the adventures of the Scarlet Pimpernel at the time of the French Revolution. But he just could not manage to relate its content to his friends, not even the simplest incidents. It was impossible to tell from his attempts at description whether it had been a farce, a comedy or a serious film, let alone whether it had a 'happy ending.' There sat the boy, obviously full of the experience of the film but unable to express it in words. His cocksure manner gave way to obvious embarrassment as he failed to make himself clear.

It is not only most important for the child's own later life but also for the continuance of human culture in general, that we strive as teachers to give children a feeling for the subtleties of speech and thereby enhance their inner life. This is a realm where the foreign language teacher co-operates with the teacher of the native language. It is important that children learn to express themselves in properly constructed sentences, and not only in single words or exclamations. Working at the cultivation of speech is one of the most valuable tasks of the teacher.

The temperaments

Knowledge of the temperaments is rooted in antiquity. In recent times it has been presented anew by Immanuel Kant and Wilhelm Wundt, among others. Although many modern psychologists have considered it outdated, in recent years it has gained renewed attention through extensive research. This research has shown that the polarities choleric-phlegmatic and sanguine-melancholic correspond exceptionally well to certain basic one-sided forces of the human soul-life (see *Facts and Fiction in Psychology* by the well-known English psychologist, H.J. Eysenck).

Rudolf Steiner has thrown new light on the concept of temperaments through his study of the human being. He considers learning to know the temperaments of his or her pupils as one of the teacher's most important tasks. Let us, therefore, go on to consider examples of the four temperaments in characteristic scenes from school life. Some of the manifestations of temperament are easy to recognize.

Some characteristic examples

As a rule, choleric children revel in danger. In a eurythmy lesson in Class 1 the children were asked to join hands and quietly form a completely round circle. Inside the circle, said the teacher, the sun was shining but outside there were great dark clouds which they were going to chase away with their movements. But the children were not quiet and the circle was not round. So the teacher began to describe imaginatively how thunder and lightning would soon start to come out of the thick, dark clouds outside the circle. After an expectant pause, a choleric child said delightedly, 'Go on then. Do it!'

Phlegmatics usually take things calmly, even when by normal standards anger would be justified. During a drawing lesson in one of the younger classes, a child snatched away a box of crayons belonging to a phlegmatic boy. The lad went on drawing and commented slowly and gently, 'Oh, blast!'

Rather shocked, the teacher asked: 'What did you say just then?'

Slowly and amiably the answer came, 'I said, oh blast, because David's pinched my crayons.'

Melancholic children are sensitive but egocentric. Of all the types, they find it most difficult to forgive if the teacher in their opinion does something unjust. The children of Class 3 were lining up outside their classroom ready to go in. There was a disturbance in the queue and the teacher, thinking it was caused by a rather highly-strung melancholic boy, told him to wait outside until asked to come in. Having started off the lesson, she opened the door to call him but found that he had disappeared. A few hours later a note was found at the main entrance to the school. It was obviously from the little truant and said: 'There is a teacher called [her name was given a comic twist] and she said a person was talking when he was not.'

Sanguine children usually take life very lightly. Walking along a passage, a teacher came across two giggling little girls hiding in a corner. When asked what they were doing there in the middle of lesson time, they said that they had been sent out of their class. 'But why were you sent out?'

'Oh, our teacher wasn't feeling very well this morning so he sent us out at the beginning of the lesson.' On being told to go back to their classroom they commented with further giggles, 'He probably isn't feeling *that* much better yet!'

It is not always very easy to distinguish sanguine children from the rest, since virtually all children have a certain amount of sanguinity in their make-up. With their urge to pass abruptly from one experience to the next, children are born impressionists. It is this characteristic which lends such irresistible charm to their letters and essays. Here is just one example from an essay written in Class 7 (age 10): 'Martin Luther had many children. He said: "Here I stand, I can do no other"!'

Four teenagers

The temperaments also have their serious side and they can be the cause of quite severe problems at puberty if the tendency towards one of the four is too marked. A brief description of four young people will help to make this clear.

Penny was a sanguine. At fifteen she was a slender, well-grown girl with a round childish face, fair hair, and brown eyes which flitted from object to object in search of something that could hold her attention. She was already falling violently in and out of love at the age of eleven, usually with boys considerably older than herself. At fifteen, she was staying out late with her current boyfriend who was a member of a jazz band. Her parents, who were nice, respectable people, had insufficient contact with Penny. They once tried to persuade her not to go to the band's evening rehearsal, but the scene she made was such that they were not likely to try this again. During lessons she alternated between great enthusiasm

The four temperaments are not just a theory. Teachers experience anew every day how they are expressed in children. In many cases it is the temperament that is the key for the understanding and treatment of a child's most striking characteristics. The temperament is revealed not only through the choice and composition of colours, but in the method of painting and the final forms.

Colour exercises typical of the four temperaments:
Page 86 — Choleric
Page 87 — Phlegmatic
Page 88 — Melancholic
Page 89 — Sanguine

manifested in questions and exclamations, and complete apathy. She kept pace well with the rest of her class, thanks to her intelligence and a considerable portion of impudence.

When she had not done her homework her excuses were usually quite convincing but often turned out to be untrue. When confronted with this, she was briefly ashamed but recovered quickly. She loved water, swam like a fish, and in many ways reminded one of a water sprite, unapproachable and unpredictable. But she also had other, deeper traits. She had considerable character. When difficult decisions had to be made at home, it was quite often Penny who spoke the final word, with great prudence and good sense. If there were no external distractions she could work very energetically. Which would prove stronger — Penny's temperament, irresponsible and unpredictable, or her true nature hiding underneath?

Samuel's temperament was melancholic. He was tall and thin and had a dreamy expression. His mother died when he was five and his father started occupying him with mechanical gadgets when he was very young. As a small child he frequently choked while asleep and awoke almost suffocating. His digestive system was weak and he suffered from stomach cramp.

When he joined the third class of a Waldorf School at the age of nine, he was a small, almost wizened little book-worm. During his first interview, a bulb went in one of the lamps. This precocious little professor said, 'I expect there's something wrong with the wiring. If you show me the circuit diagram I'll soon put it right.'

He loved his new school and had a particularly good relationship with his teacher. He usually sat quite still during lessons, listening intently, though his bodily ailments sometimes distracted his attention. The most noticeable change in him was the development of quite exceptional imaginative powers. He was capable of losing himself entirely in the descriptive parts of his essays, often forgetting what he was supposed to be writing about. When he was seventeen, he was still a tall, slim boy with a dreamy expression. His artistic abilities had grown, his drawing was evocative and his love of music absorbing.

He entered deeply into all the artistic activities of the school. This provided a healthy balance for his ineradicable 'professorial' tendencies. His favourite subjects in school were chemistry and biology. He did a lot of studying on his own, made up his own experiments and was capable of giving lengthy lectures stuffed with figures and formula. Apart from the things he learned, his favourite subject in life was himself. He was introverted and egocentric in a quite naive way. And yet on the other hand he had a very deep sympathy with all those who were weak and oppressed. Which of his traits would become dominant as he grew older — his egocentricity and introversion, or his interest in the world and his sympathy for those who suffer?

Emma was phlegmatic. As a child her greatest delight was derived from food and babies. She loved to visit families with smaller children, with whom she played for hours. Once she joined some children of her own age in giving a puppet performance. Her puppet was a princess who was supposed to be anxiously awaiting the outcome of a battle between a dragon and an elephant. Instead the little princess bored her audience to tears with a lengthy lecture on recipes and cooking. When aged about eleven, she was with a group of youngsters who were discussing what they would do if they were allowed to spend ten minutes in a toy shop, choosing as many things as they liked. Emma sat still while the others revelled in descriptions of all the toys they would quickly take. At length she said longingly: 'If only I could stay in the shop a bit longer!' Going for walks with other children she would dreamily bring up the rear. Her performance in school was average and she was conscientious about homework. But her ability to express herself was poor and her understanding often unclear. At fourteen for a short time she was transformed. Her eyes became vivacious and her glance filled with sudden desires. Her

A choleric sees the flood as powerful and dramatic.

dress was provocative. But soon she returned to her placid ways. At the age of seventeen, she had a kind of voluptuous beauty. Only her temperament did not fit the picture. Had Emma not been sent to a Waldorf School, she would probably not have been able to cope adequately with secondary education. But it was exactly the studies of the older classes and also the artistic activities which she needed in order to be jolted again and again out of her inner lethargy. What did the future hold for her? If she developed into an active human being she would be able to do so much good with her harmonious and easy-going nature. But with her tendency towards the comfortable and the trivial there was a danger that she might sink into passivity.

Eric was choleric. At the age of eight he locked his mother in a cupboard when she attempted to forbid something. Much of his upbringing lay in the hands of his two elder brothers, also cholerics, who were constantly fighting each other. Their favourite occupation together was sailing, and Eric had come near to drowning several times. But he loved danger. At home he was unmanageable and no school would keep him for long. He had an unfailing eye for the weaknesses, embarrassments and uncertainties of adults and used his observations mercilessly. In the end he was

A sanguine shows a great variety of colours and details.

sent to a Waldorf School abroad. Fortunately he found himself in the hands of a teacher for whom he developed a genuine respect. The goodness of his nature began to emerge more strongly. He was fair and helpful to other children as long as they respected his superiority. But he could not bear to fit in with a group for long and hated school excursions and other collective activities. From time to time he became deeply depressed. On entering the upper school he was at first interested in all the subjects offered and took pleasure in co-operating and working. But gradually his unruliness broke through again to such an extent that his exploits included throwing a book at one teacher, hitting another, and demanding the right to choose the subjects he wished to study. This latter was even supported by his older brothers who claimed that he was 'so mature.' Only his final year at school passed without any violent incidents. At seventeen, he was very strong, had red hair and looked thickset and uncouth. His protruding eyes almost give the impression of being in some way an additional pair of limbs. What would happen to Eric now that he had left school? Would he remain the eternal rebel, ever dissatisfied? Or would he be able to tame his temperament and put his intelligence and his leadership ability to fruitful use?

A melancholic produces a carefully thought out and systematic picture.

Using our knowledge of the temperaments

What options are there to help children, through education, to cope with the one-sidedness and excesses sometimes caused by the temperaments?

First of all it must be emphasized that it would be in vain to try and suppress the manifestations of a child's temperament or persuade the child to 'pull himself together.' These are forces which must find an outlet and be lived to the full. The educational measures suggested by Rudolf Steiner are manifold.

For instance, he recommends that the teacher should arrange her class in four groups, each of one temperament (of course, without the knowledge of the children). It is not difficult to understand why the melancholic children like sitting next to one another: they are not likely to be annoyed or perhaps even punched by their neighbours. But what of the others?

According to Steiner, the sanguines and cholerics rub off their liveliness on one another and calm down after a while, whereas the phlegmatics grow bored with each other and try to become more lively. The following once occurred in the middle of a lesson. After sitting for months qui-

A phlegmatic creates a peaceful seascape.

etly and peacefully besides a little soul-companion, a phlegmatic boy jumped up in exasperation crying, 'Oh, it's so boring sitting next to Jane, please let me sit somewhere else!'

Steiner made many other suggestions. Without any theoretical psychological knowledge, children can be helped to look at themselves. In a lecture given on August 22, 1919 *(Practical Advice to Teachers),* Steiner said:

> Let us suppose you are telling your class about the horse. You notice that a sanguine child in the group is thinking about something quite different. You try to make the child aware of this by asking him a question which proves that his thoughts are elsewhere. Then you find and show to the class that one of the melancholic children is still thinking about the cupboard you were talking of at the beginning of the lesson. So you say to the sanguine child: 'You see! You have already forgotten all about the horse while your friend is still thinking about the cupboard!'

If the teacher wishes to devote a few minutes to the phlegmatic group, she can startle them into attention and make them receptive for what she has to say by making a sudden noise, perhaps clattering with a bunch of keys, and then keep them on their toes by asking them questions.

And in order to forestall an outburst of temper, a choleric can be sent out to climb a tree for a few minutes. One teacher had two cholerics in his class who needed to work off some of their boisterous energy. He made a secret arrangement with them so that the rest of the class should not wish to participate in the little plan. When he made a certain sign, the two boys were allowed to leave the room and run once round the school house. The system functioned perfectly and the two boys were much more attentive in the lesson.

Among the varied indications for educational treatment, Rudolf Steiner also mentions diet. In the case of phlegmatics who are inclined to eat too much and too often, it is a good thing to avoid eggs and egg dishes. Cholerics who are themselves of a fiery nature should be given no strong spices. It is good for sanguine children who love sweet things not to have too many sweets; whereas on the other hand many a melancholic child will benefit from an extra allowance. If a teacher can establish the right kind of contact with the children's parents, they will usually be grateful for such suggestions.

Some problems

The picture which emerges from a brief description of this kind is of necessity sketchy and simplified. Obviously examples as 'pure' as those described above are relatively rare. Most children and adults have a mixture of temperaments. One must regard the melancholic disposition as the opposite of the sanguine temperament, and phlegmatic and choleric as another opposite pair.

We would assume that, for instance, a choleric or phlegmatic person would also have sanguine and/or melancholic traits respectively but that it would be unusual if marked phlegmatic and choleric traits were to be found in one and the same person, or if a sanguine person also turned out to be melancholic. That this is indeed the case in general has been confirmed both by Steiner and by Eysenck on the basis of entirely different approaches.

Nevertheless, as a teacher one does come across exceptions: seemingly phlegmatic children who turn out to be extremely boisterous and irritable, or children who belie their melancholic expression, retiring nature and slender build with excessively restless and fidgety behaviour. In such cases it can be virtually impossible to distinguish between the traits which could be called the child's 'own' and those which have been brought about by the environment.

A teacher who had studied Rudolf Steiner's educational ideas was to teach a young class in a school in a rural area. In order to gain a picture of her new pupils, she let them all paint on the first day of school. Afterwards she sorted the paintings into four groups, those with a lot of red, those with a lot of yellow, those with a lot of blue, and finally a group with blurred mixtures of colours. She assumed that this was an expression of the four temperaments and seated the children accordingly next day. Then she gave each child a roll of lining paper to line their desks. The 'red' children immediately began a fight with their rolls, the 'yellow' eagerly set to and busied themselves with the job in hand, and the 'blues' and the 'blurred mixtures' just sat and waited for help. The teacher's assumption that the 'reds' were cholerics, the 'yellows' sanguines, the 'blues' melancholics and the 'mixtures' phlegmatics was borne out in an almost comical manner.

However, when the same teacher moved to a Waldorf School in a large city the same experiment did not lead to such clear results. By direct observation it was also equally difficult to 'sort' the children into groups. They were too 'nervy' and though most of them did grow calmer as time went on, it remained difficult to discern a dominant temperament in most cases. This is a common experience of many Waldorf School teachers.

What is temperament?

Having considered a number of concrete examples we can discuss the most basic question: what actually is temperament? To get at an answer we shall proceed from two basic facts.

On the one hand temperament is very deeply rooted in the human being. Deliberately changing a temperament is one of the most difficult tasks a person can undertake. From the examples we have shown it is obvious that the manifestation of the temperament can break forth in an intense and clear-cut way, and that a particular inner predisposition can even be bound up with a special physiological characteristic (especially clear in the cases of Samuel and Eric; see section 'Four Teenagers' on p. 85). We may have observed that many cholerics show a thick-set build. The intimate connection between a harmoniously rounded stature and the phlegmatic temperament, and between a lanky, thin figure and the melancholic temperament has often been noted and has been confirmed through the investigations of Ernst Kretschmer.

On the other hand it is worth noting that a person's temperament often changes a good deal during the course of life quite apart from their own doing. In general, each period of life exhibits its own characteristic temperament. Just as a tendency to be sanguine is usually inherent in every healthy child, so in every young person one finds outbursts of a choleric nature, in the adult a touch of serious melancholy, and in the elderly a mood of phlegmatic reflection.

Thus deeply rooted in human nature, and yet subject to change, the temperament is a complicated and mysterious phenomenon. From where does it originate? Rudolf Steiner describes how the four aspects of the human being become manifest. According to how the requirements of the child's physical body, life-forces, soul life, or innermost self — the actual spiritual individuality — predominate, so the temperament appears to us as phlegmatic, sanguine, choleric, melancholic. In an adult in whom the interaction of body, soul and spirit takes place in a different way, the manifestations of the temperament also change. The often very striking variations in temperament which occur before or during puberty are related to the inner readjustments we are talking about. A more detailed description of the laws underlying this particular process of development would lead us too far at the moment (see Rudolf Steiner, *Discussions with Teachers,* lecture of Aug 21, 1924).

The relationship between temperament and life-forces

If human beings as a whole are involved in the manifestations of our temperament, there is nevertheless one part of our being which is marked by our personal temperament in a special way and which is especially noticeable. It concerns that level in which the etheric powers are to be sought, those powers which keep the physical body alive and give it its form. The memory and habits of a human being are, as Steiner has often described, woven into this field of power (see *The Education of the Child)*. From this perspective we can see that the effects of the temperament are very influential and often reveal themselves in a basic way. The temperament itself is related to powerful supersensory structural forces. Whoever realizes this can also understand that the climate, the earth, the customs, the language and the cultural atmosphere of a region or a country can so strongly influence the inner bearing of the person concerned (especially if they have grown up there) that one may speak of a characteristic 'folk temperament' of the inhabitants of a specific region — although there may, of course, be marked exceptions.

Observed in this way, the difficulty of finding a dominant temperament among nervously disposed children points to a really serious symptom of our times. That such children are fidgety is no indication of inner strength — liveliness is not the same as nervousness. On the contrary, Rudolf Steiner described in a lecture of January 11, 1912 how aimless involuntary movements of the physical body indicate a weakness in the active 'etheric field of energy'; meaningful movements indicate that this 'field' is influencing and controlling the physical body in a healthy way. Teaching methods which tediously cram dead facts into the pupil's head result in an intensification of this tendency — simply because the feeling human soul is not connected to the outer activity. A weakness of this kind can be found in many children today.

In the light of this uncertainty it is becoming increasingly clear that it is not simply a question of directing the children to somehow 'control' their temperaments. The point is rather for the teacher first of all to approach the different temperaments vigorously and with full consciousness as he stands before the children in the classroom. In the sections 'Introducing arithmetic' (page 124), 'A relationship with colour' (page 63), and 'The human being and the animal world' (page 143), examples are given of how teachers can address themselves to the individual temperaments in the most diverse subjects. Nowadays it appears more important than ever that teachers should stimulate the vitality of their pupils through really lively teaching. When this happens, experience has shown that the predominant temperament suddenly reveals itself and often from a quite unexpected direction.

One simple example will serve as an illustration. A fifteen-year-old boy entered Class 9 of a Waldorf School. He had not got on very well with his classmates at his previous school. At the beginning he was shy and uncommunicative and sat almost numbed in his seat. If anything disturbed his brooding, he often became frightened and shook uncontrollably. It seemed that he was of a melancholic temperament. After a while, however, he became talkative and turned out to be a happy sanguine person, who more and more through his droll jokes got the class to laugh. His vitality increased and his improvement lasted.

The temperament of the teacher

Though it is not always easy to apply Rudolf Steiner's observations about diagnosing and dealing with the temperaments in practice, there is no doubt that his descriptions are both valid and useful. The teacher who wishes to help her pupils to cope with their temperaments must learn to control her own as far as possible. She must keep her own fully developed one-sidedness within bounds and awaken those qualities which have hitherto been dormant in her.

The demands made on her in her dealings with the various temperaments meas that whenever possible she will have to ask questions and speak about her subject so rapidly that the sanguines will have to make an effort to keep up; with such human fascination that the melancholics will forget themselves; so dramatically that the cholerics are really interested and the phlegmatics shaken out of their apathy.

The point is not to work *against* the temperament but with it, to go along with it a certain way, but then gently to harmonize and change it.

A teacher should also be able to develop the following moods and feelings in himself:

— the phlegmatics should be aware of his genuine human interest in them, however uninterested he may appear to be outwardly;
— the sanguines should perceive as well as his ability to flit from one impression to another, his seriousness and his perseverance in observing the world;
— the melancholics must observe his ability to overcome the difficulties of life with the help of good humour;
— the cholerics must experience his cool self-control, even when they have an outburst of temper.

The teacher's self-education

Nobody can educate themselves to perfection. But to attempt to do so and to think about it consciously can be a great help, and once in a while something can be achieved.

Most of us are in the habit of behaving largely according to what we think is our own nature or the mood we happen to be in. 'I am what I am, I can't go beyond my own limits' or 'I can't help it, I'm in a bad mood today.' But this is not enough if we wish to educate ourselves even a little. If they wish to react in a way which is necessary for the good of their pupils, teachers must have the *will* at least sometimes to raise themselves above their temperament or momentary mood.

One of the most useful shocks a teacher can give his pupils is to react in an unexpected manner. It can be a tremendous effort for a choleric teacher to remain absolutely calm if one of the children persistently disturbs the lesson, a situation that might formerly have moved him to anger. And yet this reaction, so different from the expected outburst to which the children are perhaps all too accustomed, can open the way for a quite new and fruitful relationship between teacher and pupils.

A really thunderous reading of the riot act by a teacher who is normally calm or passive can be equally effective and fruitful. What matters is that she has to *force* herself to behave in the way she does.

The case of a melancholic teacher in one of the higher classes is another illustration. Being melancholic, his desire for clarity and order meant the pace of his lessons was too slow and the children spent a good deal of time chatting and making unnecessary remarks. And in spite of the slow pace, the lack of concentration meant that some children complained of not being able to keep up. This situation came to a head one day when a girl announced that she was not learning enough and had decided to leave school, a step which several of her classmates were also considering.

The teacher decided to try and give his lessons a more 'sanguine' character, more speed, more facts, more colour, and more unexpected aside remarks. As a result the children became more alert, nobody mentioned leaving school any more, and despite the greater speed no one complained of being unable to keep pace.

Parents can also help their children if they learn to control themselves and do not fall into the trap of reacting to the child's temperament. A very choleric girl once made a tremendous scene and then slammed the door as she left the room. Her father calmly called her back and asked her to close the door quietly. She walked out and slammed the door again, and the whole scene was repeated once more. But her father still remained calm, called her back yet again and then gently lifted the door off its hinges and propped it against the wall. The girl was speechless, calmed down at once, and the normally good relationship between father and daughter was able to run its course once more.

Differentiated religious instruction

Nowadays many people are of the opinion that in their early years children should be spared any religious instruction and that, in any case, they ought to have a strongly 'objective' religious education in school. At some future time they should be able to decide whether or not they wish to follow a religion.

An experiment

We should like to conduct a thought experiment. Suppose that Mr and Mrs Smith have arrived at the view that their children should decide for themselves whether or not they want to become interested in music. They think a musical education would intrude upon their children's freedom. Thus it is denied them. The parents carry out their idea to all its practical consequences: the gramophone, the piano and grandfather's violin are sold. The mouth organ lands in the dustbin. Father stops singing in the bath. The children go to a school whose teachers maintain a similar standpoint, according to the direction of the highest educational authority. The pupils must read and listen to numerous facts about musical styles, epochs and the great masters of music. In addition they must learn something about elementary music theory. But some things they must never do. They must not sing, play an instrument or listen to music.

The Smith children reach the age of puberty and begin to select their own interests. Through their own free time and association with friends they cannot avoid coming into contact with various sorts of pop music, which they perhaps enjoy. However, the music instruction in the school was, for them, dreary and boring.

Their path to the great musical tradition is irrevocably closed. If they should by chance hear a movement from Beethoven's *Missa Solemnis* or a piano sonata by Mozart, then it is only a sequence of meaningless sounds to their ears.

The Smith parents had an admirable motive; to give their children freedom. The measures taken, however, produced precisely the opposite effect. Their freedom was curtailed. The children will never blame their parents for this. They have no idea of what they have been deprived. Should someone be so tactless as to ask them their opinion of a composer or a musical genre, they would generally answer with a shrug of the shoulder, 'I'm not musically inclined.'

Should the ideas of Mr and Mrs Smith be practised by a great many families and at the same time be introduced into the central school system, then the consequences for the musical life of the country would become obvious in two generations; concert halls would be virtually empty; music shops would have to close; and most musicians would have to pursue another profession. The lives of many people would be profoundly influenced in a culture which had made a clean sweep of its musical life which had taken centuries to develop. In short, in the field of music we should find ourselves in a situation which in certain respects is reminiscent of the one we have at present in the field of religion.

Religious predisposition

Even though the thought experiment is extreme, it gets to the heart of the problem. We know very well that the innate talents of children need care and attention if they are to develop into useful abilities. This point has been especially well established in the field of intellectual development. There is good evidence that parents can strongly influence the development of their children's intelligence in a positive manner by playing with, and above all speaking to, them during their first years of life. It would never occur to a psychologist to recommend to parents that they refrain from playing and speaking with their children in hopes of thereby enabling their children at a mature age to decide for themselves whether or not they wish to develop intellectually.

Many people today are complacent about religion — 'I'm not concerned about whether or not there is a God,' — or discontented — 'I should very much like to pray to a higher power but it's impossible for me.' This is not because of any innate absence of religious interest but rather because their education was lacking in this respect.

No one would maintain that letting children sing and play the recorder during the early years of their lives is incompatible with their future choice of interests. If it is pursued as a matter of course, then early training in music is actually the best way to secure their freedom of choice. Only when they have acquired the ability of perception and skills through practice can the children later develop into musicians or music-loving amateurs. Not until they are fully acquainted with music are they also free to arrive at an opinion regarding listening to concerts or making music themselves.

There is no reason to believe that things are any different in the field of religion. Nevertheless, as the course of history shows, one's religious experience has a greater significance for one's life-style than one's musical experience. Keeping a child away from religion is, therefore, a greater deprivation than excluding it from the reality of music.

Religious freedom

Religious freedom is not complete if it does not include the possibility of becoming religious. Here is a topical problem, which can be expressed a bit crassly in the following way: are there reasons for atheistic parents to allow their children to take part in religious experiences, even at kindergarten age, in order to assure their future freedom of choice — by, for example, praying with them?

The formulation of this question is hypothetical. Such an approach would be deeply dishonest. Of all the insincere situations into which one could place a child, this would be one of the worst.

To anyone who penetrates and accepts the anthroposophical concept of man, it becomes increasingly self-evident that one should respect elementary facts of life. The interaction between the milieu of the home and the children is significant, and cannot be judged from the standpoint of personal wishes. No one has the right of interference in this sphere.

Anyone who has experienced atheistic families in which a good and deep-seated contact exists between the parents and the children and, on the other hand, religious homes in which human relationships are warped or neglected, will refrain from making generalized judgments.

The practice in Waldorf Schools

The views which teachers in the Waldorf Schools often take in the field of religious instruction become clear when one sees them against the background of such considerations.

When the first Waldorf School was founded in 1919, it was the original idea of Rudolf Steiner to allocate religious instruction to representatives of the Catholic and Protestant churches, according to the wish and denomination of the parents. But at the same time, he was anxious to respond to the requests which were put to him by those parents without denominational affiliations: to create another form of age-appropriate religious instruction. Thus non-denominational Christian religious instruction was established.

This practice has been applied, with certain variations, in some countries. In other countries only the non-denominational religious lessons are taught within the Waldorf Schools, and denominational religious instruction is arranged privately outside school.

The irreplaceable pedagogical value of truly religious instruction can only be touched on here. It lies in the fact that a striving for depth, for transformation, and for inner growth is called on. Self-development of the young person and a reverence before a higher world are both elements that exert a positive influence.

Non-denominational religious instruction

Non-denominational religious instruction is given by Waldorf School teachers and is primarily Christian. From puberty onwards, the pupils should be enabled by their earlier religious teaching to take a mature and perceptive stand on religious questions. In Classes 1 to 4, instruction is based on stories which instil respect for God and the divine in nature and which give strong impulses for developing human qualities such as gratitude, love of the truth, devotion and a willingness to help others. In Classes 5 to 8, stories are given from the Gospels and biographical descriptions of historical personalities who have come from very different cultural and religious milieus and who have also solved their life problems in an exemplary fashion. In Classes 9 to 12, descriptions of the history of religion and the church are given, including the presentation of non-Christian religions. These age-groupings need not always be strictly adhered to. Biographical portrayals can be given as early as Class 4, if the teacher finds it suitable for the particular class. In non-Christian countries, religious education is adapted to fit the local religion and culture.

In some Waldorf Schools a religious service instituted by Steiner is held on Sundays. Participation in the 'Sunday service for children' up to Class 8, 'Youth service' for classes 9 and 10, and the 'Festival of Offering' for older students is, of course, voluntary. Parents are also welcome on these occasions.

The principle of tolerance

Occasionally the question is asked whether there is not the risk that a differentiated religious instruction of the type given in the Waldorf School can lead to unhealthy group feelings or even to intolerance.

Anyone who has worked for a few years in such a school has often had experiences that disprove such fears. It is a question of a basic principle. Tolerance, the spiritual attitude of respect and understanding for other people and their philosophy of life, runs as a strong and deep current throughout the biography of Rudolf Steiner and belongs to the strongest impulses which he has left behind as a heritage to his students. In his most important philosophical work, *The Philosophy of Freedom,* one of the most crucial passages runs as follows: 'To live in love of the action and to let live with an understanding for the will-impulses of others is the principal maxim of the free human being.' (Chapter 9, 'The Idea of Freedom').

The same motive runs like an unbroken thread through the whole Waldorf pedagogy. It is expressed especially well in a course which Rudolf Steiner held in April 1923. In one of these lectures he summarizes the aims of Waldorf pedagogy in a few words: 'Just think what flows from these two things, loving devotion in one's own actions, an understanding interest in the actions of others. It then follows that human beings can work together socially. This you can pass on from generation to generation. In no other way will you bring it forth; you must fetch it from the very depths of human nature.' (April 23, 1923.)

When the religious groups, organized according to the wishes of the parents, disappear into different classrooms, the Waldorf School then realizes a principle of tolerance and thereby helps to produce such an attitude in the pupils. Such a procedure can be felt as being quite in keeping with the spirit of the times. The widely divergent ways in which human beings think are, after all, a fact. It is of no use to try to wipe out certain views or to pretend that they do not exist. The only thing that we can do is to learn to recognize in full consciousness our fundamental inner differences and for that very reason to learn to live in full mutual understanding for one another.

Concerning the idea of freedom

Realizing that Waldorf pedagogy aims at developing moral impulses, the question might arise whether or not the students will become 'stamped' with preconceived views. The answer to this question must be a definite 'no,' but it is well worth making sufficiently clear how much must be done and borne in mind by the teacher, if young people are to be led towards a true individual freedom.

It must be kept in mind that each child, during their period of education, undergoes, as a natural necessity of development, great transformations of bodily constitution, of perceptive faculties and experiences, and of thought patterns or state of consciousness. Children must find themselves and their own view of the world through experiences in life and through social interaction. Then, through self-discovery, they must learn to find their destined human environment and his task in the world.

If the teachers have their own decisive view of the world, then do they not, to a certain extent, impose their own views on the child during this changeable and impressionable period of life?

The role of anthroposophy

If one knew nothing about Rudolf Steiner and anthroposophy, one might be inclined to think that Waldorf teachers, with their anthroposophically-orientated view of the world, would carry out their daily work out of an impulse to make converts to their own point of view. This conception is based on a misunderstanding of what anthroposophy is actually about. Anthroposophy is not a form of religion. Neither is it a system of dogmatic ideas. It is instead a *path* for attaining knowledge of the world and humanity. Whoever sufficiently pursues this path of inner development, with its exercises for developing the life of the intellect, the will and the feeling, can, through direct experience, become certain that our physical existence is permeated by a 'supersensory' world and that our inner being stems from this sphere, although people today are generally not aware of this. For children and young people up to about eighteen, it is generally uninteresting and, in any case, unsuitable in principle, for them to engage in the study of anthroposophy and the inner exercises which are connected with such a path of development.

Teachers do not study anthroposophy in order to present it directly in their class, but rather for their own development. Rudolf Steiner emphasized often and quite forcibly that a teacher, through such inner training, could fundamentally improve their pedagogical skill and ability to perceive the stages of development of the child.

The task of Waldorf education

The task of the teacher is not to infringe on the pupil's self, but rather to help the body and soul to develop in such a way that the individuality, the spirit, can eventually live freely within it. But how can one carry through such subtle differences in actual practice? Rudolf Steiner answered this basic question:

> The task of the teacher is the greatest self-denial; in the presence of the child he must live so that the child's spirit can develop its own life in sympathy with the life of his teacher. One must never wish to make children into a mirror image of oneself. That which was in the teacher himself should not live on in the pupils in compulsion and tyranny, after they have grown up and left school. One must bring children up in such a way that one eliminates the physical and spiritual hindrances to make way for what enters the world anew in each generation from the divine world through the children. One must create an atmosphere, through which their spirit can freely manifest. (*The Spiritual Ground of Education*, lecture of Aug 19, 1922.)

Whoever cannot imagine that there is a supersensory world from which the human being originates, may find such a passage incomprehensible or peculiar. Whoever sees the possibility of living within the new perspectives which the anthroposophical idea of the human being offers, will learn much from these words. What is meant by the 'self-denial' of the teacher in relation to children is for the teacher to find their own way to 'serve' the child's individuality instead of 'forming' it. But there are yet deeper reasons why any wish to convert others to a particular world-view must remain foreign to the Waldorf teacher.

The concept of reincarnation

The task of the teacher consists in shaping the teaching material, in cultivating the general habits of the pupils, and regulating the activities of the class as a whole. In no way, however, does it consist of shaping the innermost being of the child. The child's self, or 'I,' its individuality, comes from the supersensory world. When it enters physical existence through birth, it carries with it definite capacities and intentions which are not derived from heredity or environment, and which, as a rule, cannot come to full expression until adulthood. Through observing external symptoms the teacher should try to form a picture of these future, latent possibilities in the innermost being of the child. Sometimes the teacher can get the impression that in a class, personalities manifest themselves which are strikingly 'old' and 'wise.' In addition to the characteristics which are clearly determined by age, environment and inheritance, they possess something of an inner maturity in gesture and intonation of speaking which otherwise is only found in people experienced in life. Without giving way to superficial speculation, in such situations one can have the immediate and strong feeling of confronting manifestations of individuality which come from an earlier life on earth. In meeting such a personality the teacher can often feel 'younger' or even inferior. To say this directly to the pupil in question would, of course, be completely inadvisable. The inner respect must express itself in quite a different form.

Through anthroposophy one gains a respect for human individuality. This respect allows anthroposophy — in contrast to usual world-conceptions — to help teachers who wish to avoid impressing an unjustified 'stamp' on their pupils.

As a Waldorf teacher, one can only advise those doubters to whom these ideas are presented and who still cannot rid themselves of the suspicion of more or less hidden missionary efforts, to test the facts themselves or to speak to former pupils.

It must be emphasized that the things which are discussed here are seldom or never experienced as problematic in the daily work of the school. Sooner or later, the pupils discover that their teachers are 'anthroposophists,' or that they, in any case, have a special kind of world view. If they make jokes about it, then the teacher tries to answer with a joke. Any deeper interest on the part of the pupils is not the rule, as long as they are still in school. Should questions arise in the upper classes, naturally teachers must give an answer; at the same time they must strive for the same objectivity that they would use in answering other questions concerning world views. It is not their task to lead the students in one direction or the other along a specific path, but rather to place material at their disposal, which will enable them to form their own opinion.

Pupils and teachers

Through the manner of working and the human relationships to which one aspires in a Waldorf School, pupils and teachers often grow very close to one another. Is it not then inevitable that the influence which at least some of the teachers have on the pupils should go beyond the pedagogical and human effect of the classroom and extend into the realm of one's general view of life? Since Waldorf Schools have no intention of becoming 'philosophical institutions,' this question must be taken very seriously. Naturally students will be more readily influenced by a teacher they like, than by one with whom they are ill at ease. However, it is also true that they will not really admire any teacher who does not completely respect their inner freedom. From about Classes 7 and 8 onwards, one can notice again and again that although the philosophical differences between groups of pupils on the one hand and their teacher on the other become very deep (even if these differences are mutually concealed, as is often the case), human contact remains totally unaffected. People can admire one another greatly, even if they think in quite different ways. Naturally Waldorf teachers, like any other teachers, cannot prevent their pupils from taking on, in unthinking ways, small personal traits as well as more or less clearly conceived thoughts from those who instruct them. In this sense all education is 'influencing.'

If we allow pupils to receive their knowledge from computers instead of teachers, in order to free them from all unauthorized or intentionally damaging influences, they are still, nevertheless, influenced by the very fact that they become bored. An older boy said of such teaching computers: 'They're fun to play with. But they're less useful for learning, because one doesn't have to find one's own answers.'

The essential thing is that the unavoidable influence does not work in a way that creates a uniform outlook and that rather it encourages a development which is in harmony with the pupil's own personal disposition.

The First Eight Years of School

The right time to begin

The drawings and paintings of children in the nursery class are rather like the tracks left by a bird which has alighted on the snow for a moment and then taken flight again. It is a wonderful experience to dive into the world of colour but perseverance is not important. It is just the same with singing and movement and all other activities. Everything is play, the enjoyment of the experience of the moment and the final result is of no significance.

Seven-year-olds are very different. They are much more down-to-earth. If they are healthy and harmonious in their development, they can spend quite a time every morning hard at work. But they must have something concrete to work at, such as learning a poem, playing the recorder, painting a picture, shaping letters or figures. Their way of painting or drawing is very individual. Many children will sit patiently for a considerable time, surrounding a letter or a number with one glowing colour after another. Some will go on and on until they go right through the paper. The whole class will be one with their teacher in pondering about special moods of colour. What colours belong to January? Greyish-white and blue! And what about June? Perhaps green, red and yellow. And, of course, the forms must differ too in each case.

Some children can be extremely lazy and careless. It often needs quite an effort on the teacher's part to persuade them to finish covering their page. Gradually, however, one after another, the children grasp what is required of them and share in the joy of the creative process.

Psychologists are not always entirely in agreement over what can be demanded from the school-beginner. But on one thing there is little divergence of opinion and that is that it is essential that children are able to sit still and apply themselves to work.

The ability to concentrate is such a marked change in a child's behaviour that we must indeed ask how it has come about.

Formative forces

To understand Steiner's answer to this question demands detailed consideration.

From a supersensory perception, certain formative forces can be seen at work in fashioning the child's growing and developing physical body. For those accustomed to seeing organic processes in purely mechanical terms, such as the passing on of a particular complex of chromosomes, such a statement may appear intolerable or nonsensical. But Steiner emphatically states that this phenomenon is open to empirical observation and that the inherited organism is considerably modified by the working of these formative forces.

At the infant stage, when growth proceeds at a faster rate than at any other stage of development, these healthy life-bringing forces are closely bound up with the physical organism. It is through their activity that the little child is kept in constant movement during the waking state.

Gradually a part of these forces is released from working in the biological sphere and becomes available as energy on a more inner level of being. While the body is now relatively speaking at rest, inner activity can unfold in the soul-realm. It is now a time of training the memory, developing habits and inclinations, of strengthening the conscience and the character, of guiding imagination and temperament in healthy directions. These emancipated forces do not give up their formative character, they continue to be active creatively. Formerly they were at work in living matter, in the organs and tissues of the human body, in the formation of the bones and teeth. The second dentition, beginning at the age of six or seven years, marks the final stage of their working on the physical body. They must now continue their creative activity on a different level. Young school children, as they sit bent over their work books, drawing away, can well be seen as a proof of their existence.

Continuing characteristics of the young child

At the very moment, however, when such an activity comes to an end, the power of concentration disappears too. In the first class only one small disturbing event needs to occur to bring about complete disorder. Perhaps the children are told to stand up and one child happens to push a chair over. At once a number of lively members of the class will follow the example. The imitative process has immediately come to the fore. The characteristics of the small child are still just beneath the surface, ready to appear at the slightest provocation.

The remaining tendency to imitation can, however, be made use of by the teacher. Rudolf Grosse gives an example of how these forces can be used in a pedagogical way. One day his own first class was not in the mood to settle down to work. Since scolding and moralizing are not very good teaching methods, he told them to stand on their chairs and jump off. This resulted in cheerful and noisy tumult. Again and again they had to repeat this, and then follow him stamping around the classroom, a lively procession in and out among the desks. Suddenly, he turned and said 'softly.' They joined in the game, the stamping ceased. Then he whispered 'on tip-toe.' They tried to go on tip-toe, as silently as the teacher did, to their own place. He stood in front of the class, put his fingers to his lips and whispered again, 'quiet as a mouse.' Complete silence! He kept this up for about two minutes and then praised them for their wonderful stillness. What was the result? They called out the next morning, 'Can we be quiet as mice again?'

We can see in this description that the age of imitation had not completely passed. For quite a long time after a child enters the first class, the teacher can with justification call on this method, especially in the learning of foreign languages.

Rudolf Steiner makes it clear that children at the kindergarten stage do not pay much attention to what they are actually told to do in words but more to everything that actually happens or is done around them. But at the same time as the powers of their own inner life begin to unfold, they develop a capacity which will remain throughout life, and is indeed one of the most important human faculties. This is the ability to grasp what another person says and to recreate it as part of one's own conscious soul life.

Illustration of a fairy tale.

When is a child ready for school?

The answer to this question is different from country to country. In France and Germany children start school officially at the age of six, although many French children begin a year earlier. In the Britain primary school starts at five; in large parts of the United States formal teaching begins at six; in Russia and Scandinavian countries education starts at seven.

Many modern educational investigators derive from these various approaches the idea that there is no such thing as a special age when children are 'ready' for school. They base this on the fact that so far no physiological symptom has been discovered which would pinpoint any particular age for this transition. They say that the physical body is continually developing during childhood, that is from the age of four until puberty. Even the second dentition is apparently occurring earlier than it used to.

Strangely enough, the fact is seldom mentioned that Jean Piaget discovered a definite change on a psychological level at a special point of time: 'The age of seven which coincides with readiness for education, marks a decisive turning point in the psychological development of the child. Taking into consideration any aspect of the soul-life, one can observe the emergence of new inner faculties, whether on the level of intelligence, emotion, social relationship, or individual actions.'

This is the age at which children begin to be able to concentrate and work together in an orderly manner, for instance, to join in a game which is based on definite rules. The change which takes place in the thought-realm is no less striking. As we said previously, the child is not able to deal with abstractions before the age of seven. Here is the report of another experiment in addition to those referred to earlier: 'Three differently coloured balls, *A, B,* and *C,* roll through a tube. The children have watched them starting off in the order *A, B, C,* and now expect them to come out at the other end of the tube in the same order. Intuitive thought is their sure guide. But what if we now incline the tube in the opposite direction so that the balls roll back again? The youngest children do not expect the balls to be in the order *C, B, A,* and are surprised by it. Once they have learned to predict this sequence, we turn the tube over by 180. The children must try to grasp that now we get first the sequence *C, B, A,* and then *A, B, C.* But not only do they not manage to understand this, but when they have seen that *A* and *C* roll out alternatively, they also expect that the middle ball *B* should have a turn at coming out first.'

Piaget adds that the child's inability to grasp abstractions depends on a definite inner condition: 'It is simply a question of patterns of perceptions, or patterns of actions which are transposed to become mental concepts. They are pictures, imitations of outer reality.' It would not be going too far to connect this tendency to a purely pictorial kind of thinking, with a marked difficulty in learning to read and write which can be observed in many children under seven, as we have earlier remarked.

It cannot be emphasized strongly enough that Piaget's observations are entirely in line with those previously stated by Rudolf Steiner. He too stressed that the appearance of new inner powers takes place at about the age of seven, and that it is at this time that the child learns to live and work together with other children in quite a new way. It is now that the child is 'ready' for school. Rudolf Steiner points out that to be taught to read and write before this age has as a consequence a weakening effect on the physical organism, because forces are called on and used which are still needed in the realm of physical development.

The class teacher

On their very first day at school the children are met by their class teacher. From then on he or she will be there to receive them every morning for seven or eight years. It is the class teacher who gives them their daily 'main lesson,' which covers all main subjects in block periods and may also take them for other subjects.

Apart from preparing lessons, the class teacher has a number of other tasks: maintaining contact with parents; attending the weekly teachers' meetings; giving extra help to children unable to keep up, for instance in writing or arithmetic; conscientiously marking the children's work books, organizing extra-mural activities and perhaps even sharing some administrative duties.

Why do individual teachers have to carry so many responsibilities? Does their teaching not suffer as a result? Have the Waldorf Schools not noticed that we are living in an age of specialization? Why should the children not be taught by another teacher from time to time, for instance in Class 6 or 8 by specialist teachers in certain subjects?

The class teacher system certainly brings with it considerable problems. In some cases class teachers have to spend large portions of the holidays studying the various subjects they are due to teach next term. They might even seek some private instruction from one of the specialist teachers. And if they find that one or other of the subjects is indeed beyond their capacity as the children grow older, then a compromise can be made in Class 7 or 8, and a specialist teacher may be called in to teach the class, for instance in physics or chemistry.

But in spite of the need for compromise on various occasions, the class teacher system is maintained. Indeed it is one of the cornerstones of a Waldorf School's work.

In the lecture courses which Rudolf Steiner gave to the future teachers just before the first Waldorf School was founded, he described the tasks of the class teacher from many different aspects. These descriptions are so fundamental that it is worth saying a bit more about them.

Keeping pace with the children

In *The Foundations of Human Experience,* Steiner describes what the class teacher can do to keep pace with the development of the children:

> He should review the physical development of the children and remember their appearance. Then at the end of the school year or some other period of time he should review their development again and observe the changes which have taken place. (Sep 2, 1919.)

In *Practical Advice to Teachers,* he gave examples of how quite ordinary everyday occurrences can help the teacher to put to good use her intimate knowledge of the development of each child.

> If for only a week you have been in the habit of eating a sandwich at ten-thirty each morning, you will probably find that already in the second week you are quite hungry for the sandwich at the time in question. So quickly does the human organism become accustomed to a rhythm. However, not only the outer organism but the whole human being is inclined to rhythm. Therefore, it is good in the whole course of life — and this is what one is concerned with when bringing up and educating children — to look to rhythmical repetition. It is good to remember that one can return to certain specific educational themes year after year. You should thus select certain themes which you work through with the children, make a note of them and return to something similar each year. This can even be done with abstract things. In other words: in the first year you teach the children to add up in a way which is suited to the child's disposition; you return to the subject of addition in the second year and teach them more about it; and in the third year you return to it again, so that the same activity is taken up repeatedly but in progressive repetition. (Aug 27, 1919.)

A further example: during the first year the class could learn a certain poem or verse, to which the teacher would refer in the following year, perhaps speaking about it in a different way.

For instance on an autumn day the teacher could remind the children of an autumn poem they had learned one or two years earlier. Gradually the teacher grows accustomed to weaving these 'progressive repetitions' more or less imperceptibly into all lessons.

Such a way of teaching would not be possible without the existence of the class teacher who every morning, for seven or eight years, is there to receive the children when they arrive at school.

Seven or eight years is a long time, during which the children undergo a number of profound changes. And the teacher has to accompany them through these changes. In Class 1 when the children live in the imaginative, dreamlike world of fairy tales, the teacher — like a mother — has to help them with all kinds of little practical things such as untying knots in shoelaces, finding lost belongings, etc. In Class 8 she must command a reasonable knowledge of a large number of subjects and be able to speak to her group of teenagers with the authority of someone who knows how to cope with life in the world; her role has in a way become that of an older friend and adviser.

Self education

Is it not likely that the pupils would grow tired of having the same teacher year in year out? This is something the class teacher must make great efforts to prevent. She has to try and develop and change herself according to the changing needs of her children. Some teachers find this surprisingly easy. For others it is a long and strenuous struggle.

For instance, a certain class teacher was able, for the sake of his class, to overcome a serious phobia. The effort changed him so much that he was also able to form a new relationship with the children. Or there was the class teacher who could not draw and who spent night after night practising. Gradually the children in her class came to be known throughout the school as being the most skilful in drawing. Another teacher was a choleric who knew only too well that he could not always control his temper. So that his class should not have to bear the brunt of this weakness he would spend some time each morning chopping wood to 'let off steam' before going to school.

The community of the class

Gradually through all difficulties and all joys the class and its teacher become welded together as a community. There are very rare occasions when this relationship of teacher and class is unfruitful so that either the teacher or one of the children has to leave but in nearly every case, even if there are many problems, the class community is of the deepest value.

The reason for this is quite simply that such a community enables children to grow roots. To be under the care of the same people year after year gives them a feeling of having found a home on earth. For modern children whose lives are so full of superficial meetings, making it difficult to develop loyalties to other people, this may be one of the most important experiences.

As already mentioned, there is a tendency in education today to split up the unity of a class simply for reasons of expediency: varying groups of pupils move from one classroom to another to be taught by different teachers. Teachers involved in this kind of work have often expressed the opinion that it leads to a worsening of discipline and weakens the children's feeling of security and of belonging to the school. Taken to its logical extreme such a system could indeed have far-reaching harmful effects.

In Waldorf Schools all over the world it is found that no other teacher is able to establish such a close contact with a class as the class teacher himself. In moral and disciplinary questions it is his word which is heeded most seriously. If the class teacher becomes ill, it is often difficult for another teacher to take over his class. Through his constant efforts to develop himself and through his deep bond with his class he becomes the person of greatest authority to them. It is difficult to replace him.

However, as the class teacher approaches the end of the class-teacher period, he has to arrange his work so that the pupils gradually become more independent. The former strong personal link with the teacher is widened to include the whole school and this is the transition to the upper school.

Authority or freedom?

The principle of authority is often questioned nowadays. Many psychologists and young parents are of the opinion that it is good for growing children to be treated on the same level as adults as soon as possible. The desire to do the best for one's children by treating them as companions from an early age is understandable but in some cases the bold slogans of freedom and equality are used by parents to hide their own uncertainty or even their lack of interest in how their children are developing. These parents are often more concerned with their own than with their children's needs.

It is also unfortunate that the word 'authority' has overtones which link it with the ideas of constraint or dictatorship, or at best with patriarchal customs of a previous age.

In Waldorf Schools, authority has nothing to do with these overtones. It is based on an experience which cannot be denied by anyone who works with children and who does not cling to theoretical speculations, viz. that it is important for children to be in close proximity with someone whose support they can feel and to whom they can look up. This feeling of security is a source of strength of which young children can never have enough.

It is this kind of natural authority which prompts younger children to settle any argument at home quite categorically with the magic words, 'but my teacher says …' Then as the years go by and they grow older they may no longer flaunt their admiration for their teacher quite so adamantly but it is interesting to observe how seriously they take anything that comes from a teacher they really love.

Rudolf Steiner points out that genuine authority can never be achieved or maintained by any external means. In one of his most fundamental statements he said:

> It is most important that devotion and admiration for the teacher and love for the teacher should come about as of itself. Otherwise it is of no value. Any devotion which is forced or which is based upon the rules and laws of the school is of no value for the development of the human being. It can be experienced quite positively that when children are educated in accordance with their own being they are most likely to be devoted to their teacher.
> (*Rudolf Steiner in the Waldorf School,* May 9, 1922.)

Punishment

What Rudolf Steiner says about punishment should not be taken to mean that he is against everything which might be regarded as punishment or strictness. Teachers who try to educate according to the true nature and needs of their pupils must come to understand that any wrongdoing of children and teenagers hardly ever stems from a conscious effort but is nearly always the result of some degree of thoughtlessness. And the therapy for thoughtlessness is a call to consciousness and reflection.

> Many, many theories have been expounded on the reasons for punishment. But the only real reason lies in the knowledge that punishment should serve the purpose of harnessing the forces of the soul in a way which can extend the consciousness to areas hitherto untouched by it. (Feb 1, 1916.)

An awakening effect of this kind can never by achieved if the teacher acts impulsively. Today it is becoming more and more difficult to maintain discipline and to give undisturbed lessons. It is often those children and adolescents whose behaviour is most disturbing that are the ones suffering most from environmental damage. Thus even if the teacher is forced to be extremely strict, she should never give her charges reason to doubt that what she really wants is to help them.

It is perhaps unavoidable in any school that a teacher provoked beyond his limits may forget himself and react too hastily. But what is important is that he should realize that any measures which are not basically helpful or therapeutic but are the result of hurt pride are educationally valueless or even harmful.

Some practical experiences

A number of Waldorf School teachers from different countries once met to discuss the question of 'difficult classes.' Detailed descriptions were given of a number of upper school classes in which the children were either unwilling to work or actually rebellious. Various possible causes were examined and it was found that there was indeed a 'lowest common denominator.' In every case, during their years in the lower and middle school the classes had had class teachers who would not tolerate any appreciable opposition and who had enforced strict external discipline right up to Class 8. All had been well while the class teacher remained in charge but in Class 9 the problems had begun to appear, in some cases quite rapidly.

Attention was then turned to examples of classes where the pupils had been particularly enthusiastic about work and had shown great loyalty to their teachers during their final years at school. Here too all the classes had something in common, viz. a class teacher who had not been too insistent on external discipline but had been warmly appreciated by his pupils.

One example was particularly striking. A certain class teacher had a very large class, as she liked to accept more and more new pupils. During her lessons the classroom was sometimes like a stormy ocean and when the class was singing the tempest seemed to increase in fury. The teacher often had to shout to be heard and though her lessons were rich in content, her presentation was not always systematic. Yet amid all the noise the relationship between teacher and pupils was warmly human. When her pupils entered the upper school there were large gaps in their knowledge. But then they started studying with great enthusiasm and learnt remarkably rapidly, often pushing the teachers faster then they had intended to go. Class discussions were of a very high standard, both as regards intelligence and human understanding.

Observations of this kind must, of course, be regarded and treated very cautiously indeed. It would be quite wrong to assume that Rudolf Steiner's educational principles presupposed any lack of discipline. All teachers and all classes are different. What is right in one case may be impossible in another. Every teacher has, and must have, their own way of solving disciplinary problems. But amid all the manifold individual variations there is an underlying principle which Rudolf Steiner did point out and which is shown in the examples given, namely that the only desirable form of authority is the one based on mutual sympathy and respect.

From trust to freedom

Authority which is practised for the good of the children and not for the convenience of the teacher will not hinder their development towards freedom. On the contrary, children who are able to experience steady confidence in those whose task it is to educate them, will find it easier to build up the inner calm and security which will enable them later in life to unfold in a natural and relaxed way. The question 'authority *or* freedom' is, therefore, not a valid one. Authority is a necessary stage on the way to freedom.

In the western world today there are probably many children who grow up without ever really feeling respect for an older person. To regard this fact as a positive symptom of the development towards freedom in our time is an error and also an exceedingly short-sighted way of thinking. For it is usually those people who as children were unable to feel respect and admiration in any form, who in later life are less capable of genuine feeling and of making warm, human contact.

The need for images

One of the frequent prejudices held against Waldorf Schools is that the children are told too many fairy tales. To answer such a criticism it is necessary to consider in greater depth the part which pictures, both visual and imaginative, play in the lives of young children. Many people will remember from their childhood days a painting or a book illustration which was created from an artist's imagination, and they may realize that such a picture affected them more deeply than a picture which was merely depicting outer nature. Perhaps they may still be able to conjure up something of the original feeling — maybe of joyful warmth, or maybe a fearful shudder. Children's love of pictures springs from the heart and is engendered by a longing to live in the realm of human feeling.

Why is it that children have such a strong desire for pictures which are not mere copies of earthly reality? It could be argued that their hunger for pictures merely corresponds to an adult's preference for stories in magazines or thrillers and the like. But there is more to the question than meets the eye. The yearning for pictures in children is particularly strong during a definite phase of their development. Arnold Gesell has shown that the interest in comics begins to awaken in children at about the age of six, culminating at about eight or nine, and beginning to diminish at about ten.

Children have an insatiable appetite for images, which producers of comics, cartoon films and video games have exploited to the full. Unfortunately, they tend to provide caricatures and distortions. Children of about seven will quite happily act the story of Little Red Riding-Hood, or perform it with their puppets. This engages them in a more genuinely imaginative activity. If their tastes have not been spoilt by too many sensational and fantastic films or video games, they have a deeply-founded preference for fairy tales and mythological pictures.

The age of picture consciousness

In all cultural epochs and in the history of all peoples, there have been times when adults experienced the same kinship with images as children do today. The myths of ancient India, Babylonia, Egypt and those told by the Celts, the North American, African or Aboriginal tribes, all bear witness to a stage of cultural development when people reverently accepted what their priests or medicine men told them about the creation of the world in wonderful, majestic pictures.

Historically, we can observe the gradual transition from old imaginative picture-consciousness, to a more intellectually-orientated and clearly-defined thinking, particularly well in the development of Greek philosophy and drama.

Without wishing to press the comparison too far, we can say that children go through a similar process of development. Children have a kind of pictorial thinking which reaches its climax between the ages of six and ten and which then gradually changes into their newly-found interest in the causality of things, and into the ability to use abstract concepts.

Rudolf Steiner emphasized time and again the importance of meeting children's need to live in images. One of his more forceful remarks in this respect was made in a lecture in England in 1923.

What would you say if someone who in a restaurant had been served with fish were to carefully separate out the bones and eat them after placing the edible parts on the side of his plate? You would probably be afraid that the bones might choke him and you would realize that his digestion would not be able to cope with the fish bones.

Yet the very same thing happens, only on a different level, if instead of giving soul nourishment to the child in forms of living pictures which speak to his whole being, you teach him dry, abstract and lifeless concepts. *(A Modern Art of Education,* Aug 13, 1923.)

Critics of Waldorf Schools who maintain that too many imaginative pictures are given to the children in the first three years at school, have not realized that the motives behind such practice are not merely 'sacred cows,' old fashioned ideas, or even a lack of interest in the realities of modern life, but that a consistent pedagogical principle is being applied consciously, based on a knowledge of the growing child. Furthermore, such critics only look at one side of the curriculum, for in Class 3, for example, special emphasis is laid upon lessons in practical life, such as the study of house-building and farming, and in Class 4 the children are taught how to compose their first business letters.

If one wishes not to exhaust the children intellectually, but to preserve their healthy receptivity, it is essential to let them experience truly imaginative pictures. It has often been observed that pupils in Waldorf Schools who had been taught in a particularly imaginative and pictorial way in the younger years, later on showed unusual readiness to learn and understand intellectual subjects. Such

Two illustrations of the same fairy tale. The teacher tells the children a story, and they respond through their artistic activity. Their pictures are the spontaneous expression of what they have experienced through their teacher (Bergen, Norway).

pupils not only displayed mobility in thinking, but a stable and balanced emotional life as well. In order to meet the child's natural demand for the pictorial element, it is essential to permeate every lesson with imaginative quality. There is no other way, imaginative pictures must be given their due.

In a Waldorf School, the main lesson (see 'The rhythm of the day,' page 53) usually includes a daily instalment of a single continuous story, carefully chosen to fit the soul mood of the class.

Class 1: fairy tales.
Class 2: fables and legends; *The King of Ireland's Son* is told in some schools
Class 3: selected stories from the Old Testament.
Class 4: stories from Nordic mythology.
Class 5: legends from Ancient India, Persia, Babylonia and Egypt and parts of Greek mythology.

Speaking about the importance of satisfying the child's hunger for imagination, Rudolf Steiner went even further by linking a rebellious and anarchist attitude, so prevalent today, to this very same problem. Although his views may sound strange and even far-fetched to anyone who has not occupied themselves with his teachings, they nevertheless show the depth of the problem involved:

> We live at the beginning of an era — and here lies very largely the reason for the turbulent character of our present time — in which the souls as they descend from the spiritual world into earthly life, through conception and birth, bring powerful images with them. What lives in the depths of children's souls are Imaginations which have been received in the spiritual world. They seek to come forth. Thus there are forces working in the child which will shatter him unless they are brought out through an imaginative approach in education. What is the result if this does not happen? Such forces do not vanish. They spread, gaining momentum, until finally they penetrate people's thoughts, feelings and will impulses. And what kind of people result from such happenings? They are the rebels, revolutionaries, dissatisfied people who do not know what they want because they want something which can never be found. If the world is in revolt today, then it is the heavens that are in revolt; that is, the heavenly forces that are held back in the souls of men, being unable to appear in their true guise, are changed to their very opposite … into strife and bloodshed … No wonder that those who participate in the work of destroying the social order feel that they are doing something good … Such is the serious nature of the truths which we should recognize today. *(Spiritual Science as a Foundation for Social Forms,* lecture of Sep 11, 1920.)

Pictures before letters

'The powerful prince comes prancing along and bows to the proud princess.' The children of the first class are energetically repeating this sentence, stamping as they pronounce the sound 'P.' They have heard a fairy tale about the prince and the princess, and re-experience it in rhythmical recitation. Then they draw the picture with coloured crayons, the prince raising his hand to doff his purple velvet cap and bow low before the haughty princess. Gradually the form of the letter P emerges from the figure of the prince with his uplifted arms. Finally the children draw just the letter itself, but the story and the picture they have drawn or painted remain alive in their imagination. In a similar way the teacher introduces other consonants. The king raising his sword becomes the K, the tall tree with its outspread branches becomes T, the path over the mountains remains as the letter M. Vowels arise from bodily features each expressing a different mood of soul. Such movements are then arrested, as it were, in a fixed sign which becomes the written symbol for a particular vowel. Thus 'outer' sounds (consonants) and 'inner' sounds (vowels) are distinguished from the very beginning.

In this way the letter arises from the picture, and reading is derived from the activity of writing. All the letters are gradually introduced during the first school year, and the children learn to read only what the teacher and they themselves have written. Only during the second school year is reading practised in a more systematic way, and the printed word makes its first appearance.

Why do we adopt this lengthy and rather complicated approach to learning in Waldorf Schools? Perhaps I may be allowed to recall the childhood memory of my own first writing lesson. The teacher stood at the board and wrote the letters B and I. Then she turned to us and said, 'That is *bi*.' Quickly the thought shot through my head, 'But that doesn't look like a *bi*.* It just isn't true.' I felt disappointed and as if I stood at the borders of an alien new world, which I now had to enter.

The transition from the world of real things to the world of signs is more difficult for many children than we imagine. A bridge is made by engaging the child's imagination and presenting letters at first through familiar pictures. We are speaking here, of course, of the average school child, not children who have special learning difficulties.

Rudolf Steiner emphasized that children should not be forced to learn to read and write before they are really ready for it (see 'The right time to begin,' page 105), and that then they should recapitulate the same process that is to be found in the old Egyptian, Babylonian and Chinese cultures, namely the transition from the picture-element to the sign.

One may ask whether this slow process is not boring for the more intelligent children, especially those who have learnt to read and write before coming to school. Everything depends on the ability of the teacher to make the pictorial character of the letter sufficiently interesting. Such problems soon disappear when drawing and painting, as well as telling stories which excite the children's interest. When children realize, too, that this is the way in which humankind first mastered the art of writing, they even feel a certain pride and respect for their own activities. A little girl in a Waldorf School, comparing herself with some cousins who had learnt to read more quickly at another school, remarked 'Oh yes, they did learn to read, but they have no idea where the letters come from!'

Overleaf: The transition from the world of objects to that of abstract signs is a deep incision in the life of a human being. Rudolf Steiner was most emphatic that children should learn to read and write only when absolutely ready for school, and that then they should follow the same steps which were taken in the past by civilizations as a whole — namely, from pictures to letters.

---

* In Swedish 'bi' is the word for 'bee.'

The powerful king is contracted to the pale thin letter K (Stockholm, Sweden).

*Januar is-
skjegg
smeller i
husvegg*

*Juni trår
dansen med
midtsommerkranse*

Writing is here made to suit the subject matter. The 'winter' letters are angular and cold-looking. The 'summer' letters are soft and rounded, and the colours warm and glowing (Class 5, Oslo, Norway).

Speed in learning has little value. It is the depth of the child's experience that matters. How poor is the trivial content of the customary first readers used in ordinary schools — of necessity couched in simple terms because the child is just learning to read — compared with the wealth gained from the teacher who speaks with creative imagination of the world both of everyday life and of fairy tale and legend.

Fairy tales in Class One

The educational value of fairy tales has come to be doubted. It is thought that they are not exciting enough for six and seven-year-olds and that they are too frightening for younger children. However, in Waldorf Schools fairy tales are regarded as one of the most important educational means available to parents and teachers, and a considerable amount of time is set aside for story telling. What is the reason for this?

Let us begin with a typical example: a phlegmatic little girl, aged about five or six, was told the story of Mother Holle by her mother. She heard how the good girl in the story always did her work in Mother Holle's house willingly and conscientiously, and how finally she was led by her mistress to a great doorway.

There a shower of gold fell upon her. Then the door closed behind her and she found herself near her parents' home, to which she returned. The lazy maiden, who faced a similar situation without, however, being able to cope with it adequately, was also led to the great doorway. But all she received was a shower of tar. This picture of the two maidens returning home, one shining with gold, and the other covered with tar, made a deep impression on the phlegmatic child. Slowly and emphatically she said, 'I'm always going to be a good girl, too.'

With drastic vividness not found in any other kind of literature, fairy tales reveal the inmost core of their various characters. In this way children receive a knowledge of human nature which they could not understand in any other form and which, at the same time, helps them to develop their feelings for right and wrong.

Though traditional fairy tales have undergone considerable changes in being passed from generation to generation and from one country to another, many of their characteristic features indicate that they were told originally by unknown people. In addition to their poetical gifts, these original story tellers must have had deep insight into human nature and great wisdom about the world.

Many fairy tales are real works of art, deeply ethical in their attitudes, free from all petty moralizing, and created for people who have not lost their childhood imagination.

The face of evil

But why should fairy tales so often introduce all sorts of loathsome creatures which do not exist? Should we not protect the children instead of burdening them with all sorts of wicked fairies, trolls, witches and giants?

Before answering this question, let us look for a moment at the way in which these creatures are described in fairy tales.

Fairy tales which still reveal the manner in which they were told by the story tellers of old, have a simple and almost naive style with relatively few words. Their pictures are pithy, painted with few strokes. Details are sparse. Usually the representatives of evil reveal themselves only by their words and deeds.

Illustration of a fairy tale, (Class 1, Milan, Italy).

The wicked stepmother in Snow White is able to deceive the king and many other people because she is the fairest in all the land. The wicked fairy in Sleeping Beauty dresses up as an old woman before tempting the princess to spin and prick herself with the spindle. The witch in Hansel and Gretel is a particularly striking figure. She appears to the two lost children like a friendly old woman who offers them a good meal and soft beds to sleep in. An unusually detailed generalization is added to her description, 'Witches have red eyes and cannot see far, but they have keen noses which can smell human beings when they are approaching.' The witch's animal lust becomes only too obvious when she tries to entice Gretel to creep into the oven. But she gives herself away and, by a ruse, Gretel succeeds in pushing her into the oven instead.

The Scandinavian trolls are a species apart. The Norwegian fairy tale, The Troll Wedding, tells us how a young girl, who is engaged to be married, is living high up in the mountains, together with her cows. One day crowds of people come to visit her in her hut, led by the bridegroom himself. The people have brought her wedding dress, as well as table cloths and silver plates for the wedding. The festivities begin, but the dog knows instinctively that all is not well. Barking loudly, he rushes down the mountain to the village and fetches the real bridegroom who brings his gun and rescues his bride. She had not noticed that her visitors were trolls, but now she sees that all the fine food for the wedding feast is nothing but moss, toadstools and cow dung.

Trolls can appear in all sorts of shapes and disguises: as small children, gnome-like adults, or as wonderfully beautiful women. Usually they have quite specific aims. For instance, they may want to entice certain people to follow them inside the mountain. Sometimes if someone accepts food and drink from them, he is condemned to remain with them. This is a very old theme which already appears in the Odyssey when Circe entices shipwrecked sailors to her castle and offers them poisoned wine. As soon as they have drunk, she turns them into pigs and does not let them go. Because they give in to their base instincts, Circe is able to gain power over them. Those who have been spellbound by the trolls can be saved by their own, or by someone else's, spiritual awareness. Nevertheless, a sojourn with the trolls leaves its mark. Frequently those who return feel like strangers among their fellow human beings. Sometimes they may remain eccentric for the rest of their lives.

Grotesque characters such as trolls and witches with long noses or ears usually only appear in humorous fairy tales. Giants, too, despite all their fearsomeness, generally display some comical features. With the exception of dragons (in western tales) and devils, which are evil incarnate, the forces of evil are described in many fairy tales merely as possessing the power to deceive men's eyes and in this way appear human so that they cannot easily be distinguished from ordinary people.

Fairy tales and real life

Is all this not rather fantastic and quite mad? Not in the least. Anyone who has experienced how some adolescents are drawn into joining gangs indulging in drug-taking, robberies, or violence, cannot help being amazed at the similarity of these temptations in real life to those depicted in fairy tales. There are 'bewitched' people all around us; there are others whose psychological make-up resembles that of witches and trolls in the way in which they exhibit primitive cunning, insinuating flattery, animal lust and boundless cynicism.

The terrible thing about the powers of evil as described in real fairy tales is that they really exist.

Many people express the view that instead of telling children fairy tales we ought to prepare them for modern life. Children should be fore-warned so as to be fore-armed. But if we look at the present situation, we can find countless children who have been overtaken by conditions of modern life all too soon and too suddenly and who have to face a life of fear and helplessness, of disillusionment and brutality.

If fairy tales are told in the right way, unsentimentally, without intellectual interpretations and without gory details, their witches, giants and trolls can help children experience evil in the world before having to face it.

However, what matters most is that children should experience how the beneficent powers in the world rule supreme, and how they enable the characters of the fairy tales, be they kings or hunters, princes or soldiers, to develop virtues such as courage, perseverance, loyalty or a sense of justice. For in this way the 'happy end' imbues the children with reassurance and confidence that the evil in the world can be and must be overcome and that renewed strength and deeper happiness are the just reward for an honest struggle.

Choosing the right story

Children of the fairy tale age — between four and nine — can gradually be told an increasing number of tales from their own and from other people's countries. Those suitable for the youngest stage are the short and, if possible, humorous stories which can be told over and over again, preferably word for word, such as Sweet Porridge and The Star Dollars. The Wolf and the Seven Little Goats, Sleeping Beauty and Snow White are also possible at this stage provided their darker aspects are not made too dramatic but told in a light manner. After five years of age children are able to follow stories whose leading characters go on a quest as the action unfolds. However, it is advisable before choosing one's story to consider the individual disposition of each child, their background and also the season of the year.

But what is one to do if, after all, a five-year-old does feel frightened of the wolf or of some other monster as he lies awake at night? Should one calm his fears by explaining that there are no wolves roaming the land and that in real life there are no giants, goblins or witches? After all that has been stated so far, it would be obviously wrong to nullify the pictures of the fairy tale world after having given them to the child. This would seriously undermine his trust in what his elders have to say to him. On the other hand, life will not allow children to remain completely protected from experiencing the darker aspects of existence and, in any case, most children have their own instinctive glimpses of them. We must help them to come to terms with their problems. A song at bedtime, a prayer, or a little talk about something beautiful that happened during the day usually helps. A happy and much-loved story can drive away fears. One can tell children how each child has her guardian angel who will watch over her, especially at night time. One parent once gave his young son a wooden sword, showing him how the hilt of the sword had the shape of the cross, and telling him how all bad creatures were afraid of this sign. 'And if ever a nasty goblin should find his way into your room,' he said, 'you just show him the hilt of your sword and point the cross at him. You'll see how quickly he will disappear.'

But would not the remark that a goblin *might* find his way into the child's bedroom make him more frightened than ever? It is difficult to tell, but what matters is that an atmosphere of loving trust should flow between child and adult. And then it is often quite sufficient to leave the bedroom door ajar as a gesture of nearness and a close link. Almost all children go through a period when they are afraid to go to sleep in the dark because they are plagued by disquieting thoughts. The serene light of a burning candle will also help them to go to sleep peacefully. If seven-year-olds should declare that fairy tales are 'baby stuff,' they merely imitate the attitude of people around them. If they meet adults who look upon the language of fairy tales as an expression of human culture, they will never voice such a statement. When it is story time in Class 1 the children settle down in anticipation, quieten each other and listen with wide-open eyes. Sometimes they cannot suppress their comments. Hearing of the wicked deeds of a magician, a plucky and lively little boy might protest loudly: 'Isn't he horrid!' Or the eyes of a rather timid and restless little girl might light up when she hears how the poor little mouse is finally changed into a princess: 'Oh, how lovely!'

Sometimes the question pops up, 'Is this story true?' But such doubts are rather fleeting, for the fairy tale soon claims full attention. If the teacher takes care to tell only stories which express inner truths in picture form, she can say with a good conscience, 'Yes, in their way, fairy tales are true.'

If a child brings into the classroom real scepticism picked up outside school, then the teacher will have to explain that the world of fairy tales is different from the world around us, but that it nevertheless exists.

Children who are used to hearing genuine fairy tales develop quite a feeling for their quality. Made-up stories which pretend to be fairy tales but are fantastic or too realistic, are often received with disappointment and dissatisfaction simply because they have no depth and because they are inartistic. One unfortunate teacher who once told such a story to her class was met with the remark, 'And now will you us a *proper* fairy tale?'

When we really enter into the world of fairy tales and know how much their pictures have to offer, we gain a real yardstick with which to measure the 'value' of the pictures in comic books, cartoon films and the like. One could compare them with junk food which fills you up for the moment but soon leaves you hungrier than ever, or even undernourished.

Introducing arithmetic

The class teacher is talking to her six-year-old pupils in Class 1. A farmer has made a large cheese which he cuts into ten pieces. He has promised three pieces to his neighbours and needs one for his own family for tea. How many pieces are left for him to sell at the market? (This question appeals to order-loving melancholics who like to plan carefully.)

The market is very crowded. Four big, fat ladies are pushing their way towards the farmer and each buys one piece of cheese. (Now it is time to direct a question to the cholerics, who are becoming rather restless.) Strangely enough, each lady has a husband and four children, all of whom like cheese. How many people are there altogether in the four families who will be having cheese for tea?

The pushing and shoving in the market place is getting even worse. A hungry boy cannot resist the temptation to pinch a piece of cheese and the butcher's dog runs off with another. After a while the boy's guilty conscience makes him return his piece of cheese. But the farmer is kind-hearted and lets him keep half of it. The dog, however, does not return, since he has wasted no time in eating up his piece. How many pieces has the farmer now? (The crowds of people and jumble of events suggest a whole host of further questions specially suited to the sanguine children.)

Now it is time to think of all the people who will have eaten some of the lovely cheese. (Here the phlegmatics, always at home in the company of people enjoying their food, can do their bit of steady adding up.)

This example illustrates how the teacher can involve the four temperaments even during an arithmetic lesson.

The four basic processes of arithmetic are always applied side by side. In this subject the teacher can move along fairly rapidly, in contrast to writing and reading lessons.

One thing is fundamental: numbers are generally regarded as a part of a whole (for instance, the farmer's large cheese). This can be done in many different ways. For instance, a certain distance between two places can be subdivided into the required number of parts, or a king can divide his kingdom into provinces to be shared amongst his sons and vassals, and so on.

Such an 'analytical' approach stimulates the imaginative powers of the child. It is possible to subdivide a duodecimal number in many different ways, whereas the opposite way of adding up the factors allows far less freedom (needless to say it is essential to practise the 'synthetic' approach as well). There is, however, one more point which should be mentioned here.

The all-encompassing number one

Some ancient myths describe how, at the beginning of the world, the various elements were created out of one entity, such as that of Okeanos in Greek and that of the Giant Ymir in Nordic mythology. The totality sacrifices itself so that the parts can be created. When practising arithmetic, the teacher again and again returns to this same principle, by starting with the whole which is then divided up to be given away.

Children feel quite naturally that the world is a unity. According to Piaget, the tendency to regard God as the creator of all things is found not only among children who have had a religious upbringing.

In this way, arithmetic lessons can even provide an opportunity for exercising moral qualities! But they can equally well become a playground for little egoisms if one is not careful: if you get two sweets from Charles, three from Richard, and two from Mary, how many will you have? Somehow one easily slips into this kind of question in mental arithmetic instead of asking the same question the other way round: If you give Charles two sweets, Richard three, and Mary two, how many will you have given away? Why should this be so? It is because when counting, measuring or comparing, egoism tends to enter instinctively, particularly when one appeals only to the intellect. For the intellect is by nature rapacious, it wants to conquer, it is greedy for new things. Feelings and willpower are needed to counteract this by selflessness. And yet, when dealing with numbers, an objective and unemotional attitude is called for. Such observations are not insignificant. Simply by the choice of her examples the teacher has it in her power to let moral impulses permeate her lessons quite imperceptibly.

Learning tables through movement

The best way of introducing children to the world of numbers is by letting them move to rhythms, which in any case are inherent in counting and in number series.

In Class 1, all the children might follow the teacher round the classroom counting in threes, with two tiptoed steps followed by a stamp and a clap of hands:

One, Two, *Three;*
Four, Five, *Six;*
Seven, Eight, *Nine;*
Ten, Eleven, *Twelve* …

In Class 2, the children recite their tables up to twelve to the accompaniment of appropriate movements, such as clapping or jumping, and their boisterous enthusiasm can reverberate throughout the school:

Three is one times three, —
Six is two times three, etc.

As the numbers get bigger, the activity is lifted more and more into the thinking sphere:

Forty-five is *Five* times nine;
Fifty-four is *Six* times nine;
Sixty-three is *Seven* times nine;
Seventy-two is *Eight* times nine, etc.

There is no better training for the memory than learning tables by heart in arithmetic. Every series of numbers is meaningful and full of secrets which can be discovered later on.

For instance, one can start with the numbers in the nine-times table: 18, 27, 36, 45, 54, 63, 72, 81. When adding the digits of each multiple, the sum will be nine. Other discoveries can be made

Doubling and halving.

Above: The idea that the parts derive from the whole is one that has a natural appeal for children.

which fill the children with both wonder and enthusiasm.

Apart from recognizing such laws of number, one must not forget to bring many examples from daily life. In Class 3, the main-lesson periods of house-building and farming give many opportunities for weighing and measuring. The length, breadth and height of the classroom can be measured, the length and width of the playground, etc.

Beside this practical aspect, the world of pure numbers remains important and fascinating. For instance, the children in Class 3 or 4 can be confronted with the following phenomenon:

$$
\begin{array}{l}
1 \times 1 = 1 \\
2 \times 2 = 4 \\
3 \times 3 = 9 \\
4 \times 4 = 16 \\
5 \times 5 = 25
\end{array}
\left.\begin{array}{l} \} 3 \\ \} 5 \\ \} 7 \\ \} 9 \end{array}\right\}
\begin{array}{l} \} 2 \\ \} 2 \\ \} 2 \end{array}
$$

The cholerics are now in the grip of the fervour of discovery. Surely at some point the 'difference between the differences' must become larger than 2! They try out ever larger numbers:

$$
\begin{array}{l}
10 \times 10 = 100 \\
11 \times 11 = 121 \\
12 \times 12 = 144 \\
13 \times 13 = 169 \\
14 \times 14 = 196
\end{array}
\left.\begin{array}{l} \} 21 \\ \} 23 \\ \} 25 \\ \} 27 \end{array}\right\}
\begin{array}{l} \} 2 \\ \} 2 \\ \} 2 \end{array}
$$

But at last they realize that the world of numbers knows no compromise and nothing in it is arbitrary. The laws are immutable and often surprisingly different from what one would expect. They are inscribed in the blueprint of the universe. In this way, one not only awakens an urge for investigation in the children, but helps them to develop their thinking in a fitting and healthy manner.

Above: Some teachers like to use the Roman numerals when first introducing arithmetic, as they have a direct visual relationship with the fingers, and the Arabic numbers soon follow.
Below: These flower patterns can be used either for addition, multiplication, or division. Such a picture makes immediately obvious the relationship between the four rules.

Fables and legends in Class Two

The Mouse said to the Elephant as they walked over the bridge, 'Fine lot of noise we two are making as the bridge rumbles!'

Fables are usually very terse and concise. However, children are not likely to appreciate their striking worldly wisdom unless the ground has been adequately prepared by a conversation leading to the point of the fable in question.

For instance: two men go up into the hay loft to get hay for the cows. One is strong and pitches huge bundles of hay down through the trapdoor into the mangers. The other is weak and only manages to throw down a few handfuls. But afterwards he boasts about the huge bales of hay which he has given the cows. The children understand the character of each man, the one strong but thoughtful and silent, the other weak but talkative and boastful. Later you ask the children to describe what an elephant and a mouse look like; and then you can tell the fable.

The frog who wants to look as big as an ox puffs himself up until he bursts. Being unable to reach the grapes, the fox saves face by saying that they are sour anyway. The stag, seeing his reflection in a pond, admires his beautiful antlers but deplores his thin little legs. But when chased by a lion, his antlers are caught in the branches of a tree and he awaits his doom, realizing that his deplorable legs could have saved him while his magnificent antlers were the cause of his ensuing death.

Fables show us human weaknesses in animal form and neither fur nor feathers can disguise this fact. Sometimes children will laugh, sometimes they are indignant. However, if a teacher were to tell too many fables, their laughter and indignation could easily turn to mockery. Therefore, fables need a counterbalance: stories which do not ridicule but which are uplifting. In contrast to human faults being exposed via the animal, children also need to look up to human beings who have overcome their animal nature and who, therefore, are able to tame wild animals whose mode of life would destroy the orderly world. Such characters can be found in the myths and legends.

We live in an age in which legends, with their 'senseless' miracles and pious talk, are usually looked upon as being utterly boring and anachronistic. Such an opinion is quite justified in the case of legends invented for sentimental or even mercenary reasons. But genuine legends spring from a different source and they tower above their false offspring like truly creative genius over weakness, resignation and despondency.

Offerus was a giant of a man, eleven cubits tall, and he wanted to serve only the strongest master. When he noticed his king making the sign of the cross at the mention of the devil, Offerus decided to serve the devil instead. Seeing the devil bow before a cross on the wayside, Offerus sought counsel of an old hermit who told him about the true Lord of the world. But how could he serve this Lord? Hardly by praying and fasting, since Offerus needed plenty to eat to keep up his physical strength. So he carried wanderers on his shoulders across the turbulent waters of a rushing river. One night Offerus heard a child calling three times. He took him on his mighty shoulders but the child's weight seemed to increase until, in midstream, the burden became heavier than any he had yet carried across. The child on his shoulders was Christ, who carries the burdens of the whole world. In the darkness of the night the

child shone like the sun above the wild waters (see drawing, p. 132). Thus Offerus, sinking into the water, was christened 'Christ-Offerus,' the Bearer of Christ.

St Francis renounced his extravagant way of life and his promising career as a soldier. He became the minstrel of love, the lover of poverty and peace. He mortified his body, 'Brother Ass,' but retained his good humour and his love of nature. He practised self control by fasting, thus all the better understanding the hunger felt by the animals: on behalf of the citizens of Gubbio he promises the man-eating wolf a permanent supply of food; humbly the fierce animal places its paw in his hand. St Francis tamed his own restlessness and loquacity, but he loved the chattering swallows and the cooing doves who listened to his sermons.

Raniero di Ranieri, the crusader, journeys with his lighted candle from Jerusalem to Florence over mountains and through deserts. His heart changes as he guards the precious flame through all dangers and adventures. This is one of the most moving of Selma Lagerlöf's Christ legends which the teacher could tell little by little over a period of many days.

Fables and legends have been told ever since the remotest past. They show us two sides of man's nature, and how these can become balanced.

According to Blaise Pascal's wise premise, he who is able to unite and reconcile the deepest contrasts in himself is capable of achieving greatness. 'It is dangerous to show men how much they resemble animals without also showing them their own greatness. It is equally dangerous to let them be aware of their loftiness without also pointing to their baseness.'

The Old Testament in Class Three

The events, the language and the characters of the Bible stories are intimately interwoven with western culture. They can be found in the arts, in sayings and proverbs, and indeed they have become part and parcel of our world view. Deprived of the Old Testament, children would lack one of the fundamental bases for understanding our past.

But these stories have far more to offer than a mere understanding of the historic roots of our civilization, as the following incident may indicate. A nine-year-old pupil in Class 3 of a Waldorf School was unable to attend school for a while and asked his father to tell him the Bible stories he was missing. The father asked the teacher which stories were involved and then told them to his son as best he could. When he came to a passage where he had to mention the name of God, the boy was most agitated and interrupted him, saying, 'Father, you must never say "God," you must say "the Lord," just as the Bible does.'

There is no other work in the whole of world literature which, from beginning to end, deals so thoroughly with the problem of authority.

The Old Testament — from which only a selection of significant stories is told — speaks at first of the whole of humanity, then of the Semites, then of the Israelites, and finally only of the tribe of Judah. But, throughout, the principal character is the same, the Lord God himself. People break His commandments or even deny Him and He is compelled to chastise them. His punishments are often extremely severe but He is not petty. At times He even protects those who defy Him or those who commit sins. Not many of the characters in the Old Testament could approach the throne of the highest judge with completely pure hands.

How will this wily fox manage to entice the tasty bit of cheese out of the raven's beak? (Class 2, Stockholm, Sweden).

Offerus carries the Child through the waters in the night, thus becoming Christ-Offerus (Class 2, Stockholm, Sweden).

Adam and Eve disobey His commandments and thus become the forebears of human beings who have to sustain themselves by reaping the fruits of the earth.

The descendants of Cain, the fratricide, become the ancestors of cattle-breeding nomads, artisans and craftsmen. The arrogance of the attempt to build the Tower of Babel leads to the scattering of the peoples and the birth of many tongues and hence to the spread of civilization over the face of the earth. Isaac's son Jacob wins his birthright by deception, thus becoming the ancestor of the twelve tribes of Israel. Through the falsehood of his brothers, Joseph is led into Egypt, to be followed gradually by the whole of his people. Moses, who slays an Egyptian in anger, leads the children of Israel out of slavery. He meets the Lord on Mount Sinai and receives the tablets of the law, thus laying the foundation for the future religion of his people. Saul, David and Solomon are all problematic characters, and yet they are instrumental for the continuation of the work of God. With His immeasurable wisdom the Lord succeeds in bending the forces of defiance and of evil, thus making them serve the order of His universe.

The teacher can avoid much moralizing by telling the stories of the Old Testament, whose pictures are quite different from those in fairy tales, fables and legends. The narrative style of the Bible is more complex and liable to varying interpretations. The stories do not always have a happy ending, but they are loaded with moral force.

When the children are indignant about Adam and Eve, or tremble on account of the Flood, sigh with relief when Abraham is spread the command

In this picture the child has obviously delighted in letting the Tower of Babel grow higher and higher. (Class 3).

to sacrifice Isaac, or wonder at the revelation on Mount Sinai, rejoice with David, or clench their fists against Goliath and the Philistines, then they experience in great pictures the problems with which they are wrestling more or less consciously within their own souls — the new Covenant, which at their stage they have to enter into with their fellow beings, the experience of both reverence and resentment, of obedience and wilfulness, and, not least, the dim awareness that something new is happening in their own development. This is the crisis at the age of nine, the 'new age of defiance.'

Stories relating to individual problems

Stories illustrating the inner situation of an individual child or of a whole group can have amazingly far-reaching effects. In such stories children experience their own shortcomings and the consequences of their actions with the same keen interest with which they usually follow the events and adventures of a well-loved hero, without, however, realizing that they are looking at themselves. In this way it is possible to tackle personal problems or bad habits which would otherwise be very difficult to deal with. But it is most important that when listening to such a story the children remain completely unaware of the teacher's real purpose in telling it.

Among her group of seven-year-olds, a teacher once had a boy who often told lies. Thinking of him, she told her class 'The Pearl of Truth' by Zacharias Topelius. In this story the Queen of the Land of Truth has lost an immensely valuable pearl down a deep well. One by one her subjects climb down into the well to search for the pearl.

Anyone who has told a lie even only once in their life comes up again with a black ring round his mouth. Those who have lied frequently return with large black stains on their faces. During the course of the story the boy in question clearly showed that in fact he detested lies. Suddenly he blurted out: 'I nev… always lie!' A moment's reflection had turned yet another of the boy's lies into truth. The teacher apparently took no notice of this reaction and continued with the story.

The boy's exclamation bore witness to a moment of deep self recognition. At about the same time his family moved house and their way of life also changed to a certain extent. The story contributed towards a healing process which eventually led to the boy becoming more harmonious and, as a result, more truthful.

If the teacher does not know of a suitable story, they should try to make one up. It need not be a poetic masterpiece! Steiner emphasized that what matters is the teacher's effort to enter into the being and actions of the little miscreant. Though the story may be amateurish, the inner effort has a very strong effect upon the pupils.

One young and inexperienced teacher found that he could not control his very lively Class 1. In despair he sent the worst culprits out of the classroom. In the corridor they found a coal scuttle and began pelting each other with pieces of coal. Some of the young scamps burst back into the classroom and there was complete chaos. As this was the last lesson of the day, some mothers began to arrive to collect their children and witnessed this scene.

This and similar experiences profoundly depressed the young teacher. He began to spend his evenings trying to find a solution to his problem. Naturally his thoughts turned again and again to the wildest of the children. Gradually a

The god Odin and his eight-legged steed Sleipnir. (Class 4).

story began to emerge as a result. It was about a youth who had been given the task of looking after the king's sheep and whose life would be forfeited if he lost any of them. But a number of the sheep took no notice of the young shepherd nor of his dog and ran far away. Others were scattered by the wolf. After several adventures and with the help of kind people he was at last able to collect all the sheep together again and bring them back to the king.

The children listened attentively to the story of the straying sheep. Some of them expressed their indignation about the stupidity and disobedience of the animals. The parallel situation in the class was obvious, yet the teacher avoided hinting at it and the children said nothing. Nevertheless, something had changed. A link of sympathy was at last established without which no work can flourish in any class. Of course, the behaviour of the class was far from exemplary even then, but a lasting contact between the teacher and the children had been made.

Stories of this therapeutic kind can still be very effective when children are approaching puberty. A boy aged eleven once had to face a difficult home situation caused by his parents' divorce. This, on top of his own personality difficulties, made him very aggressive. One day he picked up a stone and threw it at a former older pupil who had come back to the school on a visit. At the same time he sneered at the older boy, whom he knew well and actually admired.

The teacher decided to take 'indirect' action in the hope of helping the boy to repent of what he had done. She was in the middle of a main lesson on geography, describing the spread of local industry in one of the country's provinces. She now wove into the lesson a dramatic story about two men who had been good friends and comrades at work, but between whom enmity had gradually grown which finally led to a violent fight in the street.

The children were very indignant and the boy in question interrupted, saying: 'I didn't do it like that!' followed almost immediately by: 'I didn't really mean to do it!' The teacher took no notice and finished her story. The other children in the class did not notice what was going on, but after the lesson the boy went to the teacher and said: 'I don't know why I did it, I'm going to apologize to him.' To the joy and surprise of the older boy he really did conquer his pride and apologized. This incident contributed greatly to the boy gradually becoming more harmonious.

Those who create, prepare and tell such stories, really know what it is to share in the children's inner battles with the problems life brings them.

The ninth year — a turning point

Victor was nine. He had always been easy to manage both at home and at school. One day his parents had reason to complain to the class teacher that Victor had suddenly become extremely obstreperous, refused to take part in the usual Sunday walk, and was most unruly. The music teacher, too, had been having trouble. Victor had always been quite a support in the class, but now he had been blowing his recorder upside down, and doing many other silly things. Even his handwriting had changed to a kind of miniature writing. After four or five months this phase passed. He became quieter again, and the unruliness came to an end.

At this age an intelligent child can gaze long and silently at an adult with the unspoken question as to what kind of person the adult really is.

The unconscious feeling can arise in the child that the adult has been weighed-up and found wanting. In such a situation the child's behaviour alters from one moment to the next. All respect has vanished.

Children who have been forced to experience all too often in their own lives the effects of adult insecurity, such as continuous anxiety over the smallest indisposition, giving way to the most fleeting of moods etc., can just at this age find themselves in a real period of crisis. This can show itself in attacks of fear, outbreaks of temper, or other similarly striking symptoms.

At this age whole classes may put their teacher to the test. Earlier on children were simply noisy at times. Now they will do little experiments. How will the teacher react when a snowball is fastened to the ceiling just above the spot where he usually stands, and slowly begins to drip on to him? His weaknesses both large and small are noticed and give rise to comments. They are also aptly copied. It has also been observed that children of this age can secretly imitate and ridicule in a completely heartless way, the weakness of some child in the class. If the teacher feels personally injured, or reacts with stern or unconsidered disciplinary measures, a really difficult and unpleasant situation may develop.

What is it that is actually taking place in the child at this particular stage? Rudolf Steiner describes this phenomenon as a process of emancipation with consequences of greater import than we often realize.

Even if the original instinctive experience of 'I' comes much earlier than this, age three, before the age of nine children are not able consciously to experience themselves as separate from their environment. The instinctive longing of the little child to identify itself with animals, plants, and stones, with wind and cloud and star, is often regarded as a kind of childish anthropomorphism, a more or less conscious attempt to 'ensoul' the outer reality. Steiner maintains that such terms do not do justice to the entirely spontaneous and unintellectual element in the child's mode of experience. When Piaget describes how children before the seventh year grasp reality as an undifferentiated unity, how they are not in the position to distinguish between their own content of consciousness, and that of the objects in the world around them, and then how in the period from the eighth to the eleventh year they lose their anthropomorphism, and begin to look at things in a realistic way, then he comes very near to Steiner's ideas, even if his manner of expressing himself is a little different. (Guido Petter, *The Spiritual Development of the Child in the Works of Jean Piaget.*)

During the first three school years the teacher must pay due regard to this characteristic in her whole way of teaching. Earth and sun, plant and animal must speak to each other as if they were human beings. Only in Class 4 does she move on, step by step, to describing things 'as they are.'

It is this change in their relationship to the environment that causes so many children of this age to go through a period of alienation. The fact is that they can now observe their teacher with much greater awareness than before. But they are testing 'authority,' not because they want to shake it off, but because they want to make sure it really exists.

This remark of a nine-year old choleric, about a teacher of riper years who had mastered the difficult art of being strict and kindly at the same time, is typical for this age, 'The old thing is alright — as long as you do what she tells you!'

Having saved up the realistic presentation of

reality for this point of time, the class teacher in the Waldorf School now has at his disposal a powerful tool with which to overcome the difficulties. He has a whole battery of exciting subjects, which convey new knowledge. Local geography and animal study are undertaken in Class 4; general geography, botany and history in Class 5. For now the children have reached the inner maturity they need to look with wide-awake eyes at the world of reality, armed and equipped with an as yet unused and therefore keen desire for learning.

Environmental studies

In the first years of school the souls of healthy children still live strongly in the world of pictures created by the human imagination. The instinctive wish at this age to follow everything in the environment with close interest can actually best be served by the teacher clothing the events of this world in living stories. Field and wood, stream and bank, house and garden, flower and tree, bird and fish, hold conversations with each other as if they were people. In the third class, when the children are nearing the age of nine, another approach begins. The transition can be made by the teacher by speaking of objects and activities which are common to the realm of fairy tales as well as the world around us, and therefore have something of an archetypal quality. For instance, she may speak to the children of the farmer and his plough, the carpenter and his saw, the fisher and his net, the bricklayer and his trowel.

Today or yesterday

The objection could be raised that such an approach is in certain respects not true to the facts. Would it not be more in keeping to describe to the children the working world as it is today, in a straightforward and direct way? But whenever someone actually does this in a one-sided way, they are contributing to that unattached and rather conceited attitude which is so easily engendered in children today by our modern ways of life and thought. Life itself brings it about that in most cases our pupils come to judge the world according to prevailing modern standards. We as teachers must make it possible through our consciously directed efforts that they gradually acquire for themselves a humanly balanced approach to the world, with due regard to our historical development. Our forefathers, who did their farming without tractors, fishing without trawlers and echo-sounders, were neither stupid nor impractical in the eyes of their contemporaries. We have been able to achieve more than they did, because we, as it were, stand on their shoulders. We must feel gratitude towards them. Seen from this aspect, it is entirely in keeping with the times, when teaching a third class, to make use of many such examples which have either no special time association at all or belong to a past age.

For instance, the teacher may describe the various types of grain and their special qualities

Opposite: When children are nine or ten years old they become aware in a different way of the world around them. It is important at this point to introduce subjects that provide full opportunity for their new faculties of observation and learning. In Class 3 different basic crafts are presented, and in Class 4 the study of the home environment. These are like doors through which the child steps out into the world.
The form of the cathedral is from observation, the colours originate in the child's imagination (Class 4, Strasbourg, France).

Left. It is not an easy matter to draw a map for the first time. For how can you possibly fit in all the interesting things you see on your way to school in one and the same picture? (Class 4, Antwerp, Belgium).

Right: If the wind did not continually bring fresh air from the sea into the big industrial cities, human beings could not go on living there (New York, USA).

without the wind we human beings could not live.

Watching a house being built is a memorable experience in the third or fourth class. The work of the brick layer is one of the archetypal crafts which we can still see today (Stuttgart, Germany).

and uses, to help the children distinguish between wheat, rye, barley and oats. He may describe how in earlier times corn was harvested, threshed, dried, milled and baked. He may tell the children how butter and cheese were made, how meat and vegetables were preserved, how people manured and sowed their fields, and how they built their houses. It is a good thing if every child once in their lifetime can handle implements and materials such as a butter churn, a plough, bricks and mortar etc., or at least watch them being used. The crafts and skills concerned can be grasped by younger children because they are simple. They provide a sound basis for later understanding of complicated technical processes.

When building is the subject under discussion, one particular aspect, previously not so thoroughly dealt with, becomes important, the question of weights and measures. The children's interest in this area of mathematics can be awakened when they realize that in olden times measurements of length were often derived from the human body, for instance, an inch, a foot, a yard, a mile (the Roman *mille passus*). Later they also learn the metric units of measurement — metres, litres, kilograms etc. — which are however more abstract in their derivation. It is most important that these calculations, when one reaches this point, are exactly worked out. Pupils usually find great delight in measuring their classroom, houses, gardens and fields.

In Class 4, it is clear that the teacher must introduce new and lively themes to meet the increasing awareness of the ten-year-olds. Now we come to a more detailed study of the child's surroundings. The history and geography of the town or village and its immediate neighbourhood are described. As a background activity to this study, excursions are made to farms, mills, factories, museums, churches, the town hall etc., and the children draw or paint pictures of what they have seen.

Another significant experience can be introduced in connection with this subject. The children draw a picture of their own route to school, starting from the bed where they slept, and ending in the classroom. The houses, of course, must be rather small. One has to draw this as it would look to a bird or the pilot of a low-flying helicopter. For the first time, the child draws a kind of map.

The human being and the animal world

To what extent is there kinship between human beings and animals, and what distinguishes the one from the other? In a preliminary discussion between teacher and children in Class 4, leading up to the study of elementary zoology, significant differences can arise. The children can discover that each animal is able to do something special which human beings cannot do without tools.

Animal and human limbs

Such a discussion may result in the children becoming especially interested in the differentiation between the limbs of the various animals, in comparison with human ones. For instance, a squid propels itself along by expelling the water it takes in. Its tentacles are not actual limbs, but rather like outstretched lips feeling around for their prey, which they then greedily engulf. In the case of the mole, the fore-feet, which are used for digging, are short but very muscular, the toes are webbed and flattened out to form a kind of shovel, the bare palms are turned outwards. The mole can neither jump nor climb, and therefore

The eagle is at home in the air (Stuttgart, Germany).

only creeps out of its burrow at night. Strangely enough, it is also a good swimmer. But digging is its greatest skill.

In the same way the seal, with its trunk shaped like a large drop and its legs transformed to flappers, belongs to the water in which it lives. Out of the water it is helpless and clumsy.

The woodpecker is neither a hunter nor skilful in flight. Its feet are formed in such a way that it can grasp a tree-trunk, holding itself upright to peck at the bark.

The brown bear, despite its heavy build, is quick-moving and nimble. Clutching a dead horse in its fore-paws, it can climb a narrow mountain path. Equally well it can catch up with a running reindeer, and bring it to the ground with a single blow. Quite often it walks upright, treading the ground rather like a human being, with the flat of its foot. But its claws can never be retracted. Its touch is always aggressive.

In every case animals can use their limbs only in a specialized way. It is their instinctive desires that dictate their movements; getting food, reproduction, or defence.

Here we come to significant differences between human beings and animals. Human beings are not able to swim, run, or climb as well as the various 'specialists' among the animals. But on the other hand we are versatile. We can make tools for ourselves, which often far outstrip the achievements of the animals. We can use our hands for activities which we have consciously decided to carry out, activities which from a material point of view may seem unmotivated, and stand in direct contrast to certain instincts which we share with the animals. We can perform hand movements which are exclusive to the human race, such as making and controlling machines, writing, playing a musical instrument, painting and modelling. Rudolf Steiner said, 'There is no more beautiful symbol of human freedom than the human arm and hand.'

Animals and the temperaments

Among the instinctive capacities, which human beings have in the age of childhood, and later to a great extent loses, belongs the ability to identify ourselves with the experience of a certain animal. The teacher can work with this, inasmuch as she characterizes animals which clearly represent one or another of the temperaments. If she gives a lively description, it is a matter of course that the grazing cow will especially appeal to the phlegmatic children, the pouncing lion to the cholerics, and the leaping antelope to the sanguines. Perhaps the melancholic children in the class, especially those with a hint of choler, will be drawn to the eagle.

But there are also animals which can be so described that they have an appeal to all the temperaments. The octopus or squid was painted at the same time by the whole class (see overleaf). These pictures clearly show how instinctive and how varied is the approach of the different children in the class to the same subject. It is essential that in this period children should not be led to draw in a naturalistic way, but should be allowed to express to the full their own inner predispositions. Whoever is inclined to think that the paintings done by Waldorf pupils have a common style should carefully compare this set of paintings of the octopus.

Paintings of an octopus by the same class.

Above: Form and movement are reminiscent of early cave drawings. (Class 8, Cape Town, South Africa). Below: A lion hunting for prey (Class 5).

Botany

Basic conditions of plant life

Teaching about plants can begin with a conversation between class and teacher about the importance of the sun in the life of the plant. The children's attention can be drawn to the yearly variations in the sun's daily course in the temperate zones, the first sensitive reactions in tree and bud to the increasing daylight, the great changes that come with the warmth of spring. Without making use of abstract scientific concepts, the teacher can call on the children's own powers of observation by speaking of the difference between the parts of the plant exposed to the light, and those under the earth. How colourful and delicate is the blossom, how soft and full of sap the leaf and stem, how strong and hard the white or brownish root.

The sun, however, is only one of the two decisive factors for plant life. The other is the soil, and from the soil comes moisture. A wilting pot plant which recovers its erectness and begins to grow again when it is watered demonstrates to the children the significance of moisture. The teacher may describe the leguminous plants, which in wet summers merely grow longer and longer without forming seed, and on the other hand the trees whose leaves after a dry growing season turn yellow and wither in early summer. Pine trees with their shallow roots can only exist in a moist soil, whereas the deeper-rooting firs can survive in a drier situation.

But soil fertility does not only depend on water. Again in quite a simple but concrete way the teacher can show the children the differences in the structure and composition of the soil in different neighbourhoods and point out that while some plants need quite a special soil condition, others will grow anywhere.

After dwelling on these more general aspects, examples may be given of particular plant communities which the children themselves may have observed. For instance, what sort of plants do we usually find on a pasture, and which on grassland where no animals graze, on heaths or in bogs, on mountain slopes or in fertile valleys, in different types of woodlands? What do we see growing on waste land, and what in a well-tended garden? What plants appear during the course of the changing seasons?

The child's growing awareness for the plant world which results from such considerations throws a new light on farming practices which were first introduced in Class 3. The teacher can point out, for example, what a vast difference there is when the farmer ploughs up an old-established pasture where the soil has been kept fertile for years by grazing animals and the growth of white clover, or when he cultivates a piece of ground, which through greed has been exploited by monoculture.

One of the factors that has contributed to the destruction of our natural environment is a general lack of knowledge of the basic requirements of the plant. Only when children at the right stage of their development get a real experience of how climate, soil and vegetation form an inter-related whole will they have the insight later on to help in maintaining soil fertility and a healthy plant life in various regions of the world.

The classification of plants

But how can teachers, when they want to remain in the realm of concrete observation, give the children some kind of survey over the wide range of plant life?

One possibility would be to set side by side

Above: Sketch of a fern clump (Class 5, Forest Row, England).
Below: The hard old tree trunk performs the same function for the twigs and leaves sprouting from it as the mound of earth for the plants growing on its surface. (Class 5, Stockholm, Sweden).

the different levels of plant life (fungi, lichens, algae, mosses, ferns, flowering-plants etc.), with the stages of the child's development. The mushrooms, which while growing quickly are otherwise such undeveloped organisms, having neither leaves, stems or roots, can be compared to small babies. Flowering plants with their greater differentiation and possibilities correspond to the schoolchild, etc. Such an approach, as suggested by Rudolf Steiner in his lecture of Sep 2, 1919, is not just an arbitrary comparison, but one that is especially stimulating and fruitful for the child. Gerbert Grohmann, a botanist with many years' teaching experience in a Waldorf School, has elaborated and confirmed this in his book, *The Plant*.

Another way of achieving a similar survey would be to climb, in the children's imagination, a tropical mountain, such as the Kilimanjaro. The different vegetation zones, tropical forest, mixed woodland, moss-lichen belt, permanent snow, come into view, rather as if one were travelling from the Equator to the Poles. Looked at in this way, the two hemispheres appear like two mountains joined at the base. Plant study thus leads over into geography.

The value of plant study

Such a wide approach naturally makes demands on the teacher. Not everyone has the necessary knowledge and connection with nature. Would it not be good, just in this case, to avail oneself of various teaching aids? But which to choose? To examine a few wilting plant specimens in the classroom would actually be contrary to the desired outcome, which is to experience the plant world in its natural context. To make botanical excursions for the purpose of methodical observation is a sure way to spoil the children's experience of nature. No book, no coloured slide, no film can stimulate so strong an inner experience or so lively a conversation as gathering together what the children have actually seen themselves, supplemented by the teacher's account of what is further away and less known to them. Such a course of plant study certainly involves a long time spent in preparation by the teacher.

What is the real significance of this period of study? It is indeed a subject of the utmost importance. Rudolf Steiner has repeatedly impressed on us that the decrease in quality of agricultural produce is due to the fact that we have not acquired through his education a strong enough feeling for the importance of maintaining soil fertility. As he said in a lecture of August 14, 1924, 'If we wish to know how plant and earth belong together, then we must find out to what type of soil the single plant belongs; and how to manure the soil properly can only be learned by seeing the earth and the plant-world as a unity, and the plant as something growing within the organism of the earth.'

The problem raised here by Rudolf Steiner has become ever more acute. The enormous increase in the use of nitrogen fertilizers in modern agriculture has been a potent factor in exposing farm crops to the attacks of insect and fungus pests. In turn the use of pesticides to solve this problem is causing damage which is becoming more and more obvious. Because we have not understood the natural connection between the soil and plant life, we have caused destruction on a scale never known before. If these agricultural problems are to be successfully tackled, not only farmers, scientists and governments must take part, but also, because of the resultant cost, the ordinary consumer. Exploitation of nature will gradually have to give way to a deepened understanding for the essentials of ecology. Will our children be able to

The two hemispheres of the earth as two mountains, showing different vegetation zones (Class 5, Stockholm, Sweden).

The beginnings of precise botanical drawings (Class 5, Stuttgart, Germany).

think and act rightly in this sphere if the basis for this understanding has not been prepared through their early education?

Environmental studies

When, in Class 5, studies of the immediate environment pass over into geography proper, the children enter a realm of knowledge which in Rudolf Steiner's view is one of the most important:

> Teaching the child in this way, we place him into space, and he will begin to be interested in the world, in the whole wide world. And we shall see the results of this in many directions. A child with whom we study geography in an intelligent manner will have a more loving relationship to his fellow men than one who has no feeling of what proximity in space means; for he will learn to feel that he lives alongside other human beings, and he will come to have regard and respect for them.
>
> Such things play no little part in the moral training of the children, and the lack of attention to geography is partly responsible for the terrible decline in recent years of the brotherly love that should prevail among men. (*Education for Adolescents,* June 14, 1921)

The teaching of geography is one of the most important means of ensuring a sense of responsibility in later life towards the natural resources of the earth and their fair distribution for the benefit of people as a whole, rather than to the advantage of political or industrial power groups. There is hardly another sphere of study through which we can appeal so strongly, without the need to moralize, to the sense for 'brotherhood' in economic matters, as the study of geography in early adolescence.

The effect of the environment

In what way does our natural environment influence us? What is life like on the shores of the Arctic Ocean, where sometimes a boat has to break through the ice? How does it feel to live in a volcanic area, faced with earthquakes or flowing lava? The attempt to experience inwardly the most varied conditions of human life provide interesting and important themes for artistic activity.

The drawing of maps presents quite a new task. The transition from a simple sketch-plan of the neighbourhood, as was drawn earlier, to an actual map marks an important step in the child's development. The map shows little or nothing of what we actually see around us. To understand its meaning, one needs an appreciation of abstraction. This is something that usually only evolves in the child by the eleventh or twelfth year.

The best way of understanding a map is to draw or paint it. Different elements, such as a desert, a tropical forest, or a mountainous region, demand differing artistic treatment. For example in northern Europe the origin of Holland as land wrested from the sea, and its present contours, can be experienced through the intermingling

Above right: Fritjof Nansen's ship battling its way through polar ice.
Below right: Volcanic eruption.
The contrast of the subject matter in these two pictures is shown in every detail of form and colour (Bergen, Norway).

Having painted such a map of the Netherlands, it will be easy to remember how much of the land was reclaimed from the sea (Class 5, Leiden, Netherlands).

Finland is the land of a thousand lakes (Class 5, Helsinki, Finland).

Has the painter here realized the stark differences between Norway and Sweden from the cultural, as well as the geographical aspect? (Class 5, Stockholm, Sweden).

water-colours; blue is much in evidence in painting Finland as 'the land of a thousand lakes;' or depicting Norway, with its complicated structure of mountains and valleys, demands intricate detail.

Economic geography

In Class 5 a larger area is studied which forms either a regional or economic whole.

In Class 6 the power of thinking is beginning to awaken and with it the understanding for the laws of physics and chemistry. Geography lessons contribute facts that enlarge the children's inner horizon. They must be led into the realm of mineralogy, meteorology, astronomy, and especially to the consideration of the economic factors affecting the different regions of the entire globe.

Most Waldorf Schools are in temperate regions with relatively congenial conditions for plant growth and for intensive industrial development.

Of course, the children must learn to know their own surrounding in all its different aspects. But it is almost more important that they should become familiar with the details of everyday life and the special problems of people who have to struggle for their existence in quite different environments, for instance in tropical regions.

Cultural aspects

Economic considerations are continued in Classes 7 and 8, for at this age children delight in learning new facts, and often take an especial pleasure in statistics, graphs, or lists of names. Another new aspect too now enters in. The cultural traditions and the spiritual directions of the various peoples come more and more under consideration. It can be sufficient for the teacher to bring to the class certain examples which illuminate and characterize in a striking way the cultural climate of some particular region. In this context passages from various travellers' accounts of their experiences among the different peoples can be read and discussed.

History

Many people today have little sense of history. Interest in historical relationships must first be awakened. For only out of an understanding of the past is it possible to do justice to the present and to shape the future. Instruction in history in the early school years takes on special significance here, because it often produces lasting and effective impressions.

The historical approach was established in the curriculum of the Waldorf Schools from the beginning. It must be focussed on human, rather than national, history.

In Class 4 the children are introduced to the history of their immediate neighbourhood. In Class 5, however, this direction is not maintained, and national history is not the next step. The approach becomes immediately worldwide. But how can the interest of ten or eleven-year-olds be kindled for the remoter aspects of the history of humanity? Where should the teacher start?

Stages in historical evolution

The earliest religious documents give an indication of definite stages in the development of ancient peoples.

In the *Bhagavadgita* the holy Yogi sunk in meditation is presented as the highest aim of man. In the Persian *Zend-Avesta* other virtues are preeminent: the industrious farmer with his prosperous herds of cattle and flourishing crops becomes the ideal. In one of the Babylonian myths of creation, the human being's foremost task is to build temples to the gods. In Homer's epics, after the death of the valiant Achilles, the central figure is the clever Odysseus, who conquers Troy through his divinely inspired cunning and overcomes the many trials and tribulations that beset him on his homeward journey.

These examples illustrate four great stages in the history of humankind. The first was the religious attitude of the early nomadic civilizations, wholly turned towards the gods and away from the earth. Then came the devotion to the soil of the first tribes to settle down and cultivate the ground. A later stage was the development of an artistic culture, as exemplified by the river civilizations of the Middle East and their great monuments. And nearer our own time came the Greeks, with their newly awakened powers of organizing life through the faculty of thinking.

This evolutionary stream, flowing from east to west, and in time giving rise to our own form of civilization, had its origin in north-east India about 10000–8000 BC. It proceeded by way of Iran to Mesopotamia and Egypt, where the first great works of architecture and early writing arose about 3000 BC, and ultimately spread throughout the whole Mediterranean world. While there were many civilizations in different parts of the world, it is to a large extent the ones described here, which have laid the basis for the present western civilization.

When the teacher of Class 5 describes this development in a lively and imaginative way, she will find that the children become fascinated by this great canvas of historical evolution. The ancient myths and epics, which the children have heard at an earlier age, now assume a new significance as the backdrop of actual historical events.

Subjective or objective presentation?

There is always a problem when the subject matter of a lesson is presented primarily through the teacher herself and not through textbooks, and this comes to the fore especially in the teaching of history. The question arises how far one can achieve an objective approach.

An example may illustrate how this requirement can be met in Waldorf teaching methods.

History teaching in Class 7 should comprise those events in the fifteenth and sixteenth centuries which make it the dawn of a new era: the Renaissance, the Reformation, the great new discoveries in the fields of geography and astronomy. It is obviously impossible to confine oneself to a mere catalogue of events and to exclude any feeling of participation on the part of the pupil in the attempt to be objective. If you want to arouse the interest of thirteen-year-olds in Luther's 95 theses pinned to the church door at Wittenberg, in his appearance at the Diet of Worms and for his religious reforms in Saxony, you have to describe vividly the symptoms of decadence in the church of his time and especially Luther's own bold initiative. How shall the teacher describe this? Shall he portray equally dramatically his religious narrow-mindedness, his belief in the supreme power of the state, and his lack of understanding of what lay at the base of the peasants' revolts? Viewed historically, this would seem justified, but if this were too strongly emphasized, the children would not be able to sustain their admiration for Luther as a character.

This kind of situation presents a real dilemma. The prevalent idea today is that there should be

Hannibal's march across the Alps. (Class 6, Antwerp, Belgium).

no 'heroes.' Yet young people have a great need for personalities whom they can admire. If this is not satisfied in the classroom, and their enthusiasm for real things is not kindled, then no other objects of worship are available except those put forward by advertisements and mass media, which soon lose their glamour and are exchanged for other 'stars.'

A class teacher who faced the problem cited above approached it in the following way. First she described the Reformation in a sympathetic light, and presented Luther with an obvious undertone of appreciation. After a few days the whole class had adopted this attitude, and were loud in their denunciation of Luther's opponents. Now the teacher moved on to describing the Catholic world. She concentrated on the fierce battle that the Pope and the other Catholic leaders had to fight against the Turks. She portrayed in full detail the atrocities perpetrated by the Turks in the conquered territories, and the complete lack of help on the part of the Protestant princes. She also described vividly the brave and knightly John of Austria, half-brother of Philip of Spain, who led the Catholic fleet to victory against the Ottomans at Lepanto in 1571. Now the mood of the class changed entirely. One of the indignant questions was: 'But surely that must have meant that many people turned to Catholicism?' Of course it is then also essential to remind the class of the great treasures of scientific knowledge and artistic skills which came through Islam from the East from the time of the Crusades onwards.

If we wish as teachers to awaken in children a sense of what is generally human and not just nationalistic, then we cannot take as a starting point the glorious past of our own nation. The teaching of history must stand on a completely new basis. Even at eleven years of age the child can grasp the significance of a worldwide perspective, when the great cultural epochs are presented in a broad and colourful panorama against the background of actual historical events.

Drama

What is the significance of drama for the child in the Waldorf School? Of course, there are all kinds of plays. There are the brief scenes recited in the first class by the high, wavering childish voices of seven-year-olds and, at the other end of the scale, there are the classical dramas of Shakespeare, presented in the upper school with the youthful fervour of adolescence. It is often the custom that Class 8 performs some major piece before entering the upper school and that Class 12 presents some outstanding classical or modern drama. Here, however, we shall only comment upon what is presented in the way of plays at monthly or termly festivals.

What does Class 2 perform, for example? It might be a fable, or a legend, or a little poem which has been made into a drama. The class forms a chorus. One or several of the children dress up — and at once it turns into a dramatic presentation. Often they are all dressed up and then it becomes for them an unforgettable experience.

The most remarkable and perhaps most important dramatic presentations are to be found in the middle classes, somewhere around Class 4 or 5. At that age it is important that the plays are not banal, but have depth to give 'spiritual food' to nourish the children. Prose dialogue is much too difficult to handle and in any case, rhythmical speech in itself already possesses the quality of

The lower school term often finishes with putting on a bigger play. Scene from Henrik Ibsen's Peer Gynt *(Class 8, Tübingen, Germany).*

'spiritual food.' For example, let us enter the fifth class and observe:

> Shame on you, sons of Argos, you children!
> I trusted in you,
> You who with brave arms rescued our ships!
> But when you shun the danger of mortal combat,
> Then the day has come
> When the Trojans will compel us with force!'

There stands Hector, bathed in light, and there stands fleet-footed Achilles. And those children standing on the tower (of chairs placed on a table) must be Zeus himself, 'the cloud-shaker,' and lovely Hera. Here the *Iliad* comes to life! Their eyes are sparkling and their cheeks are glowing. The rhythm carries the voices so that the room resounds. It is quite sufficient if Agamemnon simply takes a step forward and brandishes his wooden sword a bit. All enemies fall like ninepins at his attack.

Or let us take a look at Class 4, where they are dramatizing Nordic mythology. The floors of many a Waldorf School have seen innumerable giants fall from the blows of Thor's hammer Mjolnir. The chorus first represents one character, then the other, and are responsible for all the props needed (a wall, a forest, a house, a street). Whoever momentarily does not act, simply melts in with the rest of the chorus. While it might be tempting to introduce naturalistic effects, this would go against the particular demands of this type of theatre.

On the other hand a dramatic presentation can tolerate a touch of the extreme and comical. A German Class 6 once practised a presentation of King Arthur and Merlin the Magician. They were acting in English and had learnt their pieces up to the dramatic moment when the sword in the anvil revealed its meaning. Then the teacher thought that there ought to be horses on the stage. The class was deeply insulted when he suggested they drape material over hobby horses. But the teacher explained that the heroes would be able to mount swiftly and move across the stage using their own legs. Eventually, these stylized 'suggestions' of horses proved to be the only appropriate solution.

Stage props often show remarkable ingenuity. Yard-long gilded horns on Thor's goats, a painted cardboard sheet that represents the side of a ship at the Battle of Salamis, a seven-headed dragon with seven smiling wide-eyed childlike heads, each with a collar out of which a stuffed dragon appears — all this makes an unforgettable impression.

The Battle of Salamis! That was a wonderful play! These children, who stood as still as candles while reciting their verses, were suddenly Greece personified, as can be seen in classical sculpture, or heard in the epic of Homer. The whole chorus was clothed in white and had the character of a power of fate, in whose hand it lay to conceal events (when it grouped itself at the front of the stage) or to reveal them (when it drew to the sides). This magical element is the quintessence of what happens on the stage when children perform.

If these plays simply occurred once a year, for example, as part of a programme at the end of the school year, then the impressions would be of no lasting value. Through regular festivals, however, the plays become an everyday part of the school. They must be rehearsed well in advance of the actual presentation, and the other pupils experience them as spectators. In this way the plays serve as an instrument of education.

Through looking on and participating, through words, gestures, rhythms, and movement of all kinds, feelings are awakened which otherwise might have remained dormant throughout one's whole life. A feeling for style, for rhythm and form has significance for the whole of life, and is not merely a superficial aesthetic effect of the moment.

Geometry

In the Waldorf Schools children are often taught to draw the most beautiful geometrical forms with the help of a ruler and compass, sometimes as early as the fourth or fifth class. Actual geometrical construction, however, is not introduced until Class 6.

Most of us usually associate the concept of geometry with long and difficult series of formal proofs. Here, however, something quite different is intended. Geometry can be *experienced* long before one has to *prove* anything with it.

What happens if one constructs a regular eighteen-sided figure and connects each point with the other? What happens if one intersects the radius of a circle six times and draws circles around the six intersecting points with the same radius? Or if one uses the same principle to construct twelve or more circles? What figures develop when one draws a system of 'rotating' semi circles into a large circle with each semi circle having a different centre? Approached in this way geometry becomes a voyage of discovery in a world of forms of infinite richness.

However, how does one find the path from the poetry of construction to the prose of truth? The theorem of Pythagoras can serve as an example of how these two worlds may be bridged. If the

Experiencing geometrical laws by construction and colouring is the beginning of a voyage of discovery.

children draw a rectangular triangle and construct squares on each side and cut both small ones according to one or other of the models in the accompanying pictures, they will immediately see that the entire large square can be covered by the shapes cut from the two small squares. The pupils can be encouraged to form the basic triangles of the whole construction in as many ways as possible. The principle always holds true. The areas of both small squares always exactly cover the large one.

Although such assignments still remain completely within the realm of the pictorial and concrete, they serve as practice of what is to come later. One should not then go on to the actual proofs until the children have reached the stage of development in which the need to explain causal relations has awakened and with it the joy in abstractions such as are to be found in algebra. This stage begins only around the twelfth year.

Visible proof of Pythagoras' theorum by cutting the squares to match the areas.

The twelfth year

Linda always seemed to be a reliable character. Her notebooks and practical work were finished with care and attention. Her general behaviour was always good-natured and friendly. In Class 6, at age twelve, a striking change took place. It began by her experimenting with a number of quite different writing styles: one with upright letters, one in which they slanted backward, one with letters slanting forward, one with large letters, and one with small ones; she even tried writing upside down. The next phase was experimenting with her face: eye shadow, rouge, new expressions, etc. During class she became more and more talkative and refused to sing or recite. Previously she had shown considerable grace in eurythmy and gymnastics. Now these exercises became a strain for her. If she was not actually busy with something, she preferred just to lie on the floor. Her moods and her limbs had suddenly become lethargic. Her moods changed quickly, however, depending upon what was going on around her. A little joke was all it took to make Linda happy again.

After the crisis of the ninth year, most children enter a harmonious period. Ten-year-olds are often very active and good-natured: 'When a ten-year-old is at his best, he gives such a well-balanced impression that he appears as the finished expression of nature's creative powers.' (Arnold Gesell, *Youth, the Years From Ten to Sixteen.*)

At the age of eleven and above all at twelve, the picture changes. The bones becomes heavier, and movements, especially in the case of boys, lose their gracefulness and become jerky and uneven. The tendency to rebel increases. The deep inner transformation, which appears as an accompanying phenomenon of puberty, has not only its dark side but also its bright side. Pupils of this age have a sense of responsibility and intellectual powers which the teacher need only encourage in order to see the beauty and strength of this period of life come to expression. Loneliness and true friendship, self-interest and devoted interest for others, death and love, which previously existed only in the unknown depths of feeling, now become a real personal experience. The independent life of feeling awakens and changes the relationship to the body, to the environment and to ideas and ideologies. It reflects in the ability to love and be interested in the world, as well as in the ability to reason and to judge.

In these years more and more specialized subjects are taken up in class; subjects which require independent thinking and individual initiative. Homework increases in its scope and becomes a responsibility which the young people begin to understand and appreciate.

Science

The physicist Walter Heitler wrote about the effect of scientific thinking on the modern world:

> Today when we work in the realm of atomic science or cosmology, or even the most modern area of physics, the physics of elementary particles, this no longer has the least thing to do with human life. On the other hand intellectual thinking is developed to an exceptionally high level … If scientific thinking of this type is carried to an extreme and consumes a large amount of human activity, then it is per-

haps understandable that it often, although not always, must be at the expense of other things, for example, the realm of feeling. *Here perhaps one can speak of a certain kind of destruction of the human soul. If one looks carefully enough one can actually observe this phenomenon.*

Of course, it is not so serious if this is limited to a small number of scientists. It does, however, become a serious matter if these scientists exert a decisive influence in public life. To some extent this is already often the case. But I would consider it alarming, if, as is perhaps partly the case already, this direction of abstract thinking were to extend over wide circles of the population — that is to say if one educates young people in this direction from the start, and if one sees to it that as many people as possible devote themselves largely to abstract thinking …

It has been suggested that physics instruction begin with the fundamental building block of matter, that is with electrons, protons, etc. Then the atom is gradually built (naturally only in thought), and out of the atom comes molecules, and out of molecules finally a piece of chalk or a stone that falls to the ground. That is just the opposite of what I would most decidedly recommend. The point of departure should be phenomena as they are actually experienced; observation is then supplemented through experimentation, and only then are the abstract concepts developed. Concepts in chemistry such as atoms and molecules should only come at the end.

Physics

A phlegmatic twelve-year-old girl, who was otherwise uninterested in her school work, came home and eagerly placed a number of conical glasses on the table, filled them with water to different levels, struck them with a fork, and poured water in and out, until she has worked out a little musical scale. 'What did you do today?'

'Physics, for the first time!' she beamed with joy.

There are probably few subjects which have as stirring an effect as physics. Children often get very enthusiastic about it. Physics instruction begins in Class 6 with phenomena from the most diverse fields of investigation.

It is good to start with acoustics. Most children have had some experience with musical instruments. Then one widens the field of observation by using unknown instruments. Only gradually does the physical treatment of acoustics develop from these artistic musical experiences. Experiments are begun and the most diverse objects are hung on a string, then struck to test their sound. The tonal qualities of different types of wood or plates of the most common metals are compared and arranged according to sound and pitch. The children should be given the opportunity to make as many discoveries as possible themselves. Finally a string is spanned across a sounding board, and in such a way that the vibrating part can be shortened or lengthened through a crosspiece that has been placed under it (a monochord). The children who can play the violin will immediately realize that one can produce tonal intervals by shortening the vibrating string. For the others it will take a bit more time to make this observation. However, since this deals with a very basic experience, one should wait patiently to see what they can discover on their own. When does

> Der Sand ordnete sich zu wunderbaren Figuren.
> Wir haben beobachtet:
>
> Vierstern — Achtstern — Sechzenstern
>
> Tiefer Ton — Höherer Ton — Sehr hoher Ton
> der Grieß gliedert sich wenig. — der Grieß wird mehr geformt. — der Grieß wird noch stärker geordnet.

Some of the well-known Chladni sound-forms produced through the vibrations of various musical tones. (Class 6, Stuttgart, Germany).

the octave sound? When you shorten the string by one half. If $2/3$ of the string vibrates then the musical interval of the fifth is heard, if $3/4$ then a fourth, and if $3/5$ then a sixth, etc. For the time being one can be satisfied simply with measuring the length. The number of vibrations — which, of course, the children cannot perceive immediately — are discussed later.

One can spread fine sand on a sheet of light metal which has been held securely in the centre and stroke the edge of the metal sheet with a violin bow. The magnificent Chladnian sound patterns arise through the dancing grains of sand. Here too there is great value in the fact that children experience how sounds can work creatively by producing forms in the sand. One draws as accurately as possible which figures arise from which sounds. The connection between the number of vibrations and the forms they produce is thus already visibly experienced at this point.

Then the field of optics is considered. As an example of a readily observable and impressive experiment one can show the pupils the Goethean archetypal colour phenomenon. The colour of a luminous or dark object changes strikingly when it is observed through an opaque or 'cloudy' medium (coloured panes of glass, liquids, clouds of smoke). The following experiments epitomize the phenomenon.

If you drop soapsuds in a transparent dish of water, a cloudy solution will appear. A light placed behind the dish will cause a warm, reddish colour to arise. If you place the light to the side of the container then you see a cold blue colour against a dark background. Now the teacher can remind the students that on beautiful evenings we often experience exactly the same phenomenon. The setting sun is a brilliant red while the sky on

When you blow across the mouth of a test tube, a note sounds that varies according to the amount of liquid it holds. This picture shows how fully the pupil has entered into the experiment. (Class 6, New York).

Mars, the god of iron, looks down on Manhattan. This picture arose from the consideration of the role of iron in modern civilization (New York).

the horizon is a deep blue. Clear objects observed through a translucent medium appear yellow or red. Dark objects seen through a light medium appear blue. The children have thus experienced a law (an archetypal phenomenon in the sense of Goethe's theory of colour) which they most likely would not have arrived at through their own thinking, but which was readily perceived through the experience of their senses. Thus the powers of observation are strengthened. In the same term, or at least in the same school year, the pupils are given a first glance at the other areas of classical physics by conducting experiments in the theory of heat, electricity and magnetism. Mechanics are not discussed until Class 7, while in Class 8 some basic concepts in hydraulics, aerodynamics and meteorology are developed, and all other areas are gone into more deeply.

Chemistry

At the beginning of chemistry instruction the students learn how the process of burning in different natural materials can take place in quite different ways. Why do some materials burn with a bright flame while others quickly turn into glowing embers? Why such dense smoke? Why does a flame make soot? One can set up a series of experiments to show the different ways in which fire manifests itself. It is astonishing to see the crackling flames of a hard log and to observe the hot intense inner glow of sawdust, though hardly visible from the outside (the heat that is developed in this way is so intense that pottery could be fired by it). One calls forth the bright charm of sanguine children by setting fire to old dry reeds and watching them flare up quickly. Other chil-

Blast furnace (New York).

dren are more interested in watching the wavering bluish flames as they slowly and gradually consume alcohol which has been mixed with water. To begin with it is not the great scientific results that most excite the children. It is more important to see that, if possible, every child can experience the way in which one's thinking can bring order to the often confusing things we experience in the world. One can view these phenomena as polarities like this:

```
            violent crackling, explosive burning
                            |
blazing, leaping            |            wavering, subdued
flames          ————————————+————————————          consuming
                            |
                            |
            hot glowing turning into charcoal
```

The material is not treated intellectually until the day after the experiment. The children raise questions, discuss them and propose further experiments. Through common research they investigate the role of air in any type of combustion. They are led to the discovery of oxygen. The children also have numerous experiences from everyday life to relate to the issues at hand. Most of them have made a fire at one time or another and know how to put one out. Or they may know how to start a fire in a damp forest. Chemistry can form a central part of the children's experience and remain so throughout their lives. It can span the bridge to the world around them, including the industrial world.

Gradually one expands the study to include other processes of nature (the cycles of calcium and of water in nature) as well as to industrial processes such as the manufacture of glass, the smelting of metals and their importance to our civilization.

When the development of modern industry is described in the history lessons of Class 8, then in chemistry special emphasis is placed upon that metal which — next to gold — has played the most important role in our history: iron.

Engineering and modern industry could only unfold to the extent that iron production and technology made it possible. Without Henry Cort's puddling process for producing wrought iron, invented in 1784, early industrial development in England would hardly have come about. Without the modern developments of steel production (Bessemer's blast furnace, 1856; the Siemens reverberatory furnace, 1865; the Thomas process of purification, 1878) we would not have been able to build ocean liners, railway networks, cars, modern agricultural implements, or modern cities. Every person should know, at least in principle, how iron is produced in a blast furnace.

The stars as we see them

Is it true that the children of today — who become acquainted with modern space research at an early age — can really feel 'at home' in the universe? At first glance this would seem without question to be the case. They 'know' as a rule incomparably more about the moon, Mars, Venus, and our whole solar system than their counterparts of a hundred years ago. That one calculates the distance to the fixed stars in terms of light years and that one recognizes no limits to the universe, they have surely heard as well. But to what extent can one really feel 'at home' in the cosmos of modern-day astronomy?

The popular scientific view of the cosmos as a hostile and lifeless vast emptiness really affects us and, above all, affects our children. We become somewhat estranged from the earth and its tasks through the powerful demands made upon our imagination.

If future humankind is to be spared from wasting a large part of its time in dreamy gazing at television programmes of the coming flights to Mars and Venus then we must try to arouse in our children as strong a love as possible for the earth and the responsibilities it presents.

Through its data on the moon, Venus, Mars and Jupiter, space research itself can make an important contribution. Never before have we had the occasion to be so fully and gratefully aware of the special properties of our earth, with its atmosphere and temperature conditions and its regular water-cycle. It is the task of the school to ensure that this insight does not remain merely theoretical. In the Waldorf School astronomy is a part of geography. It is only natural to compare the living conditions of the earth with those in the rest of the solar system down to the last detail. But perhaps even more important is the way in which we observe heavenly phenomena in the first place.

With twelve-year-old children a teacher can quite easily reach a rather unusual agreement: for the time being we shall decide to put as little trust as possible into any scientific authorities. We shall proceed only from what the senses and human understanding can tell us. We shall follow the courses of the stars as we see them from the earth. We shall attempt to imagine the paths they take when viewed from the equator. What does the movement of the stars look like from the poles, from the tropics? We shall observe the phases of the moon and the changes of the sun's path through the changing seasons.

This phenomenological approach can be continued as a natural sequence in the upper classes. Pupils can be given the opportunity to draw the planetary paths, at least in part, as Ptolemy saw and comprehended them, in order to trace historically the unfolding of modern astronomy.

They can witness in retrospect the moment when Copernicus, for purely geometrical reasons, hit upon the idea of drawing the planetary paths with a heliocentric construction; when Galileo first discovered the moons of Jupiter through a telescope and therewith offered visible evidence that there are stars which describe non-geocentric paths; or when Kepler, while drawing the elliptical planetary paths, had the feeling of looking into the secret creation of God, the world geometrician. Perhaps observing and intellectually comprehending the laws of heavenly movements and of the seasons form a necessary first step to *really* feeling 'at home' on the earth as well as in our solar system.

Right: The movements of the stars, as observed from the Equator, above — looking north or south, below — looking east or west (Copenhagen, Denmark).

Stjernebevegelser ved ekvator.
I syd: fra venstre mot höyre.
I nord: fra höyre mot venstre.

Stjernebevegelser ved ekvator.
i öst: rett opp.
i vest: rett ned.

The Last Four School Years

Puberty in today's world

Pamela is 14, but she looks 18. She is cheerful and unaffected. Around her mouth she has a determined look. The quality about her which most people think of is her unrestrained need for independence. At 13 she had a job as a stewardess on a large ocean liner.

Although she is quite gifted, in school she is, generally speaking, lazy and uninterested. Her parents are indifferent, that is, they make no demands on her. Pamela's relationship to her mother is not especially close. She understands her father, however, and they get along well. She likes to talk to him about all kinds of things. Although not especially pretty, she seems to be attractive to the opposite sex. Her behaviour is by no means reserved, but rather somewhat uninhibited. At the age of 15 she suddenly wants to have her own flat. After some opposition her parents finally consent to her wish.

A twenty-year-old boy moves into the new flat with her. He is rather superficial and does not share her intellectual interests at all. Pamela gradually breaks off their 'engagement.' He moves away, but keeps coming back. She feels sorry for him, and renews her attachment to him. But soon she breaks up with him again. On the telephone she shares all this with her father, but explains that she wants to handle this affair alone. Often, when she is alone in the evening, she telephones her father. The hour is late and she is afraid of the dark. After some complications she succeeds in permanently freeing herself from the boy. She is not yet 17 years old.

Then follows the next step in her development: she begins to study Catholicism, reads, makes notes, attends courses. She loves discussion, but her thoughts are completely unoriginal. She simply repeats what she has learnt. At the same time her need to believe is great. Her eyes are filled with rapture whenever she listens to someone whose views she finds pleasing. If she is confronted with other ways of thinking, she withdraws into herself, becomes quiet and closed-up. At an age when intellectually gifted young people usually try to attain inner independence, Pamela quite willingly submits to an absolute authority.

At the age of 15, Pamela entered a Waldorf School. Both she and her parents felt that this helped her gain a new interest in learning. In spite of periodically distressing personal problems, she usually did her work enthusiastically.

Pamela's situation seems to be a special case and yet in certain respects it is a representative one. One may notice especially the strong contrast between early maturity on the one hand (independence, the 'engagement,' the need for her own views) and certain remnants of childhood on the other (the need for fatherly contact, fear of the dark, faith in authority).

Accelerated physical maturity

Puberty arrives through a series of decisive physical symptoms. The body grows rapidly, the muscles and bones are strengthened. Often there is a gain in weight followed by a loss in weight. For good reasons it is assumed that all these changes are caused by the increased secretion of sex hormones, which usually sets in a few years before puberty.

Nowadays these changes begin earlier, as reported through the industrialised world. These phenomena seem to have begun to appear during the last century and were investigated scientifically in 1935, when E. Koch, a medical officer in Leipzig, first verified their existence statistically.

People are taller than in the past. The average weight at birth is higher. As a rule, the second dentition and sexual maturity appear appreciably earlier. Many psychologists talk of accelerated intellectual development as well.

What is the cause of all this? Here opinions differ greatly. Scientific discussion has been especially lively in Germany. A group of researchers, including W. Lenz, maintain that the only important cause of early maturity is the increased consumption of fat and protein. According to another theory, one which the pediatrician B. de Rudder has energetically advocated, the phenomena are not to be explained solely on the basis of nutrition. Rather are they due to the entire process of urbanization, especially the unprecedented increase in sense impressions, both in number and intensity, which influence the child. Advocates of this theory have naturally pointed to the fact that an increase in body height in small children (as opposed to an increase in body weight) continued independently of the lean years of 1945–47, according to research done in large German cities.

Even if the causes of this acceleration have not been conclusively explained, their results are visible for all of us: children grow-up faster nowadays.

Is it really so simple? In order to shed light on these questions we need to look at the issues from a different perspective.

Physical and emotional maturity

Since the decisive physical changes in puberty occur before the psychological, one would almost believe the former to be of secondary importance. Many psychologists make this assumption. According to Rudolf Steiner, however, this is not the case. He points out that as early as the twelfth year, or even sooner, the natural gracefulness of the young child gives way to jerky and awkward movements in boys, and a certain heaviness and lethargy in girls. He emphasizes that the very same inner powers which had manifested themselves as a kind of 'musicality of the limbs,' now undergo a metamorphosis and reappear as new abilities in the area of the life of feeling and imagination. In *The Education of the Child,* he describes how the biological changes occur whenever these inner powers free themselves from the body and gradually awaken as new emotional capacities.

For Steiner this is the essential aspect of puberty. The physical ability to reproduce corresponds to the ability to reflect inwardly, thus experiencing and understanding what is alive in the whole of humanity. The purely physical attraction to members of the opposite sex is only the limited expression of a wider capacity for love, which — when it develops in a healthy way — manifests itself in a deep interest for everything in the world. Where this interest is lacking, because of the emphasis on the physical instincts, one finds stunted emotional development.

Steiner considered the expression 'sexual maturity' far too narrow and wanted to see it replaced by the term 'earth-maturity.'

The inner powers with which the teacher is concerned in children of this age can often express themselves with surprising strength in healthily developed personalities. Whoever has a serious conversation with a sixteen or seventeen-year-old can sense a maturity which a few years earlier was not at all present. Then the young person was still childlike in their thinking. But now there are few questions in the area of science, art and the humanities which do not arouse this keen interest.

There is one phenomenon above all which is striking among highly gifted adolescents. Their awareness of time and its demands, their acuteness of thought and ability to formulate often attest to a consciousness and an inner maturity which are impressive. However, these same individuals often become very 'mixed-up' in their mutual relationships, especially on the erotic level. The awareness of their rich inner endowments and the idea, prevalent in wide circles, that sexual maturity is equivalent to adulthood, often cause them to overestimate their level of maturity and lead them into difficult situations. The case of Pamela is typical.

However, there are other groups of young people in whom the discrepancy between physical and psychological maturity reveals itself even more clearly. The frequent teenage mania for clothes, hairdos and pop music, and their manner of social relationships, carries with it a certain charm or is at least entertaining. Even the older generation may feel this. Such traits often originate from an understandable opposition to the narrow-mindedness and lack of imagination of the older generation. But the sudden appearance and flux of new styles in fashion also has another important side. The press, the radio and television are hugely powerful at communicating and perpetuating such trends. In their thoughts, as well as in their free time, many young people nowadays busy themselves to a great extent with things 'one must do' because 'everyone does them.' Thus an instinct for imitation is nurtured and preserved, an instinct which actually belongs to the early childhood years.

Not only relatively harmless teenage styles, but also really serious anti-social symptoms are spread and intensified through thoughtless imitation of patterns of behaviour which are picked up from the mass media or the immediate surroundings: joy rides in borrowed or stolen cars, teenage crimes, sexual aggressiveness and misuse of drugs and alcohol.

Problems of puberty and the education of young children

The case histories of criminals or social misfits are, as a rule, tales of fundamental human qualities which have been neglected through inadequate upbringing and education, and show in most cases a lack of emotional contact with the immediate surroundings during the earliest years of childhood. Many other less serious problems of adolescence can be viewed as a result of deprivation in early childhood.

During a pedagogical course in Arnhem in 1924, Rudolf Steiner touched upon this problem. He emphasized how various attitudes can be preserved throughout later life, although these attitudes actually belong to an earlier age and are usually outgrown under normal circumstances. Two such attitudes are the readiness of the preschool child to imitate, and the need for authority that is present in children before the age of puberty. The physical body continues to grow, but the emotional element, at least partially, remains at a level which is much more childish than the biological age would indicate. In another lecture of the same year, Steiner gave an example of how such a mismatch can come about. When the ability for abstract thinking is awakened at the advent of puberty, the thought processes must receive constant nourishment from a richly developed life of will and feeling. If young people suffer from inner impoverishment because the deeper levels of the soul are insufficiently developed, they grope in a void with their newly-acquired intellectual capacity. They do not then orientate themselves in the new environment with the help of their thinking but rather through imitation and belief in authority.

> It gives him an instability which causes him to engage in all kinds of mischief, to imitate all sorts of things in the early teens, whatever suits his fancy. Mostly it is something which does not please the others who, as it happens, are more concerned with the utilitarian aspects of life. He does it because he was unable as a child to live properly in the element of imitation. All this occurs at an age in which he really should have some measure of self-control. Thus we see many young people past the age of puberty wandering about, looking here and there for some kind of support and thereby dampening the experience of inner freedom. *(The Roots of Education, April 17, 1924.)*

It can hardly be doubted that many young people suffer from true emotional impoverishment and thereby find themselves in a situation which reminds us a great deal of the one Rudolf Steiner describes above. Should his diagnosis prove to be correct, then it would be high time to reconsider the education of the child. To have models to imitate during the pre-school years and an authority to respect during the elementary school years are deeply-rooted needs, which exist within every human being and must be satisfied during childhood if the desire for imitation and a lack of judgment are not to follow children for the rest of their lives. If by a 'free' education one means a pedagogy which seeks to influence the child as little as possible and thereby neglects to fulfil these two basic needs, then the paradoxical result of such an education is a lack of inner freedom.

What the school years can mean

Can schoolwork itself contribute to a more harmonious development for those children who suffer from emotional impoverishment as a result of that which they experienced or missed out on during their early childhood years?

A concrete example may shed light on this question.

During the first years of his life Martin was greatly neglected, until he finally came to a foster mother, a sincere and intelligent woman, who was very kind to him. However, because she was out at work, there was little extra time to spend with him. He often roamed about in the streets.

The foster mother wanted him to have more personal attention and was advised by a friend to try to send him to a Waldorf school. Martin was healthy and mature enough to begin school and was admitted to the first class. The look on his face was evidence of the neglect he had experienced in early childhood, but also revealed his keen intelligence. In arithmetic he was one of the best pupils. On the other hand, his speech development made very slow progress. Only in the fifth class did he learn to read. From time to time he was rough or cruel to his classmates. However, he enjoyed school and after a while became quite cheerful and open. His temperament was decidedly sanguine. When he was sixteen years old his foster mother died under tragic circumstances. Martin now stood alone in life, but was taken in by a very stable family. He seemed to recover quickly from the death of his foster mother. However, the results of childhood neglect now became obvious, most especially in his unconcealed egoism. He loved chocolate and was, for example, perfectly capable, while a guest in the house of a strange family, of sneaking into their larder before the meal and completely devouring the entire chocolate dessert.

In his limited conception of life, he considered subjects such as mathematics, science, modern history, current events and practical crafts to be worthwhile. Although extremely lazy, he often achieved surprisingly good results, thanks, among other things, to his extraordinarily good memory. His ability to express himself in words remained rudimentary. He had no physical defect which might affect his ability to read and write, such as dyslexia, but he simply neglected his written work. His spelling and sentence construction were often remarkably poor. He was completely uninterested in artistic subjects, sometimes being downright insolent in these lessons. In classes in which the teaching did not directly interest him, he would often sit with his mouth open, even occasionally sucking his thumb, and with a passive facial expression under his short, unkempt hair. His moral concepts were few, simple, and confused. If he considered it necessary, for example, he would lie unashamedly. Outside of school he associated for a while with a circle of friends who had certain criminal tendencies. It later emerged that he avoided being drawn into any kind of criminal misdeeds. Since he was easily led, there was a period when people wondered whether his development would ever take a turn for the better. Above all, everything in him revolved around his deep need for personal contact. He never withdrew into himself. If a group of his friends were talking with a teacher in the corridor, Martin would always go up and join them, put his hand on their shoulders, and enthusiastically join in the conversation. The teachers knew how important it was for him and gave him as much of their time as they could. Several years after leaving he once said, 'The school was my home.'

When he was in Class 12, the first signs of a change could be noticed, a change which gradually took root. Martin became markedly industrious. He began to develop a consideration for the needs and problems of others. Sociability turned into genuine warmth. His interests broadened widely. He pursued cultural questions intensively and critically and became a regular theatregoer. He got a place at university, lived very modestly, and was a very successful student.

Summary

The stories of Pamela and Martin can no more 'prove' the specific value of Waldorf education than can other accounts of individual cases. They can, however, help to shed light on the practical objectives of the work in a Waldorf School.

There is no doubt that Pamela acquired more serious work habits after she had changed over to the Waldorf School. In other respects her life could not be changed very much. Her experiences would probably have run their course, even if she had attended another school. With respect to Martin, however, it must be said that his experience in the Waldorf School seems to have been of greater significance. Moreover, it was important that he had attended the Waldorf School from the first class onwards. However, the later school years are by no means insignificant either. If he had left the Waldorf School after Class 8, for example, then the effects of his school years would certainly not have been so profound and would not have carried him over crucial periods to the extent that they did.

One cannot repeat often enough that Waldorf Schools exist for healthy children with normal talents and that they are not institutions for 'problem children.' But here, as in other schools, there must be a place for children who find themselves in difficult circumstances. It is quite clear in such cases that a Waldorf School has a greater impact if the child can enter it early, preferably in the first class, if she can go through the 'crises' of the ninth and twelfth years under the protection of the loving authority of her teachers and with the companionship of her classmates, and if given the proper 'spiritual nourishment,' she can develop real and independent interests and thus prepared, make the transition to adolescence. For the crises of puberty must be controlled before they break out. It is often difficult or impossible to help students who only enter the Waldorf School for their last four years.

The description of Martin also confirms another principle. The most important thing for the inner development of the older pupil is continuous contact with responsible adults. At a time when the spiritual process of maturation is, for various reasons, easily obstructed or distorted, this contact is more essential than ever.

Contrasts in Classes Seven and Eight

Young people of the age of 14 or 15 find themselves in a period of contrasts. At the start of drawing in black and white they immediately experience both polarities as phenomena which they interpret in themselves as symbols of light and darkness. The pupils learn to master the world of light and darkness by differentiating various types of light (the light of the sun and moon, street lights etc.). The final achievement of this training is learning to do a human portrait.

Other subjects, too, answer the needs felt in the time of puberty. In eurythmy which otherwise shows flowing forms, this is a time for strict spatial awareness through doing rod exercises which require great skill. In schools where Bothmer gymnastics (or spatial dynamics) is taught, there are exercises emphasizing the experience of the body.

Many schools use this time to organize practical work experience — for instance a class trip to a farm. This gives the boys and girls an opportunity to work in a practical way, contributing something positive to the world and learning to judge their own strengths and weaknesses.

From Class Nine to Class Twelve

There are important mental abilities which usually do not awaken in human beings until they reach their teens; for example, the ability to develop special interests of their own and personal taste, and the striving for independent judgment in important questions. The constant readiness to imitate, discussed in the previous chapter, which no doubt is an important factor in society today, makes it difficult for a teenager to develop and maintain emerging individual abilities.

Are the prophets of doom right when they predict that the mass media will, slowly but surely, produce 'mass' people, who have nothing but collective impulses? How is the individual to

Above: Exercise in shadow-construction.
Below: An imaginative drawing arising from the inner experience of light and darkness.
To experience the surrounding world and especially the people in it as 'black' or 'white' is one of the characteristics of adolescence. It can be helpful in these years to bring this to an objective experience through the use of charcoal.

A perspective drawing from observation.

find their own life-style in face of this stream of strong, often suggestive influences?

The instruction imparted to the pupils in Classes 9 to 12, that is in the Upper School, can in this respect be a significant help.

A 'scientific' education

Strictly speaking, one can arrive at an independent judgment on a question through an attitude which may be described as scientific. No prejudicial opinions may be entertained, no emotions may disturb quiet observation.

One does not need to be a scientist to adopt this principle. It is enough to strive to live and to think in a really modern — that is in a conscious — manner. To this extent, our epoch can justifiably be called an age of science. How many people are there today, however, who actually live in such a way that they take a position on questions without passion, without being led astray by their favourite thoughts, by catch phrases with no substance, or by the 'results of research' which in reality are often only weakly-supported hypotheses? It is a tragic irony that the unheard of scientific advance which more than anything else has led to the erasing of old beliefs, at the same time has brought about a belief in authority which, for its blindness, can be compared to the old forms of religious belief.

Instruction in the upper classes of a Waldorf School will contribute to laying the foundation of an attitude to life which, not only on the surface but also in the depths, is scientific in the sense in which it is meant here. The very first steps along this path are, as we have seen, already laid down in the last years of the class teacher period. There are fundamental changes in the teaching methods which go in the same direction, but which lead significantly further.

At this point, teaching is taken over by specialist teachers knowledgeable in their own subject. At this level the teacher no longer has a self-evident authority. To be sure, it is important that the pupils have a respect for their specialized knowledge and pedagogical capabilities. Teachers must be ready, nevertheless, to explain fully whatever they say both on an academic and on a human level. All statements may be queried, and all serious questions are worthy of detailed consideration. Classes, therefore, often consist to quite an extent of conversations and discussions.

The science periods (biology, climatology, geology, chemistry, physics, mathematics etc.) are of course particularly suited to exercising the powers of observation and thinking. The experiments of the teacher and the pupils play a fundamental role in teaching right on into Class 12. Great precision is necessary in carrying out experiments, otherwise the results can be quite misleading. When conclusions are being reached, no step should be taken which is not confirmed through the observed phenomenon. In mathematics, as far as possible, the pupils should, above all, understand the operations which are being carried out; the practice of actual mathematical processes which is of course important, takes second place.

In the cultural areas of history, the history of art and literature, and geography, the situation, at least in part, is quite different. When one, for example, speaks of social, economic, and political questions, of individual destinies and works of art, then the listener, especially through a lively description, can be personally moved. Basically, the task is often one of helping the pupils overcome purely subjective sympathies and antipathies and, equally, of instilling in them a feeling for human destiny founded on knowledge, to which they were previously oblivious and which would have meant little to them at an earlier stage. In other words, one strives for an objective approach even in the sphere of emotions.

The material which is offered to the students in the upper classes is very comprehensive. Independent effort is increasingly required in writing and illustrating the subject matter of their lessons in essays, and in preparing oral presentations. In addition individual projects are chosen, researched and presented. Some pupils choose a subject from the realm of arts or crafts, while others investigate a scientific problem or plan a special series of experiments.

Experience has shown that those students who have attended a Waldorf School from the beginning have, on the whole, a good foundation for work of this kind. A claim on their intellectual powers has not been made prematurely, and they have not been forced to take in an excess of abstract knowledge. They look forward with excitement to the new subjects and new vistas of knowledge which await them in the upper school. As a rule their attitude is that of the alert critic, not of the tired sceptic. Their involvement becomes especially active when, for example, light is thrown on human and social problems through scientific facts. Their desire to form their own conclusions often leads to the pursuit of scientifically orientated interests in their spare time.

Some general aspects

Science plays an important role in our society. According to the prevailing view if we want to prepare our children for this knowledge explosion, there is no other option than to give them 'thought models' without any detailed explanation; that is, hypotheses or theories, whose scientific foundation can hardly be grasped by the pupil. The whole emphasis of learning is thus shifted into a different direction. Teacher training, textbooks, aids and teaching methods, are orientated towards this end.

In the face of this development we are justified in asking if, with such a method of teaching, we do not force upon the pupils, perhaps even without consciously striving to do so, a ready-made view of life. Of course, one can maintain that modern scientific research finds itself in a constant state of change, which therefore (assuming that the results of such research are adequately presented) hinders the rise of a fixed view to the world. One can hardly deny, however, that the present development is moving along on definite, even more complicated courses, which determine not only the methods of investigation, the definitions and the theories, but also the questions themselves, and which strongly influence our conception of the human being and the world. When such avenues of approach increasingly become the subject of a more or less automatic and unquestioning 'learning,' then the danger of an intellectual lack of freedom is obvious.

The goal which the upper school teachers of scientific subjects in a Waldorf School place before themselves is a phenomenologically orientated style of teaching, which prefers to characterize rather than reduce to definitions, and which makes it possible for the pupils, at least to a certain extent, to understand and evaluate the foundations of various current 'models of thought' and scientific views.

Of course one might ask if the instruction in science at a Waldorf School, which received its spiritual foundation from Rudolf Steiner, is not in danger of becoming one-sided in another way. In addition to the viewpoints which have already been mentioned in the chapter on the idea of freedom, it should here be pointed out that the anthroposophical view of the world, which for the teachers forms the foundation of their concept of life, is broad-minded and tolerant, not only in the sense that it acknowledges the validity of other ways of thinking but also inasmuch as it offers real help in penetrating and understanding other thought systems. A thorough elaboration would take too long, but one brief example may clarify what is meant.

A history teacher tried to give his Class 11 pupils an idea of Marxism. He had immersed himself so intensely in his subject and displayed such enthusiasm, that for a while the pupils believed he actually was a Marxist. Such a successful presentation, of course, is not always achieved, but one can nonetheless try to realize one of the most important goals of the entire learning experience in the upper school; to teach in such a way that the teacher not only opens the door to various approaches but also makes it possible for each individual to become actively involved to a certain degree.

The social community of a class

The question arises how, in a school in which there is no streaming according to intellectual ability, lessons can be taught in a way that nevertheless stretches the abilities of the gifted pupil.

One of the basic tenets of Waldorf education is that every child with normal abilities should in principle have the chance to attend school for the full twelve years. Experience has shown, however, that certain pupils who take a full and active part in lessons in the lower and middle school, for various reasons are not able to follow the work of the later school years. Most of these young people either leave school and learn a trade or continue with practical courses which have been set up at various Waldorf Schools. But even among those pupils remaining in the class, there are, right up until the twelfth class, considerable differences in individual ability and potential. It should be emphasized that Waldorf Schools find this quite an acceptable situation. As a result of this however, there will be a wide range of actual achievement. Gifted and energetic pupils, after having completed the required courses, are ready for university. Others, although they still reveal certain weak spots in their knowledge, have as a rule reached a good general level of education and are therefore well equipped to meet the demands of modern life.

The pertinent question is naturally whether the intellectually bright children are not held back by their classmates whose gifts lie in other directions. It can certainly happen that a teacher has to go over something more than once for the sake of some pupils who have not fully understood, and thus the pace of a lesson may be slowed down. On the other hand this can serve to counterbalance a certain egoism and ambition on the part of the more gifted pupils, whose abilities can be challenged by being given special tasks. On the whole it can be said that the progress of a class is not seriously hindered by the presence of those pupils who are gifted more practically or artistically rather than intellectually, as long as each is taxed to their limits. This, of course, is only possible when a teacher really knows the individual abilities of the pupils, as is the aim in a Waldorf School.

Can the opposite not also happen, however,

that those who have no direct inclination towards scientific subjects are discouraged by the performance of the others? This danger is certainly there but the curriculum is so wide that every pupil can usually find a sphere where they can hold their own and find satisfaction. It is important to the pupils as well as to the teachers to learn to value each individual according to their own innate talents, especially as they will soon be part of the wider social life in the world.

The role of art in the upper school

Throughout the upper school, instruction in eurythmy, recitation, painting, drawing, modelling and skilled crafts still serves to counterbalance the scientific and intellectual demands of the curriculum. Art finds a new meaning in the life of a human being at this age. They can now, more consciously than before, work their way into the materials which are used in the different forms of art (tones, sounds, colour, wood, clay, metal, etc.). History of art is a subject in the curriculum of the upper school. Many pupils occupy themselves with art during their free time. Gradually they become more and more aware that life is becoming richer and more diversified, that there are definite psychological-aesthetic laws with which they can only become familiar to the extent that they are artistically active and observant. At the same time opportunities arise to understand, enjoy, to make sound judgments, and in time — regardless of one's choice of occupation — to develop an individual taste and lifestyle.

Mathematics and geometry

Class Nine

By the time they make the transition into the upper school, if not before, the majority of pupils become aware of how important it is to have a thorough knowledge of mathematics. They realize that the door to more theoretical and practical vocational training is only open to those who have a good mathematical grounding and indeed that mathematics is regarded very highly in modern society. This could be viewed as a fair wind for the awakening of new and specialized interests arising out of this subject. However, the teacher must resist the temptation to make too much use of this tendency. Throughout the school years mathematical instruction should be regarded as serving to develop the personality and should even now not be regarded as an end in itself.

The meaning of mathematical exercises has perhaps been most beautifully expressed by Plato. In *The Republic* he wrote:

> Through mathematics an instrument of the soul becomes refined and, as in a purifying fire, it is awakened to a new life force, while other activities destroy it and rob it of its power to behold, whereas it deserves far more to be maintained than do a thousand bodily eyes, for through this faculty alone is truth perceived.

But how far removed are sixteen-year-olds from such a way of looking at things?

'What use is that?' is a typical question. These young people sit in the classroom with their newly-awakened intellectual powers and yet feel under pressure to do something practical in the world. Still it is not difficult to engage them in a problem which is not at all directed toward the practical — as long as the proposed exercise addresses itself to their process of inner development.

The problem of the Hanoi towers can serve as an example for an exercise which at first directs itself to deductive reasoning and then leads beyond that. A Hanoi tower consists of a number of stones with holes through the middle which are arranged on a vertical pole. The largest stone is at the bottom and the stones become successively smaller until the top one is reached. In addition there are two empty poles at one's disposal. The question is: how many individual stones must be moved in order to build up the tower on one of the empty poles, under the condition that a larger stone should never be placed on top of a smaller one?

Assume that we have four stones. It does not take long for the students to discover through trial and error that $x = 15$ and that is how many movements are necessary to build up the tower as required. The class will at once query how many moves are necessary for any given number of stones. Several of them investigate how things work when there are fewer than four stones and conclude: one stone requires one move, two require three, and three stones require seven moves. Is there any characteristic regularity in the numerical sequence 1, 3, 7, 15 that points to a general formula? And when this clue is found does it lead in the right direction? Is the assumption correct? The students test it in the case of five stones — yes, the rule is correct!

But how are we to prove the rule for a given number of stones? We cannot just keep building larger and larger towers. This method of exploring the physical world through trial and error can only be useful up to a certain practical point. We must think, we must reason intensively until we can understand infinitely large towers. So we investigate how the number of movements increases, when we increase the number of stones by one. The five-stone tower must be so constructed that the four-stone tower is built on the second pole. After that the fifth stone must be placed on pole number 3. At last we can build the whole four-stone tower on this pole. The number of rearrangements, therefore, is $x_5 = x_4 + 1 + x_4 = 15 + 1 + 15 = 31$. The same situation prevails for a tower with any number of stones: we can take the step from four to five, from five to six, and so on to infinity. From this discovery we can write the formula for the number of rearrangements of infinitely large towers.

The greater the pains, the greater the reward. The students learn that through a process of reasoning they can reach a conclusion that is unreachable by technical means (even through the fastest computers). They have also learned to observe their own thinking. They learn to real-

Through geometry we learn to combine thinking with seeing. To achieve this we must cease to think of the point as a pin prick, the line as a bar, parallel lines as railway tracks. We only begin to have a true experience of geometry when we can wrest our concepts away from what we can sense physically.
Right: Various geometrical forms, drawn first from the viewpoint of Euclidean geometry, when we see them as we usually do as finite areas; then from the viewpoint of projective geometry, when the corresponding form reaches to infinity. The effort required in the latter case is greater, but the results are more interesting.

Vad gör en linje med ett plan? Delar det i en del.
Vad gör två linjer med ett plan? Delar det i två delar.
Vad gör en punkt i ett punktfält? Ingenting.
Vad gör två punkter i ett punktfält? Ingenting.

Två punkter i ett linjefält kan "dra isär" eller "dra ihop" linjerna. I det ena fallet går alla linjer utanför punkterna, i det andra emellan. Men eftersom punkterna är oändligt små täcks i båda fallen samma yta.

Här "delar" 3 punkter ett linjefält på 4 olika sätt. (Olika aspekter på fältet) I alla fallen blir den orange ytan en trehörning.

Med 4 punkter blev det egendomligt nog fyrhörningar av de orange ytorna.

ize when they are thinking correctly and when they are thinking incorrectly. This realization is essential. They feel that they are consciously and securely standing on the firm ground of truth when they perceive the objective nature of the problem.

As a rule pupils in Class 9 cannot achieve such a conscious awareness of thinking, some not even in Class 12. The important thing is that according to their individual abilities, they come to realize more and more what clear thinking is.

In Class 9 pupils feels an increasing need to stand on their own feet. Figuratively speaking, the teacher steps more and more to the side and the subject, in corresponding measure, comes to the fore. How suitable the practice of mathematics is to emancipate oneself from dependence on parents! For each person must find the truth for themselves. In mathematics, however, differences in the pupils' abilities play an important role. How can the dreamy pupil who is not very intellectually inclined play a part?

The teacher must find a whole spectrum of problems, from the simple to the complex. As the technical expression goes, she must 'be able to differentiate within the framework of the class.' In class they practice counting again — but in systems other than decimal. That which has become routine must now to be mastered through constant practice in the binary system. This has a liberating effect. And there are exercises of every degree of difficulty, from addition to finding the square root and the different rules of division.

Permutations, combinations and the theory of probability give the pupils ample material for exercising the powers of thinking. In geometry, through the study for example of various curves, there are similar possibilities.

Do experiences with finite curves such as the circle or the ellipse help us when we come to consider curves that run to infinity such as the parabola and hyperbola? Such surprises can be significant and instructive. The pupils gain insight into the certainty and ease with which analytical geometry with its equations solves such problems. A purely geometrical approach is as a rule more time-consuming but on the other hand is rewarding. Quite apart from the end result, important discoveries are made during the process and the pupils' interest is maintained throughout.

From Classes Ten to Twelve

In Class 10 two major sections of the curriculum are brought to a conclusion. The climax of plane geometry is the study of trigonometry. The pupils, who until now have had to be satisfied with dealing with special triangles and other geometrical figures, can now work with any kind of triangle. The pupils gain a deep satisfaction from the practical application of trigonometry in surveying. Here they learn how the theodolite provides precise angles for the net of triangles which give the developing map stability and precision.

The second section of the curriculum leads into logarithms. Negative numbers, fractions and the number zero set new tasks, developing naturally from previous work with indices. The question is then always asked if the 'old' rules of counting still hold good for the new field into which the students have now ventured. This proves to be possible, and indeed there is even more to it. They look at the four rules in a broadened perspective and, at the same time, learn the technique of mastering problems that would otherwise be too time-consuming to work out.

The joy the pupils experience in learning how to work with more precise instruments deepens their interest in exploring new areas of mathematics. After the satisfaction of mastering plane geometry in Class 10 comes the possibility of building up geometries for curved surfaces. We can calculate distances and areas on the globe, navigating by the stars, and projecting the globe, or a part of it, onto a plane, thereby drawing a map of a spherical area. The class is thus presented with entirely new situations and learns to appreciate that it is impossible to project a spherical area without distortion. It is interesting to observe, for example, that a Mercator map which distorts distances and areas is carefully created to show the correct angles; thus it is 'angularly true' and intended for tracing proper navigational courses.

Questions relating to the concept of infinity can widen one's inner horizons. Perspective drawing helps in grasping this difficult idea, as does the concept of limit and elements of the theory of sets. Are there more points than numbers on a straight line? And how is a straight line or curve 'made up' of points? The question of the 'infinitely large' and the 'infinitely small' go back to the paradoxes which Zenon of Elea formulated 2500 years ago.

Closely related to this area of knowledge is the concept of function and differential calculus which was developed and crystallized mathematically by Galileo, Newton, Leibniz and others. The concepts of speed and acceleration can be generally applied and make it possible to work out maxima and minima, an achievement which later furthered the advancement of technology.

Studies of the concept of infinity and calculus lead to abstract thought inasmuch as the problems are removed from the sensual-visual world. It is inevitable that many pupils must be satisfied with a basic grasp of the principles. Perhaps in some pupils an aversion to the x, y, z of equations may arise. They can gain a new interest through constructive tasks, as in the important field of projective geometry. A number of French mathematicians (Poncelet, Brianchon, Carnot and other pupils of the geometrician Monge) became absorbed by the possibilities of geometrical construction at the beginning of the nineteenth century and wanted to show that one can progress further by these methods than by the abstract equations of analytical geometry. Carnot wanted to 'free geometry from the hieroglyphics of analysis.'

Thus projective geometry was developed in the course of the nineteenth century. It provides the teacher with excellent material. It is surprising that it is not more widely used in general education. Projective geometry provides the pupils with exceptionally good opportunities for studying problems and relationships from different aspects. In comparison with the usual atomistic way of presentation, which thinks of a plane or line as made up of points, projective geometry presents the point as a concept containing planes or lines. The planes and the lines, as well as the point, can be looked at as primary archetypal elements.

Whoever has experienced how often young people tend to see a situation in terms of black or white, and often with deep conviction, realizes that an important task of the school is to teach the children how to arrive at sound judgments. An important part of such training is that the pupils view problems from different aspects, and best of all from diametrically-opposed points of view. Projective geometry offers an excellent opportunity for this kind of practice in which all pupils can take part. When the Frenchman Desargues

laid the foundation of this kind of geometry in the seventeenth century, he approached problems that had been raised by laypeople, chiefly by artists. These painters were looking for methods of creating perspective. 'The science that Desargues created is now one of the most beautiful branches of mathematics — perhaps because it was engendered by art,' Morris Kline wrote in *Mathematics in Western Culture*.

If we wish to avoid talking at cross-purposes in everyday conversation, or when we are trying to understand certain scientific results, then we must make clear to ourselves and to others the basic concepts from which we have built up a train of thought. In science the following question often stands in the foreground: which axioms or primary phenomena do we use as the basis? As objectively as possible we strive to recognize what is happening in the field of our investigation — be it a process of nature, an experiment, a psychological or historical occurrence. In Class 12 in a Waldorf School the pupils gain a wider perspective in different subjects. In mathematics they learn how one can derive different geometries (Euclidean, non-Euclidean, analytic, synthetic etc.) and also different kinds of algebra (generalized, Boolean, vector algebra etc.) through a skilful selection of basic axioms. Thus the researcher chooses the tool that is appropriate. Therefore, students become familiar with examples of how a mathematical creations that for a long time was only considered 'literature' for a few curious people, suddenly became a valuable tool in several fields of research, such as Boolean algebra in logical analysis and computer programming, or probability theory as applied to electricity distribution networks.

In conclusion one can say that the teaching of mathematics consists of the two elements of instruction and practice. The more intimately these two aspects can be joined, the greater will be the interest and output of the pupil. In the long run, constant practice leads to a mechanical kind of activity, while continual instruction disregards the intense desire for action on the part of the pupils. When it comes to dealing with proofs and deductions, the golden rule is that what can be directly experienced forms a middle way between an exact, pedantic description and a more general survey which, however, lacks the necessary detail.

Parallel with the solving of actual mathematical problems go informative conversations which provide insight into the way in which mathematical laws underlie nature and also the form of the human body. The chief significance of mathematics lies in the fact that it leads to an ability for pure thought and to confidence in such a way of thinking; that is, to that type of thinking that we work out for ourselves through an activity which is at the same time both subjective and objective.

Physics

Class Nine

In physics during Classes 6, 7 and 8 the pupils have studied certain elementary phenomena of acoustics, optics, heat and mechanics (including hydrostatics and aerodynamics) and have become familiar with a number of their practical applications. In Class 9, from both practical and theoretical aspects, pupils learn to understand certain facts about heat and electricity sufficiently to have a complete understanding of how the steam engine, internal combustion engine, the telephone and other basic inventions work.

The 'growth' of a pentagon — an exercise in projective geometry. (Class 12).

The way one may proceed in Class 9 can be demonstrated with an example from the theory of heat. Boyle's Laws on the pressure and volume of a gas serve to show how mathematical laws arise from the observation of the behaviour of matter. Matter does not react arbitrarily to the impact of heat. Expansion, the absorption of heat, melting and evaporation points, and boiling and freezing points are specific mathematical values which are characteristic for the different materials. Substances that are added to a specific material may raise its boiling point or lower its freezing point; indeed, a shifting of the boiling point may occur in certain cases that seems at first inexplicable.

The astonishment of the pupils over such natural phenomena is especially important and fruitful at this age. Strangely enough, water — the substance that is the most plentiful on the earth — is an exception to expansion through heating, for its greatest density is at 4 C. Thus ice forms at the top of water, allowing life to continue below. Of special significance is the remarkable property of liquids to boil at ever lower temperatures if the air pressure is decreased. Graphs of changing saturation pressures can easily be drawn. It is especially interesting to note that, while all these curves appear to start out from so-called absolute zero, on the other hand they collapse into a point, the critical state of matter, when gas or liquids can no longer be distinguished. Nature itself sets a point for each liquid below which it cannot become gas and over which no gas can become fluid.

When we work with such laws and try to bring the pupils to a proper understanding of them, we soon realize what a subordinate role mere arithmetic plays. Even if technology and industry ignore the qualitative aspect preferring to employ scientists with a good command of mathematical physics, the qualitative appreciation of phenomena is pedagogically important.

An especially interesting — but at the same time difficult — phenomenon is that of latent heat. Matter may take in considerable quantities of heat that nevertheless do not manifest themselves as increased temperature. Instead this heat transforms the state of matter. Thus, when it snows it does not get cold, because latent heat from the solidifying liquid is released and warms the surrounding area. Or we get cold when we are wet, because the heat that evaporates the water is taken from our body.

Expansion usually follows when matter is heated. Thus a body takes in heat and reacts with an expansion in volume. But what happens if the volume of gas is expanded without an increase in heat? It gets colder. It is not always easy to make this clear to the pupils, but it is an analogous occurrence; any expansion in volume requires heat. If the volume is expanded, for example, through the release of gas from a pressure tank, but the gas is *not* at the same time heated, then it loses inner energy and gets colder. Carbon dioxide can easily crystallize in a warm classroom if released from a high-pressure cylinder.

Gas, on the other hand contracts when it is cooled. A decrease in volume therefore means a decrease in heat. This, of course, explains why a gas gets warm under compression. Heat is released. That means that a solidification, contraction or a tendency to make forms corresponds to a loss of heat. Conversely an increase in heat corresponds to dilution, expansion, and a dissolution of form. In this sense one could even speak of heat as the opposite of heaviness: heat works outwardly from matter, making things lighter, more rarefied and less formed. Heaviness contracts, solidifies, and shapes.

How can heat be measured? Strictly speaking, it cannot. Heat is measured by its effect on a given amount of water. If one gram of water is heated one degree centigrade, it is called a thermal unit of one calorie. Here one can introduce a number of calculations that can usefully be carried out in the course of a mathematics lesson. Here too we meet one of the fundamental principles of Waldorf pedagogy. The most important aspect of such study is to arouse an interest in the phenomena of science and to cultivate an understanding of relationships. The mathematical aspect is of secondary importance.

Thus the whole theory of heat can be developed without ever actually explaining what 'heat' is. The question of whether it is heat that moves molecules or whether the movement of molecules manifests itself as heat, should wait for a few more years — it is best suited to Class 11. In Class 9 we should stick to those phenomena that afford sufficient occasion for wonder and experiment.

Class Ten

This age is devoted to classical physics in all its beauty and exactitude. The mathematical foundations have been well prepared. Trigonometry, quadratic equations, properties of the parabola and the ellipse, progressions, proportion and logarithms form the basis for an understanding of the physical laws of Galileo, Kepler, and Newton.

It is the awakening of expanding human thinking that, like the planetary spheres of Ptolemy, unfolds itself further and further into the cosmos. His geocentric conception of the universe was supplanted by Copernicus' heliocentric interpretation. Why? What happened here?

The pupils experience the greatest of the new thoughts. They are clearer, more logical, and the modern mind finds them more satisfying than the earlier ideas. With the help of the most perfect geometrical figure, the circle, Ptolemy painstakingly explained the paths of the planets. The pupils draw and construct some of these interesting figures, which of course manifest themselves in the heavens to our eyes in the same way as they did then. For millennia these movements have been the same. But we always view them from a new standpoint. Copernicus views them from a universe with the sun in the centre. That is easier to imagine, and the human spirit can grasp this because in the meantime we have become familiar with varying speeds and distances. But even Copernicus could not think otherwise than in circles, and it was only Kepler who, through his own particular destiny, met the great observer of the stars, Tycho Brahe, at just the right moment and was able to show that all planetary courses are ellipses. The biographies of such personalities are especially suitable to make the new element in our physical conception of the world clear to the pupils.

In Kepler's life this proof was a major event. Divine harmony was complete, for the harmony of the spheres became manifest as beauty through the mathematical laws. The cosmos proved the existence of God; it was not mere accident that prevailed in the universe. All was well ordered. Kepler's laws apply to the moons of the planets, even to artificial satellites, and the pupils can see that the laws are correct.

Once the movements of the heavens were mastered, it was clear that should a new planet be discovered, its course would not be arbitrary. A certain distance corresponds to the time required for its revolution. On the other hand, if the planet has a specific revolution then its distance from the sun could be determined.

In Class 11 emphasis is laid on exactness in technical drawings in the physics lessons, for now the pupils should become familiar with the form and function of machines used in everyday life.
Above: A D.C. Generator.
Below: An electric motor for both direct and alternating current.

At this point in the study of physics a pupil may ask that very important question which has had significant consequences in the historical development of human consciousness. Now that the celestial movements have been made fully clear, and now that the almost religious experience of a world order has arisen, the question comes up, *why* are these laws valid? What is the cause of these movements?

At this point in the development of physics Isaac Newton steps in. The falling apple through which, according to an anecdote, he became aware of the phenomenon of gravity, can be symbolic of the development of a more human consciousness. Nothing divine is recognized as the cause any longer, only so-called gravity. It is forces that move bodies, it is forces that stop them, it is forces that hold the planets in their courses or throw them off course. The forces of inertia, gravity, friction, and the centrifugal force are the foundations of Newtonian mechanics.

Newton's law of gravitation becomes the universal law of the cosmos; without ever having been there we can calculate the mass of the sun and each of the planets. This feeling of the triumph of knowledge is the note on which the physics period in Class 10 can be concluded.

If time allows, the equations of motion and the laws of forces can be further developed through the parallelograms of forces and of velocities. The ability to calculate, however, should not come before the qualitative understanding of physical laws. Here too there are many possibilities of adapting the subject matter to the different members of the class. The study of surveying and of geography strengthen the conviction that the human being is the central point of the universe — this time not geocentrically in the sense of the physical earth, but rather through our powers of thought. Newton placed the human intellect at the centre of the universe. From our vantage point on the 'dust-particle earth' we can calculate the most distant galaxies and assign our solar system its appointed place.

Class Eleven

In this class, the teacher must decide what to choose from a virtually unlimited amount of material. A vast variety of experiments can demonstrate the laws of electricity and magnetism.

How much should a person today know about electricity? In the course of a few weeks of study the teacher must present the essentials of electricity and its uses in such a way that all pupils — among them perhaps even future specialists in the field — can get something important out of it for life. Each pupil, for example, should have a thorough understanding of the electric motor, the generator, the telephone, radio, television and computer. In their daily use of these things people have a feeling of security if they have at some time investigated them thoroughly. It is of course unnecessary to burden pupils with all the details of electronic theory or of the mathematical aspects of physics which are an essential for electrical engineers.

This is an exciting study. Through releasing gas into a near vacuum and with the help of cathode-rays, one concept becomes clear: of electricity as electrons, that is particles in motion. Through the study of electric and magnetic fields we come to another concept of electricity as a movement of electromagnetic waves which takes place easily even through a vacuum. These waves move at the speed of light in all directions, millions of them, without interfering with each other. The 'empty' space of the universe turns out to be full of electromagnetic fields, and has the property of letting electromagnetic waves pass through it unhindered and unlimited. Waves or particles — what is electricity in reality? At this important point we learn the significance of the Goethean way of observing such phenomena, without asking, 'What is electricity?' but rather 'How is electricity produced?' and 'What does electricity do?'

Everywhere we are confronted with polarities in this field of study, electricity never manifests itself one-sidedly. There are always two poles called positive and negative, which Faraday called glass electricity and resin electricity. Changing electric and magnetic fields mutually create and determine each other. Particles and waves appear as a polarity and so do capacitance and inductance. An impressive illustration of the latter is the oscillatory circuit, which as a result of the polarity of inductance and capacitance gives rise to the phenomenon of resonance, by means of which we are able to pick a single one of the millions of electromagnetic oscillations, as happens in radio. Another example is the polarity of metals, which produces electric potential (voltage) in a Galvanic pile, in a photocell or in a thermocouple.

The teaching of electricity is the study of tension, of duality, of polarity. The discoveries of Oersted and Faraday, for example, can be seen at work in the microphone and telephone-receiver or in the polarity of an electric motor and generator.

The phenomenon of electricity is many sided and far reaching. What, for example, can we measure with electrical meters? Everything except electricity. We measure heat (or more precisely the expansion of a heated wire) or we measure the magnetic force that arises through electricity. The electricity itself seems to disappear the moment it is produced. It is transformed into heat and energy. Electricity is invisible — we possess no sense-organ for it — and the moment it is created it transforms itself into other physical forms. Even electrical fields of static electricity do not manifest themselves as pure electricity, but rather as mechanical forces. Even a battery contains no electricity, and in electric sparks we find glowing matter. Above all else, however, we should not withhold from the pupils of Class 11 the duality of phenomenon and theory, but make a sharp distinction between those experiments that represent a part of the world that can be perceived with our senses, and such images that reflect concepts, ideas, hypotheses, and theories. In textbooks experiments and theoretical concepts are often mixed, and in describing experiments that have been carried out we should take pains to distinguish clearly between observation and theory. Methods of research on the one hand, and on the other the modern scientist's view of the world, are a continuing undertone in the classes of the upper school.

The unity and harmony of Class 10 has now been definitely lost. Class 11 is dominated by polarity, duality, tension. Is it then impossible to gain a clear insight into the nature of electricity? Perhaps this period of study can close with such a question.

Class Twelve

The phenomena of optics such as those of mechanical waves serve as an introduction to the study of physics in this class. Reflection, refraction and diffraction, polarization and interference are properties of light, which bring clarity to a number of phenomena we meet every day. At the same time they form the basis for an understanding of the significant role which the dualistic conception of light has played in the history of physics. A man such as Newton adhered for a long time to the corpuscular theory, although the wave theory of Huygens had already been accepted by most people. It was only after additional evidence presented by Fresnel and others concerning the phenomena of diffraction and interference that the followers of Newton finally gave up the idea of particles. Light 'is therefore a wave.' But in which medium? A wave could only be conceived as being analogous to a wave of water. But the human mind was not entirely satisfied with this invisible, unweighable 'substance,' until the further paths of research into electricity and optics finally met: Maxwell explains light as an electromagnetic oscillation and classifies this oscillation among those already known. When X-rays were finally found to be subject to interference, all known waves arranged themselves in the electromagnetic spectrum.

This unity of phenomena, however, did not last long. Max Planck made decisive discoveries. And the quantum theory which quickly arose no longer leaves any doubt: light must be thought of as particles (photons). Thus in the end, light also manifests itself dualistically: either as wave or as particle. The difficulties of comprehending physical occurrences finally reaches its climax when we describe to the students the development of the model of the atom to its present state of knowledge. Even matter itself shows interference characteristics and must, therefore, also have the characteristics of a wave. Wave mechanics arose. Dalton thought out the first model of the atom, and this set off an interesting line of development. If we want to attempt to observe the behaviour of atoms, Rutherford's famous experiment is a good example. He sent rays through a thin gold foil. The rays were deflected at some points in a way that led Rutherford to identify electric concentrations as the nucleus of the atom. Thus Rutherford discovered the atomic nucleus, and his idea is still valid today. The atom consists essentially of nothing.

Niels Bohr then proposed a new concept of the atom, which took into account new phenomena of quantum physics. In *The Part and the Whole*, Heisenberg said about Bohr: 'It was immediately apparent that Bohr had achieved his results not through calculations and evidence, but through intuition and guesswork.'

Bohr himself said, 'The point of departure was not the idea that the atom is a planetary system in miniature and that one could here apply the laws of astronomy. I have never taken it that literally. But for me the point of departure was the stability of matter, which from the viewpoint of modern physics is a pure miracle ... Because of the stability of matter, Newtonian physics, within the atom, cannot be right; it can at best occasionally give a clue. And no clear description of the structure of the atom can be given, since such a description — just because it is to be clear — must make use of the concepts of classical physics which, however, no longer suffice to describe what is happening.'

Heisenberg asked, 'Will we ever be able to understand atoms at all, then?'

Bohr replied, 'Yes, but at the same time we shall learn for the first time the meaning of the word "understand".'

Despite this, subsequent students of Bohr and Heisenberg have described the atom model in such a way that it has become absolutely real for the student. Chemists, for example, work very well with the concept of the atom which in theory is already outdated, but which still completely satisfies their requirements. The task of the school, however, should be to awaken in the students a strong experience of the secret, well-structured nature of matter and to bring them to a closer understanding of the difficulty of really comprehending matter.

> Even when modern science speaks about the forms of the atoms, the word 'form' here can only be understood in its most general meaning, as structure in time and space, as a symmetrical property of forces, as the potential of linking up with other atoms. In the case of the atom, concept and the thing itself will no longer be separated because the atom is actually no longer either. (Heisenberg.)

It is not necessarily so that something as complicated as the atom will be better understood if we make a 'simple model' of it. Obviously such a simplification often gives the possibility of calculating physical processes; on the other hand, it carries with it a tendency toward unreality. For every 'model' has its limits of validity and can turn into a lie, if we are not conscious that such limits exist.

With respect to this, Walter Heitler remarks, 'I find it unjustified when teachers try to present higher, abstract areas of science in simplified form in the high schools, when such areas can only be properly understood at the university level.'

We should never forget that most pupils hardly ever return to a study of physics in later life. The impressions we pass on to them of the difficult fields of scientific conceptions of the world should be impressions for life. Even those who later do take up the study of science should be fully aware of the fact that the greatest of today's researchers are still wrestling for understanding, a fact of which those working only in the field of applied science are often quite oblivious.

Chemistry

How is it that we daily come into contact with chemical phenomena, that chemical processes of many different kinds take place in our own organism, and yet many of us remain strangers to fundamental concepts of chemistry throughout our lives? Does this have something to do with the difficult nature of understanding chemical phenomena or does it derive from our methods of teaching?

Nowadays teachers, parents, and not least of all pupils, are confronted with such questions more than ever before. In many countries the chemistry curriculum is taught with the aim that chemical processes can be grasped ever more quickly by making the pupil conversant at an early stage with the world of models and formulae which, it is assumed, is as real as the physical world. Any experiments performed mainly serve as demonstrations and proofs of these more abstract concepts.

What happens when a teacher in a Waldorf School introduces the children in Class 7 to a wide range of actual phenomena. It ensures, for example, that the phenomenon of fire is not limited to the controlled flame of a Bunsen burner. It makes it possible for every child to have the opportunity of holding their breath before the crackling noise and consuming force of a fire, and to be carried away by the greatness and beauty of the experience. Chemical phenomena constantly threaten to overwhelm us. That is their nature. It is necessary to classify the phenomena to relate them to one another without, however, denying them their validity as pure phenomena. Through experiments on a large scale the teacher awakens wonder and the pupils long to understand what they have observed. Experiments in school are more readily comprehensible than direct experience in nature. This is often because they answer a particular question which we may have about the world around us.

It has cost humanity a great effort to reach an understanding of a number of chemical processes. If one did not let the pupils share in basic discoveries they would miss important experiences. It is, therefore, essential that the teacher gives the pupils ample opportunity for discussion and carrying out their own experiments.

Right into the upper school the teaching of chemistry not only adds to the pupil's body of knowledge but also furthers their inner development. In the course of experiments the great chemical polarities of acid and alkali reappear again and again. But there are also opposites of other kinds, such as the metallic and the non-metallic elements.

Of course, many experiments and a good deal of mental effort are required to bring the different phenomena together in an intelligible way. Is an alkali always connected with a metal? Have acids always to do with oxygen, as Lavoiser thought when he called it *oxygenium,* acid producing? What part do non-metallic substances play in the chemical interaction of matter? One tends all too quickly to deduce rules from experiments, only to find soon afterwards that there are various exceptions. In such a situation a hypothesis offers an easy way out, and with the help of corollaries to this hypothesis one can tolerate the exceptions a bit longer. But is there a methodical way of building up a concept of nature, in which such exceptions can have their proper place? This would have to be a way free from any hypotheses, and which takes special interest in all the exceptions to the general rules.

Upon close examination Lavoisier's ideas about the role of oxygen in the formation of acids did not prove generally applicable. After all there are the hydrogen halides which have all the distinctive properties of acids and yet come into being without the participation of oxygen. Which substances in such a case give rise to acid formation? Fluorine, chlorine, bromine, and iodine, elements of a special character, whose nature one can learn to know more closely through observing their exceptional behaviour. In fact they constitute a special field of chemistry.

In this way, especially in Class 11, the need gradually arises to come to a careful classification of matter and also of the basic chemical processes. There are different possibilities of arrangement, and each can reveal something interesting. If one looks at the periodic table of the elements or other groupings, it becomes increasingly clear that nature manifests itself in polarities, and is enhanced through their mutual interaction.

Many students can comprehend this intellectually without any great difficulty; however in a mixed-ability class it is often necessary to present pictorial examples. The essential element of a picture is that it reveals its validity on more than one level. After the relationship of alkalis and acids to other natural phenomena has been worked out, in a fume cupboard the teacher can add a small pellet of solid sodium hydroxide to a small quantity of concentrated hydrochloric acid in a dark coloured container. The mixing of the two results in a harsh hissing sound and violent dangerous splashes. The mixture quickly heats up and boils wildly and noisily. Only gradually do things quieten down. One notices that many pupils feel relieved once the tumult has subsided. Finally it becomes completely still. After a period of cooling down, a salt precipitates out of the solution. Out of the chaos arise well-ordered crystalline forms.

Smell, colour, sound — the wealth of observable phenomena must be put on one side when reducing a chemical process to a formula. This path from a multitude of sense-impressions to an abstract definition has been trodden by humanity in the course of history, and in the chemistry teaching of the top classes it is broadly retraced.

The illustrations on this and the facing page are taken from the main lesson books of two girls in Class 11 studying sulphur.

Left below: Sulphur is heated in a test-tube and when it had caught alight it is swiftly poured into a glass of cold water that is illuminated from below. There is a turbulent reaction. The lump of sulphur hisses and smokes and flares up, until at last it collapses to the bottom.

Left above: Mixed with iron filings, flowers of sulphur burn steadily, with an intense glow and showers of sparks. What is left is a lava-like crust, a compound of iron and sulphur.

Above: Three forms of solid sulphur or compounds of sulphur.

Just as in the course of the history of chemical discoveries, so in the teaching of chemistry the need arises for careful terminology and readily comprehensible classifications. On the whole standard chemical symbols are quickly grasped and learned by the pupils. In their eagerness many even make a game out of it. An understanding of the ratio required in chemical reactions is more difficult to master. Yet the interaction of chemistry and mathematics offers interesting and important opportunities to learn about proportions.

Even in other fields of the study of nature, such as biology, proportions are a significant factor. Chemical formulae are an expression of relationships between weights. But it is by no means easy to grasp this intellectually. That is why at this stage the more abstract concept of models in chemistry made their appearance. Usually in teaching today the simpler way is chosen, using atomic models which have simply to be accepted without being fully understood. An understanding of the origin of these models requires hard-won experience in experiments and an advanced mathematical knowledge. An important question faces the teacher at this point: can the pupils remain free in respect of what they are being taught? Through the premature introduction of models which are not properly derived, students are led to a false belief in authority, from which it is difficult to free themselves. In some schools this starts very early, but such a method runs counter to the basic scientific method of building on observation. In addition, nature itself recedes even further from the students' experience.

The history of modern chemistry reached a decisive turning point at the end of the nineteenth century. Even in the first half of that century, Faraday had striven to present phenomena. His experiments were often true discoveries, because they revealed the true being of nature. In Faraday's presentation there is much that can be of value to the teacher, for example, in the field of electro-chemistry. We experience the effect of certain forces in chemical reactions, but still have no direct sense experience of the forces themselves. Even here there are models (for chemical compounds) which offer themselves as a substitute for physical reality. Chemists such as Wilhelm Ostwald tried to purge science of unnecessary mental constructs. However the chemistry of today is no longer comprehensible without the use of hypothetical models. So even in a Waldorf School this approach is justifiably used in appropriate instances. One can learn a great deal from the study of such one-sided thinking which tries to get behind the phenomena. Many students are also aware of the wider problems, for instance with the world of synthetic preparations, which are no longer part of natural cycles and act as poisons. But it is not just a matter of rejecting modern technological chemistry. Chemistry will continue to develop. For this to happen, however, greater insight is needed into the interaction and transformations of matter in the environment. We also need more precise knowledge of the subtle effects these interactions have on human beings, a knowledge which is only gradually being acquired.

This awareness leads to an appreciation of the dilemma of modern chemistry. Chemistry gives us a great deal of power, but it estranges us from the world, in so far as it is not in harmony with nature.

Technology

The Waldorf School would not be fulfilling its aims if it did not prepare for life today by teaching technology. Technology is dealt with in many subjects, though in the main lessons primarily through observation. In particular, pupils who will work in more practical professions need the opportunity to come to grips with practical technology. Practical subjects are often taught as arts and crafts lessons. How this subject is covered varies greatly in different Waldorf Schools. Some of the aspects covered in the upper school are:

— basic surveying and mapping which demand accuracy;
— machine and car maintenance;
— spinning and weaving as a basis for textile studies;
— gardening including grafting;
— computer studies;
— practical insights into money and financial markets.

Some schools have a period of practical work outside school. This can be in the form of class trips for surveying or working on a farm, or individual work experience in hospitals, kindergartens, businesses or factories.

The aim of this practical work is not just to give a taste, but to widen the students' horizons and train their willpower. Work experience can have an effect on the choice of career of young people. For instance, some had never thought of farm work, but after work experience, take up a career in agriculture out of a feeling for its profound importance. Some may find their working conditions difficult but begin to realize that the work requires strict rules and discipline. They may see their time in school is much freer, and return from their work experience with renewed vigour to work more diligently, and perhaps also resolve not to be insensitive to their colleagues. And even those who never again work in the fields will have gained insight into a reality which may otherwise have remained hidden.

Some Waldorf Schools go much further in these practical realms than has been indicated here. They have parallel streams for non-academic students who can learn practical skills, qualifying in different trades.

Geography

Classes Nine to Ten

The earth is our home, but it has become increasingly clear that through our actions we have profoundly influenced those conditions which are necessary for the continuance of life, and we are even in a position to destroy our planet. The question of the inner attitude with which we regard our earth has never been so important as in our present age.

Geography teaching in the upper classes of the Waldorf Schools is designed to contribute towards a genuine and scientifically well-founded appreciation of the entire earth.

While regional geography has provided most of the subject matter in Classes 5 to 8, pupils in the upper classes gradually come to consider processes which encompass the whole earth. The lessons must be planned in such a way that the pupils are introduced to the manifestations of nature in a hands-on way.

Geology is taught in Class 9. Instruction in the school room should be supplemented by excur-

In Class 9 the complex formation of the Alps is studied. These three diverse pictures illustrate the same geological cross-section.

sions, taking the whole class on an extended visit to a geologically interesting area. Through the process of erosion, for instance, one can clearly see that the face of the earth is forever changing. Plants and trees transform stone into fertile soil and flowing waters reshape the landscape.

The opposite of the processes of disintegration, is the building up of mountains. They create the backbone of the continents. The mountains in those countries which border the Pacific Ocean have a primarily north-south orientation, while the mountains of Europe and Asia run mainly in an east-west direction. Seen from a global perspective, they form a kind of cross. A comprehensive description of the powerful events which have produced the present characteristics of the earth is fascinating for pupils of this age.

In Class 10 pupils busy themselves with the actual surveying of a small, limited region. They make their own maps. In addition, they view the whole earth from a broad perspective. Geological discoveries of the second half of the twentieth century show the notion of the earth as merely a dead body to be obsolete. Through the shifting of tectonic plates the earth shows a continuing mobility both in vertical as well as horizontal movements, for instance in the uplifting of the Scandinavian mountain chain, and continental drift. The more we move away from the actual surface of the earth, the more intense the forces involved seem to become. First pupils study the shape of the continents. They learn among other things that the earth shows a distinct polarity between the land and water hemispheres; they sketch and paint not only the heights of the mountains but also the depths of the sea; they experience the great ocean currents and through their own artistic work gain an understanding of the living picture of the wide range of plant life which covers the earth's surface. Atmospheric phenomena, too, are thoroughly studied. The outermost layers of the earth's environment demonstrate further intensification of activity. Not only meteorites but also other substances constantly penetrate our atmosphere from outer space. While the earth loses hydrogen in a constant stream out into space, it receives a supply of cosmic substances of several thousand tons per day. Also in the magnetosphere there is a constant interplay between the cosmos and the earth. From its outermost layer to its core, the earth reflects an intelligent organization. It is an organism. Such perspectives are designed to awaken in young people a sense of responsibility to the earth and its functions.

Mineralogy is often a favourite subject of teenage pupils, especially if they can make practical field excursions and collect their own specimens.

Biology and the study of the human being

Of all the ideas we carry with us through life there are few which affect our actions so profoundly and permanently as the way in which we view the human being. Let us try to put aside all secondary considerations and turn our thoughts solely to the essential question: what is a human being?

Are we a product of our social environment? This is the conviction of the Marxists, and from this follows the idea of the right of the collectives to shape the existence of the individual.

Are we incurable egoists, ruled by our impulses and desires? This idea lies at the basis of the capitalist system, in practice if not in theory. In the modern consumer society industrialists and advertisers plan ways in which the consumer can be 'steered' by the help of 'needs' which are sustained by advertisements and indeed are to some extent created by them in the first place.

Are we a specific combination of genes? Today this is the standard scientific interpretation and one which is increasingly gaining acceptance among laypeople. Such an idea, however, also has its dangerous side. If it should become possible to manipulate our inherited characteristics, then from such a viewpoint this would be justified.

There are also other interpretations which can lead to far-reaching practical consequences: 'We are what we eat,' 'We are a higher animal,' 'We are a naked ape.'

For the very reason that our own ideas of the human being can lead to profound lifelong consequences for ourselves it is especially important that not only teachers but also textbooks used for self-study avoid premature judgments.

Rudolf Steiner's knowledge of human beings lies at the basis of his pedagogy. Does it not often happen therefore that Waldorf teachers themselves present the students with ideas such as 'The human being is an immortal being of soul and spirit who goes through repeated earth lives?' The answer is that if that happens, then it is just as unpedagogical as all other cut-and-dried definitions.

Children and young people have the right to experience how their own ideas about the human being gradually evolve. One of the teacher's most important tasks is to direct the work that each judgment made and each conclusion drawn is suited as far as possible to the material under consideration and the age of the pupils.

The biology curriculum

The actual study of the human being begins in **Class 7** with a general survey of the basic aspects of health and nutrition. Anyone who has ever read a book on medicine knows the danger lurking here — the reader comes to think they have every illness in the book! In puberty this anxiety is often very pronounced. It is important, therefore, that these questions be discussed as early as possible. On the other hand, below Class 7 most children would not be in a position to grasp the subject at all. Instruction in this sphere can be a real blessing. Never before and perhaps never again does a person eat so much and so quickly as they do at this age. Much better than long sermons on chewing or the quality of food, is to describe in a lively and interesting manner the process of digestion through the mouth, the oesophagus, the stomach, the intestines, the liver, the blood and the kidneys, and to let the pupils work out the forms and primary functions of the most important inner organs through their own sketches. Once we realize how the different organs react to unchewed, badly prepared, indigestible, spoilt or even poisoned food,

In the upper school the illustrations gradually become more precise and include exact anatomical detail.

we will be able to develop a healthy feeling for these organs for our whole life.

In **Class 8** the children are advanced enough to complete a new and important step in the study of human beings. They have in the meantime become acquainted with a number of elementary physical laws. Often with a keen interest they now discover how such phenomena have their counterparts in the human body: in the human eye, or the leverage system of the skeleton, for example. Not all functions of the human body can be explained in mechanical terms, however. Direct observation is key and we should not go further than saying that there are certain activities in the human body which are understandable in physical terms.

The curriculum is such that the upper school teacher who becomes responsible for the study of human physiology and biology in general in Class 9 can adjust the class work to the previous knowledge and needs of the children; they can also fill in gaps or review and expand on especially important sections. Teachers can weave in descriptions of animals and nature and compare the ways in which animals and human beings are related to their environment.

In **Class 10** a new stage is reached: the functions of the human soul and spirit are introduced. What actually takes place in the physical and conceptual life of a person when they pick up a pencil? Through such simple examples the structure and function of the nervous and muscular systems can be illustrated. In addition the different levels of consciousness are considered: the waking state in which we can perceive and think about such an act; the dream state which pervades our feelings and emotions and which are perhaps also associated with it; the totally unconscious state of the functions of the will through which we carry out the act itself. While the different organs and systems of the human being are now described in connection with one's inner life, it is clear that the presentation on this level is much more complicated than it was in Class 7.

Cytology, the study of cells, is discussed in **Class 11**. Now is the time to study, for example, the division of cells, regeneration, propagation, heredity and ontogenesis. Modern genetics can also be discussed.

During the course of this school year a survey of the plant kingdom is begun which is then continued in **Class 12**. The biology curriculum culminates in a comprehensive survey of the main species of the animal kingdom and of the whole process of evolution.

The relationship between human beings and animals

One of the most important questions is directly related to biology teaching in the top classes: what is the relationship between human beings and animals?

This question is not just theoretical. It arises naturally from the life experience of the pupils. In early childhood as well as in the early teens a person often has a fundamental need to identify with the animal world in one way or another. In Class 9 a girl asked the question, 'Why does the hedgehog have spines?' Without realizing that he himself was a good illustration of this very question, a boy well-entrenched behind a thick shock of hair and a leather jacket answered, 'To be able to roll himself up and defend himself, of course.'

Here are some more examples. A decidedly choleric pupil always wanted to give talks or do projects about the rhinoceros, never forgetting to describe the outbreaks of wrath of this not exactly gentle animal. A small shy girl, without

In the study of biology in Classes 11 and 12 the pupils become aware of the typical form or gesture of a certain plant or animal, whether it is more outwardly visible or more inwardly felt. The changing moods of colour and form bring to expression various aspects of the cuttle-fish.

any outside prompting included in her nature-study notebook a kind of self-portrait, a picture of a shy doe. A phlegmatic child depicted in his notebook a careful and deeply-felt portrayal of an orang-utan resting lazily in the branch of a tree and enjoying the delicious fruit all around. This instinctive way of feeling oneself into the animal world can, of course, also express itself in a far more primitive manner.

What can a biology teacher say in summing up this whole question if she wishes to proceed in a purely phenomenological way of observation?

When Ernst Haeckel, at the end of the nineteenth century, wrote down his thoughts about the evolution of human beings, without any qualms he wrote the names of the different ape-forms on the family tree leading in a direct line to the human being. Since then a great deal has happened in evolutionary research. The Belgian paleontologist, Louis Dollo, has shown that specialized organs cannot revert and then redevelop int another specialized direction. Human beings, however, are in many ways extraordinarily unspecialized. Here the teacher can remind the pupils of the lessons in Class 4 where the hands of the human being were compared with the corresponding front limbs of mammals. It is not biologically conceivable, therefore, that the human being could stem from ancestors who evolved in their way of life and their bodily development a marked one-sidedness in the construction of the head or the extremities, for example. In modern family trees the names of the primates have for the most part been placed on side branches; and it is assumed that both humans and primates have descended from common ancestors. However, since even the most recent finds have provided no certain key to the appearance of these ancestral forms, recourse has been taken to ancestral 'models' that understandably vary considerably from one scientist to another. It is quite likely that the coming decades will bring far-reaching changes in the understanding of our origin and evolution.

But what about the obvious psychological relationship which has so often been pointed out in modern behavioural sciences? In the human being there are certain clear 'animal needs' (sexual and territorial impulses) and in many animals a number of 'human' traits (self-assertion or aggression). Through our powerful technology, however, human beings are incomparably more dangerous than any kind of animal. If one is really serious about putting human beings and animals on an equal footing then the consequences are very far-reaching. Then the most important goal of our education would have to be to learn to contain the especially dangerous impulse of aggression through sport or other harmless physical activities and to direct all base instincts into other areas.

All such questions lead inevitably to the realization that we stand before a clear choice. If we regard human beings as mere creatures of instinct, then they need constant behavioural, economic, and political directives. However, if we view them as self-conscious beings, capable of self-control and self-development, then it becomes meaningful to strive for such great goals as freedom, loyalty and democracy.

What right do we have to speak of as self-conscious beings? This question can certainly be taken up in biology classes, perhaps by means of detailed comparisons between the functions of instincts in human beings and in animals. Nevertheless, this is a problem which science alone can never answer. Just by discussing such an important question of human existence one realizes what a vital part the humanities play within the school curriculum.

History and sociology

In Classes 8 and 9 the pupils are eager to learn as much as possible about the time they live in. History teaching for these years is designed to meet such a need. In Class 8 history from the sixteenth century to the present day is discussed, with special attention given to economic history, that is the great technical discoveries and the development of trade and industry.

In **Class 9** the same period is dealt with again, but this time the cultural, social and political events stand in the foreground: the rise of the modern national states, the history of colonialism and the struggles between Europe and the other parts of the world, and the social developments of the era. Anyone who has no idea of these foundations cannot really understand what is happening in the world today. When the hunger for modern history has been satisfied, at least for the time being, then from a new perspective one can look back again at more distant times.

In **Class 10** the cultures of the ancient world are again taken up, but now from other vantage points: the significance of geographical and sociological connections for the particular lifestyles of China, India, Persia, Mesopotamia, Egypt and Greece. In these, as in the following epochs, their connection with our own time is pointed out.

In **Class 11** medieval times are the main study. This goes parallel with the history of literature. Above all, attention is paid to the different cultural, historical and religious currents.

In **Class 12** when the pupils survey the whole course of history, they can draw comparisons and consider cross-sections of particular aspects, in order to appreciate what is characteristic of any given period. Of the many special studies that might be undertaken, we shall present only one as an example.

Social life in ancient Egypt and in the Sumerian city-state was thoroughly centralized: the priest-king, who was looked on as a god, was not only the chief priest and thus the leader of the whole cultural life, he was at the same time the supreme judge and warlord and — at least in the earliest historical period — the owner of all property.

Subsequently, we see how gradually worldly rulership becomes separated from the priesthood. Kings and priests now stand opposite each other as two separate powers — sometimes as enemies, for instance, Consul and Pontifex Maximus in ancient Rome, Emperor and Pope in medieval Europe. During the transition to modern times, with the rise of the town, its guilds and corporations, a third powerful social factor, the growing economic life, begins to play an important part in the historic process. The beginnings of a threefold ordering of society, in which the spiritual, economic, and political institutions find themselves in a certain balance, were destroyed or weakened through the powerful Absolutism of the fifteenth, sixteenth, and seventeenth centuries. The unified concept of the priest-state repeats itself but now in a more secular version. With the advent of the French Revolution the power of the prince begins to change into the power of the people. The rise of democracy, which was certainly necessary, had as a tragic consequence that disagreements between kings become enmity between whole nations. With the advent of industrialization and modern communications, the democratic state of today acquires those economic and spiritual means by which it can become a threat to other equally well-equipped states. This leads to the confrontation of nations and peoples in the modern world.

From such considerations it becomes necessary to consider the different social theories which attempt to overcome this problem. There is Marxism, for instance, the dialectic logic of which anticipated the dissolution of the modern state; a world federalism which would bring together all power-blocks into one democratic universal state; the belief in a balance through mutual fear which enables the different states to hold one another in check by skilful diplomatic and technical manipulations. Rudolf Steiner's idea of a threefold social order would neutralize the danger of the superpowers by carefully-planned emancipation of both the economic and the spiritual life from the tyrannical domination of the centralized state. Which view best suits reality and which can best help in our present situation? The pupils themselves will have to decide that. The task of the teacher is to point out clearly the problems of the modern world and also the most important suggestions which have been advanced as a solution.

The main task of the teaching of history in the upper school is, of course, to present a broad overview. Often there is not enough time left to go into the destinies of individuals. Nevertheless biographies are very important. Through such studies to which the pupils themselves may contribute in the form of projects, one thing becomes very clear. The inner core of the human being — however one may judge their deeds — need not remain a passive onlooker of events that happen more or less automatically. This inner being carries its impulses into the historical process and can, if the conditions are right, give a new direction to a whole stream of events. But the inner being can also remain passive and thereby miss a decisive opportunity.

Brief biographies which bring to expression a tragic human problem, can stimulate in the students unexpectedly positive reactions. A boy whose emotional life had become severely disturbed as a result of a difficult early childhood and who consequently completely neglected his school-work, one day heard about the life of Bismarck and the severe depression that accompanied him throughout many years of his political activity and the consequences of which he mastered only with the greatest effort. A few days later the pupil came up to the teacher and said: 'That Bismarck — he was a remarkable man!' After that he seemed to gain a new inner strength and during the rest of that period produced excellent work.

The arts in the upper school

As their powers of thought develop in various spheres, many of the pupils in the upper school are no longer satisfied merely to learn the method of certain artistic techniques. They want to know what gave rise to them. A study of the different forms of art is taken as a main lesson period, in the same way as the sciences. Literature and poetry are treated in this way in Class 10, and music in Class 11.

The visual arts

In **Class 9** the life and work of Leonardo da Vinci may be the theme. The teacher reports briefly on his accomplishments in the most diverse fields (painting, drawing, sculpture, architecture, poetry, music, botany, mathematics, mechanics, anatomy), and describes his almost unique ability to remember an image seen only once — for example that of a human face — and then to reproduce it in a sketch in great detail as if the object were present in the room. He may end with an aphorism in which Leonardo's dry down-to-earth wisdom is clearly expressed: 'Whoever cannot achieve what he wants should want what he is capable of.' To be confronted with extraordinary human greatness can fire the students with enthusiasm but it can also be a sobering experience. A pupil came with a question which reflects the whole uncertainty of that age, 'How do you know what you are capable of?'

It is not easy to answer such questions. Nor is it always necessary to do so. Often the most important thing is to engage the young people in the classroom on a purely human level so that important questions concerning life in general can spring up spontaneously.

The teaching of art in Class 9 also deals with the history of the visual arts from ancient times as far as the time of Rembrandt. In studying the transitions from one style to another the teacher can draw attention to significant riddles of human development. In sombre and heavy Romanesque architecture and the boldly-conceived Gothic cathedrals which in their upward thrust seem almost to overcome the forces of gravity, two contrasting moods of soul are reflected. A wide spectrum of feeling is expressed through the development of painting. The imaginative picture world of the medieval artists with its background of piety and devotion is followed in the south by the overwhelming enjoyment of the world of the senses expressed in the paintings of the Renaissance and in the north by profound and often enigmatic landscapes as exemplified by the works of Grünewald, Dürer, and Rembrandt. The dramatic contrasts between light and shadow in Rembrandt's paintings can provide a basis for interesting colour studies.

Romanesque and Gothic cathedrals (upper school, Hamburg, Germany).

In the art lessons of Class 9 one of the tasks set can be to work through colour relationships in the contrast of light and shade (see also page 218).

History of architecture

In **Class 12** the history of architecture is studied. From the vast field of available material one example will be given here, which can lead to an understanding of the problems of modern architecture.

The Spanish architect Antonio Gaudi (1852–1926) saw in the straight line the expression of human reason, and in the curve the reflection of the activity of a creative deity. He sought his inspiration in nature, in the teeming richness of the realm of plants, and thus created a bold, often fantastic, world of form. The brilliant and remarkable impulse which came to expression in his art was carried to an extreme and lost itself in the non-architectural, naturalistic plant-ornamentation of Art Nouveau. In energetic reaction to this manifestation of decadence, Le Corbusier (1887–1965) at a specific phase of his creative work condemned the curve altogether — he called it the 'path of the donkey' — and wanted to create spaces in which the straight line ruled alone as an expression of reason. With his one-sided striving for rational utility ('machines for living in'), he became the founder of modern functionalism. The use of computers and of prefabricated building components have carried such ideas to an extreme, which threatens to force the town-dweller into living in a uniform, completely soulless space.

The attempts undertaken since then (not least of all by Le Corbusier himself) to 'humanize' modern architecture once again by introducing a strong element of movement, bear witness to the difficulty of finding a valid alternative to the language of form generally used today.

Are we condemned, therefore, to decide on one or the other of these two chief directions in architecture, or is it possible to find a middle way? This is the point at which it is appropriate to mention the direction taken by Rudolf Steiner in this field. He was of the view that the activity which was to take place in a house should come to expression in the whole shape and structure. Whoever wants to build 'functionally' must not only seek solutions which are flawless from a technical aspect but which also are the expression in architectural terms of the soul and spiritual needs of the person who is to live or work there. Accordingly, in the second Goetheanum he wished to realize an architectural impulse which could be described as a 'search for balance': an effort to bring the movement which is manifest in the individual surfaces and lines to a unified and harmonious whole.

The history of literature

Why do we need poetry? Do we not live in a time in which reality, in many respects, surpasses all fiction, and in which the real problems of our fellow people must be incomparably more important than the fictitious fate of any hero in a novel? What is the point of a thorough study of the fields of poetry and the other aspects of writing, or the history of literature in a contemporary curriculum?

One could, of course, answer the question by saying that only modern literature is studied in order to show how the problems of our time forcefully come to expression in just this medium. There is no doubt that many young people would welcome such an approach. Others would realize more or less clearly that the perspective which

From history of architecture.
Above: Gaudi, Sagrada Familia, *Barcelona. Below: Frank Lloyd Wright,* Falling Water, *Pennsylvania.*

one gains through such an approach is not entirely true. The question is really this: is the literature of the past a cultural burden which we drag along from generation to generation only out of conservative regard? Or have perhaps the classical writers something to say to us which can rarely be found in contemporary writing? In fact the great problems of our time are not experienced and artistically expressed in all their ramifications only by modern authors. The literary material which is used in the upper classes of the Waldorf School shows very clearly that the motives and personalities of writers of the past can often be especially relevant and interesting for young people of today.

In teaching literature, just as in the teaching of history, individual writers and their works from the end of the eighteenth and the beginning of the nineteenth century are considered. Gradually the students realize how exceptionally rich such a study is for an understanding of our own time. As the storms of the French Revolution and the Napoleonic Wars broke out over Europe, many people thought a time of apocalyptical upheaval had begun. These decades, chaotic though they were from a political aspect, turned out on the cultural level to be a true 'Golden Age,' an age in which a wealth of musical, philosophical and, above all, poetical gifts came to expression at the same time in Europe. Many people in this era knew a great deal of loneliness, human conflict, broken promises, anxiety, fear of death, doubt in God and the world, as well as of war and famine. But they often had the ability to formulate their suffering and deep inner problems in artistic terms, which in form and content were landmarks then and will remain so for some time to come. An outstanding example is Goethe, who in this context should not be looked at as a German, but rather as a European cultural figure.

A brief example will show how impressive the intense intellectual activity of the leading cultural figures of that era can be. A teacher in a literature period in **Class 9** had described how Heinrich von Kleist, with his strong sense for the real consequences of Kant's theory of knowledge which is so full of resignation, decided to give up all research and to devote himself as a poet to the 'beautiful illusion.' One pupil found this view of life in which there was no way of achieving a knowledge of true reality ('the thing in itself') simply unbearable. Her arm shot up quickly and she asked with deep feeling: 'How did Kant actually die? Did he commit suicide?' The seriousness of life which is expressed in such a period finds its counterbalance in the treatment of humour and humorous poetry.

In **Class 10**, at the age of 16, the students experience the transition from a lifestyle closely bound up with the family to independence. The main theme in the study of literature now depicts the same change, as it has come about in history. In the oldest version of the *Edda,* Gudrun decides in the battle between her husband and the scions of her own clan in favour of her blood relations, although they had once slain her lover Sigurd. In the later sagas and in the *Nibelungenlied* we are told how this same personality — whether she is known as Gudrun or Kriemhild — carries out a terrible revenge on her own brothers because of her murdered husband. Between these two interpretations of an ancient theme there lies a powerful historical change: the experience in which human individuality frees itself from the bonds of blood relationship and becomes an individual in its own right. A similar ancient Germanic theme, which comes to expression in the *Edda* and especially in the Icelandic sagas, such as the saga of *Burnt Njal,* is the striving of the individual to remain steadfast in the face of loneliness, sorrow and death. In such scenes one can glimpse the birth of an ideal which later, in ever new metamorphoses, reappears in western history: the emphasis on individualism.

In Class 10 one period of teaching is devoted to basic literary forms. The different schools of creative writing, poetry and its various metres and styles from ancient times to the present can here be observed as representative of the different states of consciousness in the different epochs. In the construction of dramas, epics and lyrical poems, certain basic artistic and psychological principles of each age can be discovered.

In **Class 11** the point of departure is a study of medieval literature, above all that epoch which stands out in the world of knightly tales as an early and powerful parallel to the story of Faust: Wolfram von Eschenbach's *Parzival.* Parzival's course of life goes from the simple-mindedness of childhood and youth, through uncertainty, defiance and doubt to a spiritual rebirth, to a deepened and satisfying experience of the self. The journey through life which Wolfram depicts in his epic has something which is valid for everyone. Whoever studies these three stages closely will recognize them as possibilities in the life of every human being. Pupils and teacher can now both see how many authors of the past there are who have basically remained at the level of 'simple-mindedness' through their whole life, how many modern authors have never gone beyond the experience of 'doubt,' but that there are also a group of important literary personalities who have lived through the earlier stages and then, towards the end of their lives, in one way or another have reached the stage of 'spiritual rebirth.' Faithfulness to the chosen goal determines one's destiny, the path of individual development, in spite of all obstacles in the way, and the single human being who has trodden this path can eventually be of service to humanity as a whole.

In **Class 12**, after a survey of earlier literature, modern literature is discussed. In many schools this activity begins with Goethe's *Faust,* who can be taken as the prototype of the struggling modern human being. Nietzsche, Ibsen, Tolstoy and Dostoevsky then form the transition to modern literature, which encompasses both the sufferings and the greatness of our own era.

The selection of examples may vary, but it should always be such as will acquaint the pupils with literary creations which are a genuine expression of their own period and, at the same time, point towards the future.

In much of modern literature there is the underlying theme, expressed with many variations and often with genius, of despair over the inability of modern people to find a way out of their difficulties. This pessimistic attitude is often considered, especially by young people, to be honest and in keeping with the times. If in abeyance to this opinion we restrict ourselves mainly to twentieth century works, it is impossible to give a true picture of the development of the art of literature, and the ways in which human beings have faced their problems in the past. The perspective becomes even wider and more realistic if we also introduce the literature of different nations as well as of former ages.

A girl of Class 11 has drawn and painted scenes from Wolfram von Eschenbach's epic of Parzival in the style of medieval illumination.

Drama in the upper school

In one of the upper classes — the tenth or the twelfth — a complete, full-length drama is undertaken. The pupils now experience what it means to work not out of the natural love of acting of younger children, but out of a conscious artistic feeling for style. The experiences which both the producer and players may undergo was related by the drama teacher of the Waldorf School in Stockholm, Louise Björneboe, as follows:

> A key word in the classical theory of drama is 'empathy'! To creep into a role, to become so deeply involved in it that you suffer to the same extent as the person you are representing. The beginning of all love is interest. Compassion is enhanced interest. At this point a pedagogical problem arises. How can the teacher help the pupil in such a way that she does not tire but maintains her interest in the part she is playing? One will succeed in this by continually discovering new shades of meaning and new nuances of expression. Then the role becomes a real character, it comes to life. This interest, which can grow into compassion, is something different from the amateur interest of wanting to get on the stage to act out one's own self. The empathy which is spoken of in the ancient theory of drama goes much further — a suffering which passes through a dramatic climax and reaches a release, a solution. The Classical Theory of drama also spoke of catharsis, of purification and refinement as the final phase of the dramatic experience. These concepts have been interpreted in many different ways in the course of the centuries ... But in the dramatic work of the twelfth class the pupils can get an idea of what this actually means. Indeed, each pupil will perhaps notice that in struggling with a certain role he has become a different person. The class as a whole may go through a change because the pupils get to know one another in quite a new way. The pupils stand in a more objective relationship to their own personalities as well as to those of their comrades. In the course of this work much has come to pass — in fact, a kind of catharsis.

Only after puberty are the pupils able to represent on the stage a personality totally different to themselves. This new experience can bring about what young people especially need, namely the ability to participate in the destiny of others to such an extent that now and again they may forget their own personal problems.

Next page: An exercise in drama. Classes 10 and 11.

Music

Whoever has been present at an assembly in one of the larger Waldorf Schools knows that the choir and orchestra play an important part in the life of the school. If it is one of the schools in which a real musical life has developed over the years, then the pupils in the upper school play some of the symphonic works of the great composers. In musical education, of course, an attempt is made to get even the relatively unmusical pupils to sing in tune. The purely 'phenomenological' study of the nature of different intervals and keys plays an important part. Characteristic folk songs from different parts of the world are practised — often in connection with particular subjects of study, such as history or geography. In order that the pupils may come into a direct and living contact with music, which then becomes a lifelong interest for many of them, the musical examples, as far as possible, are given through live instrumentation or song. The question of the effect of technical aids (recordings, amplification, etc.) becomes a central theme of conversation.

Side by side with the practical experience, music theory and especially the history of music is a particularly important factor in Class 11. The characteristics of different currents and styles give occasion to touch on central questions of the world of art and of human life.

The archetypal dichotomy of Apollonian and Dionysian* elements in ancient Greece was experienced first in the realm of mythology, and then made its mark in the whole Hellenic cultural life, especially in music. In the musical development of the West one can see this polarity come repeatedly to the fore. During periods in which the Apollonian mood predominates, there are still individual artists who represent the opposing element, for example, G. de Machault in the musical life of the fourteenth century, and Monteverdi at the beginning of the seventeenth century. Classical western music belongs to the treasures of cultural life and has as such been cultivated in a continuous tradition. The great masters of the Baroque and Rococo period, including Mozart, viewed music as a 'play of forms moving in sound.' Their basic attitude to art and to life in general was, in spite of the intensity of feeling expressed in their music, essentially Apollonian. One of the first to represent a radical approach was Beethoven. He was in full command of the whole range of traditional musical forms, but again and again consciously broke through them, especially in his last period of creativity.

In the time that followed, an affinity developed between music and poetry, as for example in Weber, Schubert, Schumann, Berlioz and Liszt. In the operas of Richard Wagner the endeavour to blend the different arts, drama, scenery, instrumentation and song reached a climax and in its power and universality achieved an effect on the audiences which went beyond anything known hitherto. In his last years Wagner strove intensely for release from the world of passion and emotion. Did he actually achieve this in *Parsifal,* or is it true, as is often maintained, that even in the purely sacramental parts of his opera an unbridled emotional element comes to expression? Since the Parsifal theme is a kind of thread in Class 11, such a question can well be dwelt on.

With few exceptions — among which especially Mendelssohn and Bruckner should be mentioned — the basic nature of the Romantic composers can be described as predominantly Dionysian. In modern music we discern evidence

---

* Apollonian relates more to the life of thinking and outer form, hence 'classical' in a musical sense. Dionysian relates to the inner life of personal feeling and impulse, hence is connected to what is called the Romantic School.

of the Apollonian element which, however, finds its source of inspiration not primarily in the sphere of religion, as with the old masters, but rather in the realm of science and technology. In the case of Schoenberg this tendency often appears in a more mathematically structured form; in the case of Hindemith and Stravinsky more as a naive musical form. It becomes clear that once again a radical change is taking place in the world of music. With all their modern freedom of form, contemporary composers seldom look on their work as products of personal creative artistry. They do not create finished compositions; they 'give an account of some musical material.' Their human attitude is often unassuming and experimental.

It is also worth studying the music of other cultures such as those of India and China, which stand outside the mainstream of western musical evolution.

Painting

After working in black and white in Classes 8 and 9, the pupils in Class 10 return to colour. The following words of Rudolf Steiner can serve as a guide for the present task:

> One should realize that we do not have to set up a special kind of painting for the children, but when one finds that they, in some way, are going to grow into painting, then the principles must be derived from a living painting-art, not from pedagogically contrived methods. The real artistic element must be carried out in the school, not a reasoned thought-out process … *(A Modern Art of Education,* Aug 17, 1923).

The examples of paintings reproduced here show how one can try, without directly following any one style, to penetrate the world of colours as great modern artists have done. They have grasped the characteristic nature, for instance, of blue and of yellow, of the warm and the cold colours, the powers of form and expression which are latent in the colours themselves. Goethe's theory of colours is an inexhaustible source of inspiration for this experience. It gives rise to free colour compositions.

The experiences in working with watercolour in the lower school have been by no means exhausted. The technique of layer-painting (or veil painting) produces new and especially interesting colour effects. Each shade of colour is applied separately and has to dry. It remains transparent: that is, what has already been painted shimmers through the next veil of colour. The new creative possibilities thus available stimulate the imagination. The picture takes shape as a process evolving from colours, not as a preconception which one has in mind from the beginning.

In Class 11 the attention of the pupils to their environment is redirected. The young people now experience the colours in their surroundings as eloquent phenomena. Still-life and figure painting are practised. The Impressionists and the Expressionists with their diametrically opposite attitudes are represented in the pictures. The culmination of this study of painting is reached in Class 12 when the pupils paint the human countenance.

Further crafts and practical activities

In the upper school arts and crafts subjects are often given in main lesson blocks, which means that there are several weeks to devote more inten-

Free exercises in colour as a revival of painting after the period of working in black and white tones. Above: Cold and warm values of the colour blue (Class 10). Below: Tensions in the sphere of yellow (Class 10).

A profile (Class 12).

A colour exercise (Class 12).

sively to different aspects. Initially the subjects are more practical but in the later classes become more freely artistic. Painting, described above, is one aspect of this curriculum. The following list can gives a picture of the kind of activities which may be offered.

Class 9: clay modelling, joinery, dressmaking, basket weaving with cane, black and white drawing, technical drawing of simple geometrical shapes, gardening.

Class 10: health and hygiene, first aid, practical chemistry, care of trees, technical drawing of more complex geometrical forms, pottery and ceramics, stone carving, spinning, artistic drawing.

Class 11: modelling, painting, metal work, cardboard work, practical physics.

Class 12: book-binding, musical instrument building, pottery, stone carving, descriptive and projective geometry.

It will generally not be possible for each student to take part in all these activities; usually there is a choice. It is not the breadth of experience which is important here, but the possibility of acquiring a skill and developing it.

Spinning lessons (Class 10, Bexbach, Germany).

The School in the Modern World

The industrialized school

Since the Second World War education has changed in many countries. There is a tendency to see the role of schools to provide a well-trained labour force. As manual labour has been replace by machines, and industry in western countries has declined, there is a growing demand for well-educated office workers and managers, as well as a huge increase in research. This has led to a knowledge explosion in the last few years with more young people than ever before continuing to tertiary education at universities and colleges.

As research and technology and life in society become ever more complicated, general education has to provide factual information in a far greater measure than previously. Our present age is characterized by rapid changes and thus demands that large sections of society continually carry their education further, and the principle of 'continuous personal development' is now widely recognized in many professions. The most important task of the schools, therefore, cannot be merely to dispense knowledge as such, but rather to teach the art of learning.

However, the pressure from the economic side of society for more education has led to schools almost being seen as production units that can be organized in a rational way like any other. In the name of efficiency there is greater standardization, wider use of teaching aids, films and computers, and teachers cease to give instruction themselves and changes their role to merely guiding the pupils and organizing and supervising their work. The classroom is replaced by a set of flexible learning-units with suitable equipment. Each pupil has to learn to work more and more on their own and not concern themselves with what others are doing. In order to provide these numerous subject-groupings economically, schools are becoming larger. Human relationships and social contact are no longer part of school experience. What will become of human beings, of mutual relationships, and of the most essential sphere of learning — learning to understand one's fellow human being?

In the meantime we live with the consequences of these 'industrialized schools.' Young people have a feeling of alienation and isolation, which leads to a breakdown in society and in its extreme to antisocial and even criminal behaviour. The effects on young children are more severe. They are exposed to far too many one-sided sense-impressions while receiving insufficient stimulus for the life of feeling and will-activity.

There is now a growing realization that this is not ideal, and the role of the teacher is being taken more seriously again. Not only in Waldorf Schools where these tendencies were resisted but also in state schools, there are countless teachers who are by their presence creating an atmosphere of joy in working, of security and friendliness. We can have only the greatest respect for the work of such teachers.

The independent school

In the industrialized countries there are within the framework of the school system three groups of people who actually belong together, but who have been forced apart by the way society functions today.

A good many parents tend to feel that their children are slipping away from them. Leisure activities and standards of behaviour that are foreign to their parents have assumed an increasing significance in the lives of the younger generation. Nor do the parents have real contact with the school. While there are parents' evenings, and perhaps a teacher will phone a parent on occasions when something is not in order, there is strictly speaking no problem which is not solved within the framework of the school, without the help of the parents.

Many teachers may also suffer from insufficient contact with their pupils. The demands of the curriculum, the methods of teaching, as well as deeply-rooted prejudices, build barriers which are not easily surmounted. The fact that teachers and pupils are forced into opposing roles only serves to show how far the school has departed from its educational task. No doubt many pupils consciously or unconsciously long for a more human contact, not only with their parents but also with their teachers. However they suffer from the unwritten law that they must stand apart from the world of adults.

The social significance of the Waldorf School

Something is needed to bring these three groups together. In this respect Waldorf Schools are a good example. Parents who take part in founding a Waldorf School take on a great burden. When funds are scarce — and that is almost always the case — then parents must be ready to make sacrifices. During the early years of a new school they must be ready to help out in construction and decorating of buildings. Bazaars and school festivals need to be arranged. At parents' evenings, through lectures and courses, they gain insight into the actual work of the school, perhaps even into the anthroposophical foundations upon which the special teaching methods are based. By sharing in the life of the school, the parents are able to find the strength to help to carry the burdens. A close contact with teachers arises. In many cases even true friendships develop. The needs and viewpoints of the parents are to a large extent taken into consideration in the life of the school and in the common concern for the children. Parents are also represented on or sometimes even run the administrative body, and they often represent the rights and needs of the school to government and education departments. The children thus feel that their parents are working for *their* school in a concrete and visible manner.

The teachers take an enormous amount of work upon themselves, lengthy teachers' meetings, discussions with parents and pupils, general meetings, as well as meetings for parents of a particular class, late evenings preparing lessons and marking books, financial worries, negotiations with education authorities, lectures and discussions for the general public. Life is not made easier by founding a Waldorf School but it becomes much more interesting!

The pupils may indeed meet certain difficulties, for instance if they have to move to another school, or when they leave school and join the ordinary working community, because they are accustomed to a more holistic, spiritually-orientated environment. They encounter the same conditions in society as do other youngsters. Their manner of responding to them, however, is strikingly individualistic, and they often have really wide interests. Above all, their particular kind of education has helped them to develop a quality which is of inestimable value, and that is the ability to trust in their fellow human beings. As an adult one can easily enter into a conversation with them. School plays a real role in their lives. As a rule they love their school. Many feel as secure at school as they do at home.

This is a social function of the greatest significance. In our current social environment the independent school that can cultivate the human aspects of life is an indispensable element.

Whoever has played a part and shouldered the burdens in building a lasting and truly deep feeling of community between children, parents and teachers, will know that this has much more profound and lasting effects than superficial measures such as establishing a café in schools, setting up educational democracy, friendship campaigns, and similar activities. One can feel the greatest sympathy and respect for many of these efforts towards reform. But a lasting relationship can only develop slowly through the experience of both pain and joy, perhaps under financial difficulties, superhuman burdens of work and irritating human conflicts — but never through theoretically-conceived arrangements. The reward of this solidarity can be summed up in one word. It is a word which is used here not because it sounds attractive but rather because it expresses a reality which is just as difficult to bear as it is inspiring to live with — freedom.

The problem of examinations

Experiences in a number of countries has shown that Waldorf pupils who follow the necessary course of study can do well in the traditional examination system. Through its many years of practice and its wide experience the Waldorf School movement can show well-established results. They demonstrate the possibility of combining in the Waldorf School concern for the individual with a systematic discipline of learning.

How Waldorf Schools relate to state examination systems varies in different countries and from school to school.

Anthroposophy and Waldorf education

Waldorf education, the art of education founded by Rudolf Steiner, is not merely the sum-total of pedagogical methods, but rather a way of viewing the whole of life. What gives the Waldorf Schools their unique quality and special value is the fact that the group of teachers responsible for the school have the same spiritual aims. To be aware of these aims is not an obligation, but rather an inspiration. Teachers cannot really fulfil their tasks without continually deepening their knowledge of Rudolf Steiner's theory of child development and following the anthroposophical path of inner self-education.

Does this mean the Waldorf School movement can only unfold its activity within very limited circles'? No! Neither anthroposophy nor Waldorf pedagogy is, by its nature, exclusive. Both address deep inner needs of our time, needs that cannot be disregarded, and which become more pressing with each passing decade.

It is conceivable that far-sighted education authorities in various countries might encourage and finance the founding of national or regional Waldorf Schools and yet leave them sufficient educational freedom. The state schools in the canton of Bern (Switzerland) in which Waldorf teaching methods are used, about a hundred in number, are an interesting example. Large-scale experiments of this kind could be fruitful in other places too.

At the same time, however, it must be realized that the true spirit of Waldorf education can only come to full expression within an independent and free school for which parents and teachers carry joint responsibility.

Establishing Waldorf Schools

In many countries the laws and legal practices put obstacles in the way of the founding of Waldorf Schools. An interesting and important task for official and individual groups whose representatives have realized the unique social significance of the Waldorf School must be the attempt to remove such obstacles. One of the difficulties of founding an independent Waldorf School is that parents who wish to send their children to such a school contribute to the life of this school through school fees and other fund raising efforts. At the same time, however, they have to finance the official state schools through a part of their taxes.

In those countries in which independent schools receive no public funding for their activity, there is the danger that the rights of parents to choose a school for their children which is in keeping with their religious and philosophical convictions may in practice be available only to those who are financially well-off. This situation is contrary to the social aims and origin of the Waldorf School, and is certainly considered deeply unsatisfactory by many people. But so far there has not been a unified international consensus which might call for a new solution to these matters. Once a comprehensive idea of a new social order has been established according to the real demands of our time, as they were presented at the beginning of this book with the idea of the threefold social order, then the foundation will be laid for the unfolding of an independent cultural life. A constructive reformation of society can only take place on such a basis. Independent Waldorf Schools in which parents, teachers and pupils work together are, in this sense, centres where the most important pioneering project of the present and future are taking place.

A worldwide school movement

The death of Rudolf Steiner on March 30, 1925, did not interrupt the pedagogical work which he had started. It was carried on by his students and began to spread. His lecture tours in various countries were fruitful in that a whole series of independent Waldorf Schools were established in the 1920s: Hamburg in 1922, The Hague in 1923, London in 1925 (this school later moved to Forest Row, Sussex); Basle and Hanover in 1926, Berlin in 1928, Dresden, New York City, and Bergen (Norway) in 1929. After the Second World War a new growth of Waldorf Schools began, and now (in 2008) there are over 1000.

A brief survey is given here of the development of the Waldorf School movement around the world.

Germany

A large part of Rudolf Steiner's activity took place in Germany. Thus it was only natural that the Waldorf School movement unfolded and flourished most vigorously in this country. Visitors were frequent at school functions, and the pedagogical lectures given by the teachers were well attended. In 1935 the National-Socialist Government forbade the German Waldorf Schools to accept new pupils and in 1938 forced most of these schools to close down. This blow struck the Waldorf School movement at a stage of thriving development. In 1945 the work was able to start anew. Shortly after the end of the Second World War a number of former pupils and teachers gathered in Stuttgart and cleared away the debris of the bombed central building of the first Waldorf School. At that time wherever a Waldorf School teacher landed, whether as a result of the war or as a political refugee, parents came to them and various Waldorf Schools arose immediately. Today in Germany there over 200 Waldorf Schools with over 80 000 pupils. In almost all schools there is a Class Thirteen for those pupils taking the state school-leaving examination.

A remarkable attempt to realize anew the concept advocated by Rudolf Steiner of a comprehensive school, by including vocational training, was undertaken by the Hibernia School in Wanne-Eickel in the Ruhr district. Founded in collaboration with a factory, the school quickly became independent. Not only does this school provide a general education for all pupils, artistic activities up to Class 12 and in one special department preparation for university entrance, but during the later school years it offers training in specialized professions such as kindergarten teacher, laboratory assistant, gardener, cabinet-maker, machinist, tool-worker, mechanic, or electrician. Similar arrangements for helping pupils to make the transition to a profession while still at school were established in Nürnberg, Kassel and Bochum.

Switzerland and Austria

In Switzerland too Rudolf Steiner's educational ideas have found a good response and the work was able to go on during the Second World War. Besides the schools in the larger towns (over 30), there are about a hundred state schools in towns and villages in the canton of Bern, where teaching uses Waldorf methods.

In Austria the Waldorf Schools developed a bit later, and there are now about 15.

The Low Countries

The Dutch Waldorf School movement, just as in Germany and Norway, was interrupted by the Second World War. In the end however this misfortune worked out positively. When the Vrije School (Free School) was closed in the Hague in 1941 by the Nazi occupation, its three hundred pupils had to attend other schools. Things went so well when they entered and passed through these schools that the methods of Waldorf education won respect and proponents of Waldorf education came into close contact with the representatives of other school systems. Today Waldorf education is well recognized in Holland, and this has had practical consequences for the structure of the state schools. Today there about 100 Waldorf Schools the Netherlands, 20 in Belgium and one in Luxembourg.

Scandinavia

In Denmark the liberal educational policy of the country has favoured the founding of Waldorf Schools. Like all independent schools, the Waldorf Schools receive generous subsidies from the state. In Norway a number of individuals who had made a name for themselves in general cultural life became active in the Waldorf School movement. This helped considerably to generate general interest in Waldorf Schools. A law favourable to independent schools has recently been approved by parliament. In Sweden and Finland the attitude of the public and the educational authorities has been decidedly positive and open, so that knowledge of the educational ideas of Rudolf Steiner has pen-extanded to relatively wide circles.

Together there are over 120 Waldorf Schools in Denmark, Norway, Sweden, Finland and Iceland.

The rest of Europe

From the 1960s Waldorf Schools expanded in other western European countries, with over 30 schools in Italy, over 10 in France and 5 in Spain. Since the collapse of Communism, schools have expanded in the Eastern European countries with over 20 in Hungary, more than a dozen each in Russia and Romania, and a few the Baltic States, Poland, Ukraine, Czech Republic and other countries.

The British Isles

Five Waldorf Schools were founded in Britain before the Second World War, and carried on their work throughout the war with only minor disturbances. Generally, there is no state support, and the need to charge fees has to be carefully balanced to avoid social exclusion.

There are now 32 Waldorf Schools in the United Kingdom and 3 in the Republic of Ireland.

North America

The Waldorf School movement initially struggled here. The New York Waldorf School was founded in 1929. A facility for training Waldorf teachers was established at Detroit University in 1967 and in 1968 the first Canadian Rudolf Steiner school was founded in Toronto. Today there are over 120 schools — about a quarter on the West Coast — in the United States, over 20 in Canada and 5 in Mexico.

Other English-speaking countries

There are over 30 schools in Australia, and 10 in New Zealand. In South Africa there are almost 20 schools, and one each in Namibia, Kenya, Tanzania.

The rest of the world

In the last twenty years there has been an enormous expansion of Waldorf Schools in South America and in Asia. In Brazil there are over 20 schools, and about the same number again in the Spanish-speaking countries of Argentina, Chile, Colombia, Peru and Uruguay.

Japan, India and Israel have about half a dozen schools each, and there are one or two each in Georgia, Armenia, Kazakstan, Kyrgyzstan and Tajikistan, as well as in Nepal, Thailand, the Philippines and Taiwan.

As was stated in the Foreword, no doubt this overview will be out of date by the time it is read.

Financing Waldorf Schools

Underpinning all Waldorf Schools is the need to free the education from political and economic concerns.

The financial and social problems which are connected with the support of a independent school can, according to the circumstances in each country, manifest themselves in quite different ways and must be solved differently. There are countries which give no state support for the running of such schools, nor for expenditure on new buildings; countries in which schools are not even permitted to receive larger sums from private donors. Wherever subsidies are received, whether on a national or regional basis, the tax burden becomes very noticeable. However, if great financial burdens are imposed upon the parents, how is one to avoid the danger that the Waldorf Schools, contrary to their original purpose, become schools for the children of the rich? In many schools a circle of private benefactors have made it possible for less well-off children to attend the school. Even if this problem is solved, other questions may arise. If a reduction in fees or full bursaries are granted for many of the children, where does one draw the line?

To what extent should financial considerations be a deciding factor in this matter? Should parent representatives determine pupil admission on the basis of social structure or should they at least belong to the decision-making panel? To what extent may, and to what extent can, the teachers be burdened with financial and administrative tasks? The co-operation of a conscientious body of parents is of great significance in all these special issues connected with the life of the school and the struggle for freedom in cultural life.

The question of teachers' salaries also plays an important role. Since Waldorf Schools usually suffer from financial difficulties, the teachers' salaries, with a few notable exceptions, are often relatively low. They are almost always below the official norm.

If a school is to fulfil the demands made by Waldorf education, then the teachers must enter into their tasks with their whole heart and soul. A circle of people who in this way have pledged themselves with complete devotion to a common task cannot accept that certain formal criteria, such as examination results or qualifications in special subjects, would entitle them to a higher level of pay. On the other hand, there are other ways by which salaries are still differentiated: consideration for family situations, the number of children, additional social obligations, the length of the teacher's journey to school, unpaid loans they still owe from their time as a student etc. Thus the problem of salaries is settled according to individual circumstances in most Waldorf Schools. What matters is to achieve a method of fair apportionment. There are certain Waldorf Schools in which each teacher declares how large a salary they 'need.' The requests are totalled and it is often surprising to see that the required sum agrees with the amount allotted in the budget.

The questions raised here are not hypothetical but are taken from real life. People who wish to start an independent school have no choice but to come to terms with these questions.

Teacher training

An encouraging sign for the future is the fact that more and more young people want to train to become Waldorf teachers. Such training centres exist in many countries. The training includes a study of human development and a study of methods of teaching, which forms the basis of the work at a Rudolf Steiner school, as well as participation in a variety of artistic courses. Practical teaching periods at a Waldorf School are part of the course. It should be emphasized that a teacher-training course of this kind cannot be thought of as replacing special studies in particular subjects. The course of instruction is designed to develop basic teaching abilities including artistic elements which will be of use in teaching at any level.

Kindergartens

In many places there are independent Waldorf kindergartens as well as those fully integrated in a school. They are members of the International Association of Waldorf Kindergartens.

Federations of Schools

Each Waldorf School is an organism in its own right. However, they all work from the same source of inspiration and stand for the same ideals. In many countries there are federations of Waldorf Schools, therefore, to represent the movement at government level, to maintain standards and provide mutual help.

Education towards freedom

The word 'freedom' has occurred often in this book. The meaning of this word should in each case be taken in relation to its context. It is more fully considered in the section 'Concerning the idea of freedom' (page 101). Nevertheless it may be appropriate at the conclusion of this book yet again to emphasize what is actually meant here by 'freedom.'

Freedom is not absolute. It always depends on the inner activity of the individual. The richer and more manifold the potential for self-expression at our disposal, and the more consciously our inner self can come to well-considered decisions, then the greater our inner freedom. When a mature adult takes responsibility for their development, then the capabilities and resources at their disposal are largely dependent on the efforts made throughout their childhood years by parents and teachers. A form of education which strives to remove as far as possible the physical and inner obstacles which can place themselves in the way of the conscious mastery of the self in adult years, can be called an 'education towards freedom.' It is hoped that the illustrations and text of this book will reveal the vast richness of possibilities which can be called forth in children through an education which works in this way. The goal of artistic activity within a Waldorf School is — and once again this must be emphasized — not to produce artists, but rather to develop human beings who can be creative in all walks of life.

The task of helping to unfold the latent inner abilities of the growing human being can only be undertaken by educators who know the person thoroughly and who have grown accustomed to the educational demands which arise anew in the daily life at school. The future of humankind depends on the extent to which parents and teachers are successful in this joint activity.

The representatives of political and business life should refrain from interference in this sensitive and decisively important process through imposing unsuitable teaching curricula and examinations. On the other hand, the state and industry should be willing to support teachers and parents willing to carry the burden of a Waldorf School through financial means, and through cultural freedom.

The contribution which can be made to the development of humanity by a truly free form of education was summarized by Steiner in a few words which may serve as the motto of this book:

> One should not ask: 'What does a person need to know and be able to do for the existing social order?' but rather: 'What gifts does a person possess and how may these be developed in him?' Then it will be possible to bring to the social order ever new forces from each successive generation. Then this social order will always be alive with that which each fully developed individual brings with him into life, rather than that each successive generation is made to conform to the existing social organization.*

---

* From the essay 'Freie Schule und Dreigliederung' (Independent School and the Threefold Social Order), in *Aufsätze über die Dreigliederung des sozialen Organismus und zur Zeitlage.*

Further reading

Basic books by Rudolf Steiner

Christianity as Mystical Fact, Steinerbooks, Massachusetts 2006.
Theosophy, Rudolf Steiner Press, Forest Row 2005.
An Outline of Esoteric Science, Anthroposophic Press, New York 1997.
How to Know Higher Worlds, Anthroposophic Press, Mass. 2006.
The Renewal of the Social Organism, Anthroposophic Press, New York 1985.

Educational works by Rudolf Steiner

Education of the Child, The, Anthroposophic Press, New York, 1996.
Foundations of Human Experience, The, General Education Course (14 lectures, Stuttgart, Aug 21–Sep 5, 1919), Anthroposophic Press, New York 1997 (previously published as *Study of Man).*
Practical Advice to Teachers, (lectures, Stuttgart, Aug–Sep 1919) Steinerbooks, Massachusetts 2000.
Discussions with Teachers, (discussions held in Stuttgart, Aug 21–Sep 26, 1919 at the foundation of the Waldorf School), Anthroposophic Press, New York 1997.
Education as a Force for Social Change, (6 lectures, Dornach, Aug 9–17, 1919) Anthroposophic Press, New York 1997.
Spirit of the Waldorf School, The, (lectures Stuttgart and Basle 1919) Anthroposophic Press, New York 1995.
Rudolf Steiner in the Waldorf School, Anthroposophic Press, New York 1996.
Genius of Language, The, Anthroposophic Press, New York 1995.

Faculty Meetings with Rudolf Steiner, Anthroposophic Press, New York 1998.
Renewal of Education through the Science of the Spirit, The, Steinerbooks, (lectures, Basle April 20–May 11 1920) Massachusetts 2001.
Education for Adolescents, (lectures, Stuttgart 1921) Anthroposophic Press, New York 1996.
Balance in Teaching, (various lectures, Stuttgart 1920–23) Steinerbooks, Massachusetts 2007.
Soul Economy Body, Soul, and Spirit in Waldorf Education, (lectures, Dornach Dec 23–Jan 7 1921/22) Steinerbooks, Massachusetts 2003.
Waldorf Education and Anthroposophy 1, (various lectures 1921-22) Anthroposophic Press, New York 1995.
Waldorf Education and Anthroposophy 2, (various lectures 1921-22) Anthroposophic Press, New York 1996.
Spiritual Ground of Education, The, (12 lectures, Oxford Aug 16–29, 1922) Steinerbooks, Massachusetts 2004.
Child's Changing Consciousness, The, (8 lectures, Dornach April 115–22, 1923) Anthroposophic Press, New York 1996.
Modern Art of Education, A, (14 lectures, Ilkley, Aug 5–17, 1923) Steinerbooks, Massachusetts 2004.
Essentials of Education, (lectures, Stuttgart April 8–24, 1924) Anthroposophic Press, New York 1997.
Roots of Education, The, (lectures, Berne, April 13–17 1924) Anthroposophic Press, New York 1997.
Human Values in Education, (9 lectures, Arnhem, July 17–24, 1924) Steinerbooks, Massachusetts 2005.
Kingdom of Childhood, The, (7 lectures and answers to questions, Torquay, Aug 12–20, 1924) Anthroposophic Press, New York 1995.

Books by other authors

Aeppli, Willi, *Biography in Waldorf Education*, Anthroposophic Press, New York.

—, *Rudolf Steiner Education and the Developing Child*, Anthroposophic Press, New York.

—, *Teacher, Child and Waldorf Education*, Anthroposophic Press, New York.

Andersen, H.C. *Favourite Tales from Hans Christian Andersen*, Floris Books, Edinburgh 2001.

Anschutz, Marieke *Children and their Temperaments*, Floris Books, Edinburgh 1995.

Barnes, H. and others, *Introduction to Waldorf Education*, Mercury, New York.

Bauer, John, *Swedish Folk Tales*, Floris Books, Edinburgh 2004.

Childs, Gilbert, *Steiner Education In Theory and Practice*, Floris Books, Edinburgh 1992.

Clouder, Christopher & Rawson, Martyn, *Waldorf Education*, Floris Books, Edinburgh 2003.

Colum, Padraic, *The King of Ireland's Son*, Floris Books, Edinburgh 1986.

Cusick, Lois, *Waldorf Parenting Handbook*, St George, New York.

Edmunds, Francis, *Rudolf Steiner Education*, Rudolf Steiner Press, London.

Grimm, Jacob and Wilhelm, *Favourite Grimm's Tales*, Floris Books, Edinburgh 2000.

Heydebrand, Caroline von, *Childhood*, Anthroposophical Press, New York.

Koepke, Hermann, *Encountering the Self: Transformation and Destiny in the Ninth Year*, Anthroposophic Press, New York.

Kornberger, Horst *The Power of Stories*, Floris Books, Edinburgh 2008.

Kovacs, Charles, *Parsifal and the Search for the Grail*, Floris Books, Edinburgh 2002.

La Fontaine, Jean de, *The Fables of La Fontaine*, Floris Books, Edinburgh 2006.

Lievegoed, Bernard, *Phases of Childhood*, Floris Books, Edinburgh 2005.

Nobel, Agnes, *Educating through Art*, Floris Books, Edinburgh 1996.

Petrash, Jack, *Understanding Waldorf Education*, Gryphon House, Maryland 2001 and Floris Books, Edinburgh 2003.

Richards, Mary Caroline, *Towards Wholeness: Rudolf Steiner Education in America*. Wesleyan University Press 1981.

Spock, Marjorie, *Teaching as a Lively Art*, Anthroposophic Press, New York.

Strauss, Michaela, *Understanding Children's Drawings*, Rudolf Steiner Press, London.

Thomas, Heather, *A Journey through Time in Verse and Rhyme*, Floris Books, Edinburgh 1998.

Waldorf School Federations

For more information and addresses of Waldorf Schools contact the federation in the country, or download a complete list from www.waldorfschule.info

International federations

Bund der Freien Waldorfschulen e.V., Wagenburgstraße 6, 70184 Stuttgart, Germany. *forschung@waldorfschule.de* *www.waldorfschule.de*
Goetheanum, School of Spiritual Science, Pedagogical Section, 4143 Dornach, Switzerland. *paed.sektion@goetheanum.ch* *www.paedagogik-goetheanum.ch*

Freunde der Erziehungskunst Rudolf Steiners, Weinmeisterstr. 16, 10178 Berlin, Germany. *freunde.waldorf@t-online.de* *www.freunde-waldorf.de*

Internationale Vereinigung der Waldorfkindergärten, Le Quartier Hornbach 15, 67433 Neustadt an der Weinstrasse, Germany. *info@ivwdeutschland.de* or *inter.waldorf@t-online.de* *www.waldorfkindergarten.org*

European Council for Steiner Waldorf Education, Kidbrooke Park, Forest Row RH18 5JB England. Brussels office: Rue du Trône 194, 1040 Brussels, Belgium. *ecswe@waldorf.net* *www.steinerwaldorfeurope.org*

National federations

AWSNA, Association of Waldorf Schools of North America, 337 Oak Grove Street, Minneapolis, MN 55403, USA. *awsna@awsna.org* *www.WhyWaldorfWorks.org*

Steiner Waldorf Schools Fellowship, Kidbrooke Park, Forest Row RH18 5JB, England. *info@swsf.org.uk* *www.steinerwaldorf.org.uk*

Irish Steiner Waldorf Education Association, c/o Raheen Wood School, Raheen Road, Tuamgraney, Scariff, Co. Clare, Ireland. *www.raheenwood.org* or *www.steinerireland.org*

Southern African Federation of Waldorf Schools, Centre for Creative Education, McGregor House, 4 Victoria Road, Plumstead 7800, South Africa. *federation@waldorf.org.za* *www.waldorf.org.za*

Rudolf Steiner Schools of Australia, PO Box 111, Robertson, NSW 2577, Australia. *rssa@bigpond.com* *www.steineroz.com*

Federation of Rudolf Steiner Waldorf Schools in New Zealand, PO Box 186, Raglan, New Zealand. *rudolfsteiner.federation@xtra.co.nz* *www.federation.steiner.school.nz* or *www.rudolfsteinerfederation.org.nz*

Waldorf Schools around the world

School hall, Stuttgart-Uhlandshöhe, Germany

Waldorf School, Mönchengladbach, Germany

School hall, Göttingen, Germany

Stairwell, Waldorf School, Karlsruhe, Germany

Rudolf Steiner School near Zurich, Switzerland

Activities at the Waldorf School in Bexbach, Germany

Rudolf Steiner School, Verrières le Buisson, France

Steiner School in Stavanger, Norway

Lessons in Charlottesville Waldorf School, Crozet, Virginia, USA.

Lake Champlain Waldorf School, Shelburne, Vermont, USA

The Hill Top Circus of Pine Hill Waldorf School, Wilton, New Hampshire, USA

Maypole at Camelia Waldorf School, Sacramento, California, USA.

Kona Pacific School, Kealakekua, Hawaii, USA

Atrium of the Waldorf School in Toronto, Canada

Solymár Waldorf School in Budapest, Hungary

Lessons at the Moscow Waldoef Schol, Russia

A class at the Waldorf School in Manila, Philippines

Music lessons at Panyotai Waldorf School in Bangkok, Thailand

Class 1 at the Free School Gwa-cheon, Korea

Craft lessons at Harduf, Israel

A class at the Waldorf School, Kenya

Nelson Mandela visiting Khayelitsha Waldorf School for Creative Education, near Cape Town, South Africa

Mount Barker Waldorf School, Adelaide, Australia

Taikura Steiner School, Hastings, New Zealand